Easy
Plants for
Difficult
Places

Easy Plants for Difficult Places

Geoffrey Smith

Hamlyn
London · New York · Sydney · Toronto

To My Father

Contents

Colour Illustrations 13

General Considerations 15

Herbaceous Plants:
Aconitum to Rudbeckia 25

Herbaceous Plants:
Salvia to Veronica 55

Trees and Shrubs:
Acer to Fuchsia 71

Trees and Shrubs:
Gaultheria to Pyrus 93

Trees and Shrubs:
Rhododendron to Weigela 113

Climbers 133

Conifers 141

Roses 151

Bulbous Plants 165

Envoi 177

Plants for Selected Sites and Seasons 179

Index 185

Acknowledgements

Line artwork by Norman Barber, Ian Garrard, Ron Hayward and Charles Stitt.

Colour photographs
Pat Brindley, pages 24, 50, 70, 96, 104, 147, 169; Jerry Harpur, pages 10 (Yeomans, Oxon), 41 (Pusey House, Oxon), 66–7 (Waterperry), 109, 144, 150 (Windle Hall, St Helens), 178; Robert Pearson 78–9 (Adrian Bloom's garden at Bressingham), 100;

The Harry Smith Horticultural Photographic Collection, pages 21, 29, 32–3, 44, 54, 58, 108, 112, 132, 158, 173; Michael Warren, pages 6, 14, 59, 63, 88, 115, 123, 140, 154, 161, 164, 168.

Colour Illustrations

A terraced garden 6
A secluded country garden 10
Mixed shrubs and perennials 14
Taxus baccata hedge 21
Aquilegia, euphorbia and rodgersia 24
Alchemilla mollis and bergenia 29
Gentiana septemfida 32–3
Herbaceous peonies 41
Papaver orientale 44
Iris pseudacorus and candelabra
  primulas 50
Verbascums 54
Saxifraga fortunei 'Wada's Variety' 58
Senecio przewalskii 59
Trillium grandiflorum 63
Herbaceous border 66–7
Acer palmatum cvs. 70
Cornus alba 'Spaethii', *Cotinus
  coggygria* and *Picea pungens* 'Erich
  Frahm' 78–9
Daphne retusa 88
Magnolia × *soulangiana* 92
Hypericum patulum 'Hidcote' 96
Laburnum anagyroides 'Vossii' and
  Rhododendron 'Pink Pearl' 100

Malus 'John Downie' 104
Pernettya mucronata 108
Pieris formosa forrestii 109
Deciduous azaleas 112
Rhododendron yakushimanum 115
Sorbus cashmiriana 123
Parthenocissus tricuspidata 132
Wisteria 137
Picea pungens 'Koster' and *P.
  brewerana* 140
Conifers in association with
  evergreens 144
Conifers and heathers 147
Roses in the garden 150
Rosa 'Mountbatten' 154
Rosa 'Zéphirine Drouhin' 158
Rosa 'The Fairy' and *Senecio*
  'Sunshine' 161
Naturalized narcissi 164
Cyclamen hederifolium 168
Erythronium tuolumnense 'Pink
  Beauty' 169
Anemone nemorosa and muscari 173
Meconopsis betonicifolia 178

General Considerations

There has only ever been one perfect garden and that, unfortunately, was lost by the perfidy of a woman and a man's taste for apples. I have seen gardens which seemed to come near the perfection of that other Eden, but in each case there proved to be a serpent which marred perfection. In any case no gardener will ever admit to possessing an ideal site, even if there were such a thing.

Site

Few people are in the fortunate position of being able to search the length and breadth of the British Isles for the best possible site to build a house. Usually it is a case of choosing a location close to a place of employment, to schools, and shops, with the garden and its requirements a very bad fourth.

One gardener I know sought to overcome the problems of his particular locality by moving his garden the width of a road and three fields from his house, into the shelter of a quarry, only to discover it a frost pocket. On some, the gods of fortune smile: their task is made easy by natural conditions only needing a little of man's artifice to make the earth produce a hundredfold from the sheltered, stored-up goodness within itself. For those so singularly blessed this book will have little or no appeal, unless it be to illuminate still further their obvious benefits, or to give an indication of how the other two-thirds of the horticultural world struggles to live.

Each and every gardener will have his, or her, own idea of exactly what constitutes a rough site, for each plot of earth must be lived with and worked before all its moods are discovered. For 20 years I helped to make a garden from half-a-dozen fields and a strip of wood-land, which was deliberately chosen, not for all the desirable features which are considered essential to a garden, but for all the factors which lay severe limitations on the cultivation of plants. For me, then, a difficult site is a piece of ground with a slope towards the prevailing wind, facing the open moors. The soil is an intractable clay which shows a distinct tendency to waterlog after prolonged rain, especially during the winter months. The workable depth of the topsoil nowhere exceeds 20 cm (8 in), overlying a subsoil of blue or yellow clay which is extremely resistant to cultivating implements. I could think of several more little refinements such as atmospheric pollution, but usually the inhibiting factors are limited to two, or the unfortunate gardener would rapidly be driven to an early grave.

Wind

Sweet are the uses of adversity, however, adding as they do a stimulus to the challenge of making a garden, for were the whole operation made easy, the rough places made smooth, then much of the excitement of growing plants would be lost. Yet man is born unto trouble, as the sparks fly upwards, and it is in the surmounting of difficulties that knowledge is added to knowledge, and eventual success is assured. So far as I am concerned the greatest single obstacle to overcome on a rough site is wind. Each time I read an advertisement for a house which emphasises the beauty of the view, a certain sympathy for the gardener of the family comes to me. My house is on a hilltop, with the most beautiful view on three sides which excites admiration from all who see it, but the price of such a view is inevitably a windswept garden. I do get a certain feeling of contentment

Opposite: Herbaceous plants, like trollius and potentillas, provide the changing patterns of the garden while shrubs give an air of permanence

during periods of heavy rain, or snow, with their attendant fear of flooding in the low-lying areas, for at least there is not that problem to contend with. The water does tend to run down hill on a sloping garden so quickly that it washes soil from beds on to paths, and this should be always borne in mind when laying out the various features. Of that other weapon of the elements, lightning, I have little experience, finding it safer to get into a cupboard or under the bed until the storm has passed.

The Meteorological Office will supply detailed information about the weather in a particular locality over a period of years, and this can be extremely helpful as a rough guide of what to expect. No one could ever complain about the climate of this green and pleasant land being monotonous, so the information can be nothing more than a very rough guide. Only by actual experience of living and working with a garden can all the peculiarities be understood: where the sheltered corners lie, the shade areas, the dry places, the frost pockets; from this understanding comes the knowledge of how best to set about improving the site for the type of plants we wish to grow.

Drainage

Having already stated that to me exposure to wind is the greatest single limiting factor to success or failure in a garden, it would be correct to assume that in any development work with which I have to deal, some form of shelter is a primary consideration. On a heavy soil with all the problems of waterlogging which crop up at regular intervals, it would be a mistake to rush around planting hedges, building walls,

or erecting fences, for suddenly one discovers that a complete drainage system is needed to get rid of the surplus moisture. Then all the walls, hedges, and fences would make the laying of a proper drainage system virtually impossible. A wet clay soil is slow to warm up in spring, and the stagnant conditions check and sometimes bring to a halt the development of an efficient healthy root system.

There are plants which can survive in a wet stagnant soil, but the range will be vastly increased if the moisture content of the soil is lowered to a proper level by efficient drainage. Land tiles are, without doubt, the best of all methods of draining any plot of land, but a complete herring-bone layout of piping needs a considerable amount of labour and skill to construct. After compromising over land drainage for some 10 years, and the endless trouble which has resulted, I would unhesitatingly advise anyone with a wet, badly drained garden to do the job properly from the outset. If possible get someone with experience to advise on the fall, distance apart at which the pipes would have to be laid, and also on the outfalls. Quite frequently test digging reveals that the land has already been furnished with a perfectly adequate drainage system, and all that needs to be done is to push rods through it to clear any stoppage interfering with the free removal of surplus moisture. In addition to the traditional clay tiles, it is possible now to buy them in porous concrete and plastic, but of the latter I have no experience. Whatever tiles are used, keep a map showing the location of both the main drain and the feeders; then should anything go wrong with the

Land tiles (1) provide the best means of draining soil and are laid in rubble (2) in a herring-bone arrangement (3) with the main drain emptying into a soakway

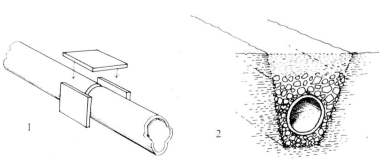

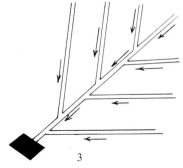

system in later years the fault can be traced, and rectified without digging up half the garden.

A free-draining soil is of such vital importance to most plants that unless adequate provision is made to ensure that all surplus moisture quickly seeps away, the gardener is working under a severe handicap from the very outset. There are several alternative methods of draining; none as permanent or as effective as tile drainage. Brushwood or mole drains have only a relatively short life, even in clay sub-soils. You can, of course, do as a friend of mine has done, and raise the general level of the garden above that of the surrounding land. Unless you really enjoy moving large quantities of soil this can be a slow, laborious business, but it is undoubtedly permanent and effective.

Knowing the garden

I am of the opinion that the ideal way with any new garden is to live with it for a year before making any major planting decisions. This applies equally both to old established gardens, and a piece of land just as the builders have left it. Only by one's own experience can all the tricks of the weather in a micro-locality be fully appreciated. The lie of the land may cause peculiarities not immediately obvious; for example a small hill deflecting a strong down current in one corner of the garden with a resulting whirl-wind effect, or a copse of trees which by abruptly interrupting the flow of wind causes a gusty condition. A gusty wind can do far more damage than a steady gale in some cases; and should be avoided where possible, or baffled out by carefully lined hedges. Sometimes I find myself investing the wind with a perversely human personality, or a warped sense of humour, especially with respect to delphiniums. Some years it will let me enjoy the full unsullied beauty of a legion of stately blue, white, and purple spires. In the following year, which promises even greater glory in purity and wealth of blossom, the whole bed will be desecrated in a single night. I have stood out in the garden at three o'clock in the morning and cursed the wind, as it stripped the heads from roses in a riot of destructive exuberance. Even more strange is the regularity with which a gale visits this garden some two or three days before our local harvest festival. I even went to the lengths of remonstrating with the vicar, but he assured me, albeit a shade unwillingly, that it was nothing to do with him.

Windbreaks

Wind, then, is, so far as I am concerned, the greatest single limiting factor with which I have to contend. The only way to combat it is to construct or plant some sort of windbreak which will temper the fury in the area where the house and garden are situated.

The direction of the prevailing wind varies from one part of the country to another, but in the majority of cases the strongest and most persistent variety come from the west. In this area it is from that direction the plant-wrecking gales come and usually they last for several days. The east wind in spring, though less strong, is equally persistent, and catches the plants at their most vulnerable stage. All the upthrust and resurgence of growth is arrested overnight, and gardeners get moody with unpredictable tempers until the return of better growing weather.

It should be borne in mind that walls or similar obstacles check the wind abruptly, forcing it upwards until it clears the barrier, and creates the gusty effect which can be so dangerous. An experience I had some years ago, when growing vegetables under cloches in a walled garden, might serve to illustrate the point. The garden was situated at the end of a road which ran due west between a row of houses up to the open moor. The wall which surrounded the garden was 3.7 m (12 ft) high, the garden itself 42 m (138 ft) wide. I had a crop of lettuce under cloches on what should have been the most sheltered bed of all, but after a night of gale-force winds the carnage, 9 m (30 ft) out from the wall, had to be seen to be believed. Some cloches were left intact, but the majority had been carried right across the garden and shattered against the far wall. Only those in the area of relative calm, immediately under the wall, had escaped. I solved the problem of this immovable object being met by an irresistible force, by putting a thorn hedge outside the wall, and dividing the garden inside with lines of cordon fruit trees and lonicera, though the latter has disadvantages (see p. 101). Walls should never be considered the complete answer to the wind problem. The ideal barrier is one which filters the wind rather than checking it abruptly. I remember being astonished, during my first day of work in an exposed garden in Cornwall, to find the main shelter belts consisted of double rows of small-mesh wire netting 15 cm (6 in) apart. They served the purpose admirably.

Frost pockets

The garden should be designed, then, not only to be aesthetically pleasing, but also to avoid the worst of the weather, and to permit maximum shelter from wind while yet still allowing free air movement, or rather air drainage, which is essential if frost pockets are to be avoided. Frost tends to move in a similar fashion to water, namely downhill to the lowest point. Should a hedge, wall, or similar solid obstacle be sited in such a way as to impede that movement, then, like water, the frost will be dammed back to form a pool of freezing air. Where this occurs it is possible to go out the next morning and see the high-tide mark on the plants themselves. Even a small gap, a gateway for instance, is often sufficient to permit the cold air to drain away.

How often will the proud owner of a new garden, beguiled by illustrations in catalogues, and the perfection of the blooms at the horticultural show stands, make frantic efforts to have the garden made and furnished the first season. If gardening teaches nothing else, it will drive home the lesson of 'patience being a virtue', again and again.

Soil working

Soil is a collective name for the mixture of finely ground rock, decaying organic matter and microscopic organisms which, combined, form the basic material with which all gardeners work. As those of us who cultivate them for pleasure or profit are only too well aware, soils can show extraordinary variations in character and quality. For all practical, as opposed to scientific, purposes, soils may be loosely classified as heavy, medium or light, according to the amount of clay they contain. Heavy soils which include a large amount of clay in their composition are retentive of moisture which makes them difficult to work in wet weather. When improved by drainage, the addition of coarse sand and humus-forming materials such as compost, farm manure, or similar organic matter, they are potentially very fertile.

Sandy or light soils drain quickly, can be worked at almost any season and warm up early in the spring. Minerals essential to plant growth rapidly leach out of them, and they become drought ridden in dry weather. A sandy soil needs regular dressings of farm manure, compost, peat, or any material which will rot down to form humus. This black material, the final stage almost in the decomposition of organic matter, serves

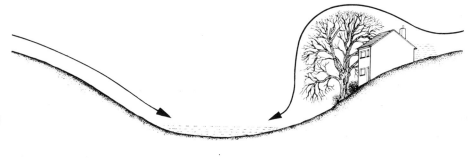

Frost moves downhill to the lowest point, where it forms a frost pocket. A solid object on a slope will impede this movement causing the frost to be dammed back to form a pool of freezing air

a twofold purpose in a sandy soil – acting as a reservoir of moisture in dry weather, and holding tight to essential plant food which would otherwise be leached out and lost.

My ideal soil would be a medium loam, well drained, on a site which sloped ever so gently towards the south.

Alkaline and acid are names used by gardeners to define the chemical composition of soils. Alkaline soils usually contain appreciable amounts of chalk or lime, whereas when the soil is acid the reverse condition prevails. The gardener working the land needs to know whether a soil is acid or alkaline. There are some plants which will not thrive in an alkaline soil – rhododendrons, heathers, and many more. On the other hand lime is an essential plant food: it makes clay soils easier to work, releases minerals which would otherwise be unavailable to the plants, and helps in the control of certain diseases such as club root in wallflowers. Lime as an aid to disease prevention is of more importance in the vegetable garden. Acidity can be neutralized by dressings of lime or chalk. Excessive alkalinity may also make essential minerals unattainable, particularly iron. Working in farm manure, peat and pulverized bark will, over a period of time, counteract an excess of lime.

Shade conditions

All gardens I have ever worked with offer some areas which are shaded. Why this should be considered a disadvantage escapes me completely. Borders which are shaded for at least part of the day enable me to grow a whole variety of plants which would otherwise suffer major discomfort if fully exposed to the sun.

There are various qualities of shade: the north side of the house in my present garden is the best. In a bed which runs the whole length of house and garage, rhododendrons, trillium, primula and similar shade-tolerant plants luxuriate in the cool moistness. In practice walls or buildings are the ideal shading agents as they offer no active competition to plant growth.

Trees, shrubs and hedges cast shadows; they also hang out branches which drip, and send out roots to deprive surrounding soil of food and moisture. However, by exercising a little care in the selection of suitable plants, the patterned shade caste by the canopy of a tree or shrub can be used to good effect.

Just one example from those outlined in the main text of the book: *Cyclamen hederaefolium* (*C. neapolitanum*) has carpeted the ground under the shade of a white cherry. The pink and white flowers are a delight in autumn, the green-grey marbled foliage a panacea against the melancholia of winter. Extra feeding ensures that plants growing in competition with tree or shrub roots are not starved out of existence. Mulching with rotted manure, leafmould, or peat to which has been added a slow-release fertilizer solves the problem for me.

Planting

What to grow depends, of course, on personal preference. We all have our favourite plants – indeed, this is one aspect of gardening which I find so interesting – though fashions change and our gardening life progresses through various stages to an ultimate maturity, yet there are some plants which share the passing years with us. The flower which delighted in adolescence commands our admiration years later. Familiarity in fact deepens the attachment.

My familiars, constant associates over four decades, include annuals, herbaceous perennials, shrubs and, of course trees. My garden would just not be complete without them and they measure for me the passing seasons like a floral calendar. Individual choice is, however, influenced by soil and climate. There is scant reward from trying to plant heathers, rhododendrons and camellias if the soil is full of chalk.

Having drawn up the final list buy top-quality material from a reputable nurseryman. Plants are available from nurseries either as lifted from the ground with bare roots, or balled with some soil left on the roots which are then wrapped in a netting made of plastic or hessian. Or the third method which I prefer, plants grown in pots or, as the trade terms them, containers. Shrubs or trees bought in containers can be planted at any time of the year as root disturbance is minimal. They still need watering and after care, as like any other newly installed shrub whether bare or ball root they may die if the soil dries out.

Dig the hole wide enough and sufficiently deep to comfortably accommodate all the roots. Fork up the soil at the base of the hole, incorporating at the same time a little well-rotted compost laced with slow-release fertilizer. Should a stake be necessary, hammer it into place at this stage. Make certain that the support is on the prevailing wind side so the tree blows away from and not on to it.

Plants lifted from the open ground may have damaged roots. Cut these back to healthy tissue. When the roots are balled up to keep the soil in place, stand the plant in the hole, check for depth, then remove the wrappings. Container-grown material should be well watered an hour before the time for planting so the compost is thoroughly soaked and adheres to the roots when the container is removed.

Mix the soil from the hole with well-rotted compost or one of the special planting mixtures now on offer before back filling round the roots, gently firming at intervals until all is level again. A good soak with water completes the first stage. After-care includes watering in dry weather and keeping the soil over the root area clear of weeds at least for the first season.

Privacy

A garden is a private place, somewhere to be safe from the intrusion of the mundane workaday world, and therefore some part should be completely screened from view. My ideal would be to have the whole lot carefully secluded and shut in, but I have never possessed a garden where this was practicable. There are many obvious artificial methods of achieving privacy, all are in varying degrees expensive, and unless the pocket runs to a wall of stone or brick, singularly unpleasing to the eye.

The screens I propose to deal with are composed of living plants, and like all living things they may prove unpredictable but never monotonous. As with all the plants in this book, only those which I have grown and proved successful on a very testing site will be mentioned, the choice then may be rather limited for some tastes.

Hedges

Beech was the first hedge to be planted, a 54 m (60 yd) stretch running more or less south to north, in an attempt to stop the westerly winds blasting the rose garden and shrub borders into the East Riding where at least they would find better soil. Since that first planting several more beech hedges have been put in and all, without exception, have proved quick to establish themselves.

The first after 15 years made a close, well-furnished barrier 3.7 m (12 ft) high: a thing of beauty at all seasons, but particularly lovely as the leaves change colour in the autumn. I had never before appreciated just how many different tones of brown and yellow a beech could produce. Now when any fresh hedging venture is considered my first choice is always beech. Further variety can be introduced by planting alternate blocks of five green and three copper or purple. Single specimens of purple are useless as they become so overgrown by the green as to make no worthwhile contribution to the colour scheme at all. People with plenty of time can start from scratch and grow the plants from seeds sown in nursery rows; drills 1 cm (½in) deep with the mast (seed) spaced 5 cm (2 in) apart in the rows. When large enough, transplant the seedlings to their permanent site, single-row spacing for the best results about 38 cm (15 in) apart. Do not clip the hedge for the first three years after planting, only shorten back any side growths which grow too far out of bounds.

A hedge of yew, *Taxus baccata*, makes a good background for a herbaceous border

Hawthorn has proved completely reliable, but cannot be compared with beech as a purely ornamental plant. It is a good deal less handsome, and needs considerably more clipping during the growing season to preserve a neat appearance. Unless great care is taken in raking up the clippings, the thorns become hard and are extremely painful when picked up in the fingers during weeding operations. Finally, it sometimes gets mildew when hard clipped, but apart from these defects hawthorn makes an excellent barrier. Space the plants 30 cm (12 in) apart, or, as I have done when money was short, 1 m (3 ft) apart, and then after four years lay the young plants in as one would with an old, worn-out hedge. Cut back newly planted bushes to about 15 cm (6 in) above the soil level.

Ligustrum ovalifolium, privet, is an easy-going, tolerant plant, in spite of the rude things said about it. There would not be so many hedges of this material in both town and country if it was not first class for the job. Unfortunately, it does need clipping frequently. Plant in single rows 30 to 38 cm (12 to 15 in) apart, and cut it hard back to within 20 to 30 cm (8 to 12 in) of the ground the first spring. There is a golden-leafed form which in mild winters is almost evergreen, and a mixed planting of green and gold can be very effective.

Lonicera nitida is a nightmare plant; having had the job of keeping a long hedge of it neat and tidy for seven years, the very name of it makes me shudder. In any case I should hesitate to use it on a windswept site in full exposure. There is a small hedge around a little parterre garden and it has stood 12 years with no sign of weather damage, but it is in a fairly sheltered position. *Lonicera nitida* will make a hedge fairly rapidly, but it needs cutting regularly during the summer; the old saying of 'mow the lawn and cut the lonicera' was not without an element of truth.

Cotoneaster simonsii makes a beautiful, but not, in my experience, very stock-proof hedge. For several years it formed part of a boundary hedge I had to deal with, and the cattle not only walked through it but ate all the parts they could reach with considerable relish and, so far as I could see, no ill effects to themselves. Where not required to be stock-proof it makes an effective screen up to 2 to 2.5 m (6 to 8 ft) high. Semi-evergreen, of a naturally erect habit, this shrub looks lovely in autumn when carrying a full quota of orange-scarlet berries. Plant 45 cm (18 in) apart, and wherever possible clip only once a year, or much of the beauty of berry will be lost.

Berberis × *stenophylla* will make a strong evergreen screen up to 2.5 m (8 ft) high, even in an exposed situation. The best planting distance is around 60 cm (24 in) apart, and in due course this will give an impenetrable screen which not even the most thrusting child can defeat. One trimming, as the flowers fade, will enable the bush to make sufficient wood to produce a further profusion of the fragrant yellow blossoms in April, which on a well-grown specimen festoon the branches from end to end. Unfortunately, to show to best advantage it needs room, and it sends out suckers. Attempts at tentative penetration of this sort can be easily discouraged by chopping back the offending shoots with a sharp spade.

Holly will, of course, make a good screen, but after 10 years of suffering I would not plant one again in my garden. Beautiful though this hedge may be, the fact that it scatters leaves in the middle of summer, which make the garden look untidy and presents a serious hazard to the business of hand weeding, makes it undesirable. Pruning or clipping is usually done in mid-May, but this still does not eliminate the trouble. However, so enduring and beautiful is a holly hedge that people stronger minded than myself may prefer to overlook the rather unfortunate habit of the plant. The distance apart in the row is again 60 cm (24 in). For those with time to wait, plants can be raised relatively easily from seed, which should be mixed with sand, left exposed to the elements over winter, and then sown in drills.

Chamaecyparis lawsoniana and *Thuya plicata* also scorch rather badly when planted on an exposed site, and the individual plants get misshapen when constantly teased by the wind. For those who feel they have a suitably sheltered site, they make fine hedges planted at 1.2 m (4 ft) apart.

Another coniferous hedging plant is the bi-generic hybrid × *Cupressocyparis leylandii;* the fastest-growing evergreen I have ever handled. Only three years have gone since a hedge of this conifer was planted across the garden, but already it is looking comfortably at home. In this age of high speed, it looks as though × *C. leylandii* will soon be presented as the instant hedge, with a warning to step back smartly after insertion or it may catch you under the chin. The foliage is in sprays, rather lighter than that of *Chamaecyparis lawsoniana*

'Green Hedger', which is discussed on p. 140, but clipping will correct this. As a single tree it will grow to 15 m (50 ft), but just 2.7 m (9 ft) across.

These, then, are a selection of the general run of hedging plants; in point of fact, any shrub will make a hedge provided it is tough enough to grow well, and will stand hard cutting.

What do we want from the garden? To most people it is the endless pleasure which comes from seeing a piece of land take heart under cultivation, the enjoyment of growing things, as an escape from the pen-nibbling, tarmacadam existence most are subjected to. Gradually as the design takes shape and as the plants mature, much will be learned about the practical applications of pruning, mulching and feeding, but these will be dealt with where they apply in the body of the book.

Herbaceous Plants: Aconitum to Rudbeckia

In the past the large private gardens were divided into carefully designed areas: herbaceous borders, rose beds, shrub and wild gardens. The area in the immediate vicinity of the house was usually reserved for the multitude of bedding plants raised annually in the glasshouse. Nothing, it seemed, could interfere with the well ordered routine, but two wars in the space of 25 years caused a social upheaval which even 40 years and more later has not reached stability. The economic factor, coupled with the growing interest of the general public in gardening, has completely changed the concept of design. From this re-thinking has evolved the mixed border, and the association of herbaceous plants with shrubs to the mutual benefit of both. I have never realized the full potential of *Iris sibirica* and its hybrids until I planted them against a background of the yellow *Rosa* × *cantabrigiensis*. The colourful annuals, too, gain in beauty when used throughout the whole garden, rather than keeping them segregated in formal beds in neatly regimented lines. As more and more of rural England is built over with steel and concrete, so will people turn to informality in garden design as a relief from the rigid formality around them.

The herbaceous, shrub, bulb, and rose catalogues are veritable mines from which can be excavated an inexhaustible supply of gems to bring colour to every garden, no matter in what site or situation. Almost inevitably as the years go by, one section will find favour over all the others; with some people alpines become the ruling passion, or shrubs, herbaceous plants, orchids or roses. Whatever plant eventually is honoured and loved, it is certain that the pleasure discovered in its cultivation will more than repay the effort involved.

Herbaceous plants have a reputation for demanding constant attention – lifting, dividing, staking – and yet without the brilliant colour they bring throughout the season no garden landscape is really complete.

Aconitum

The common names of aconitum indicate the antiquity of this beautiful plant in cultivation. Helmet Flower and Monkshood are two which are self explanatory, but Wolf's Bane needed a certain amount of research to discover the connection between two such widely different entities. Finally I discovered that a poison extracted from the thick, fleshy roots was used as a bait to kill wolves in olden days. Indeed, so many remarkable tales are related about the deadly properties of not only their roots, but also their flowers, leaves and even their scent, that it is a wonder any gardener could survive their cultivation for more than a year. Be that as it may, I have grown aconitum in one form or another for the last 20 years, but hasten to add without eating any portion of the root, stem or flower; hence my survival. In a windswept garden their strong wiry stems are much less vulnerable than are those of delphiniums to which they bear such a marked resemblance. Most of the cultivars I have tried grow well under shady conditions, and enjoy a moist soil. *Aconitum napellus* has given several useful hybrids, and in my experience the best is 'Bressingham Spire'. The habit of the plant is pleasing, and the flower spikes well shaped, tapering at the tip. Its deep blue flower spikes average 1 m (3 ft) tall in moist soil. *A. wilsonii* 'Barker's Variety' is rather coarse for any but the

Above: Aconitum 'Bressingham Spire' has well-shaped flower spikes

Opposite: The horse-chestnut-like leaves of rodgersias contrast with the greenish flowers of euphorbia species and purple-flowered aquilegias

range of colours offered. Sufficient indication of the plant's resilience was given when a group I forgot while dividing the main planting lay under a forsythia right through one summer, only to recover when hastily replanted in the autumn.

Caltha

Caltha palustris, known as May Blobs, Butter Blobs, Kingcup and Marsh Marigold, rejoices in the doubtful distinction of having the most primitive flower in the British flora. Primitive or not, having seen a field full of these bright golden flowers in Upper Teesdale on a warm, perfect spring evening, I shall always find a place for it in my garden. This is a variable plant, but the cultivar described as *C. palustris* 'Flore Plena', which grows to about 30 cm (12 in), with bright green leaves and double orange-gold flowers, is the best I have found. It does not require special soil, but death is inevitable unless there is adequate moisture present. I grow it with other moisture-living plants such as astilbes, and *Primula denticulata* which flowers at the same time, and whose mauve-blue pompon flowers combine so well with the yellow of the Marsh Marigold.

Campanula

Campanulas, be they alpine in habit, or stronger-growing herbaceous plants of the meadows, are essential in any well planned garden. These flowers figured largely in cottage gardens, and have been in cultivation for centuries. Some become pernicious weeds, but there are many of less rapacious habits whose inclusion in the border can give nothing but pleasure. *Campanula carpatica* is more of a plant for the rock garden and is a variable species; some only grow to 20 cm (8 in) while others, more ambitious, reach 38 cm (15 in) in height. For the named cultivars careful division or cuttings of basal shoots offer the best means of propagation. Of those I have tried, 'Hannah', a free flowering white one, has proved itself reliable. 'Jewel', a cultivar of *C. turbinata,* is my special favourite, with large, upturned, blue

cups, almost translucent when planted high up so that the sunlight is seen through them. Both bloom from June onwards through the summer. *C. lactiflora* is a tough, vigorous plant for the rough and tumble of the border, or even the competition of tree roots in the woodland. Of the tall forms, I prefer the deep violet-blue 'Prichards Variety' to the rather insipid pinks. An extremely attractive one which on casual acquaintance bears little or no resemblance to the type plant, is the dwarf *C. lactiflora* 'Pouffe'. I have grown it as a ground planting under the pink-flowered shrub rose 'Belinda' for five years now, and find it a pleasant companionable front-of-the-border plant. Only reaching 30 to 38 cm (12 to 15 in) in height, the mound of light green foliage is almost hidden in June under a profusion of lavender-blue flowers. The type species *C. lactiflora* readily comes true from seed where this is considered necessary, and the named cultivars are increased by division or basal cuttings in spring. *C. portenschlagiana* from Southern Europe, which I grew for years as *C. muralis,* and *C. poscharskyana* from Dalmatia, are linked indissolubly in my mind as vigorous, easy-going plants for quickly covering bare and difficult ground. These are two which for many years a friend of mine contemptuously dismissed as 'the stinking Jims', for what reason I could never discover. Both grow 15 to 30 cm (6 to 12 in) high, depending on whether in shade or full sun, and both are hardy and have an almost weed-like persistence.

Campanula portenschlagiana has erect light blue-purple bells and flowers from June to August. There is a white form which, in my experience, is not quite so vigorous but well worth planting as a colour contrast. *C. poscharskyana* has lavender-blue flowers over a much longer period – in favoured seasons from June until October. There is a cultivar with not quite the ground-hogging qualities of its parent, named 'E. K. Toogood', a neat hummock-former with darker blue flowers. Both are excellent because of their easy-

Opposite: A strong contrast in shape and texture – bold leaves of bergenia and sulphur-yellow flowers of *Alchemilla mollis*

going disposition, and look well used as a carpet under one of the golden-leaved dwarf conifers. Propagation is simple, one just removes pieces with a trowel; a rather endearing trait when covetous friends visit the garden.

The best groups of *Dicentra spectabilis* are usually seen in cottage gardens

Cephalaria

Cephalaria tatarica, or as most people would have it, including the eminent J. C. Loudon, Giant Scabious is another indestructible plant, but is only for the medium or large garden. I have grown this for years in a very windy part of the garden and nothing seems to perturb the plant's solid equanimity. On mediocre soil the lemon-coloured scabious flowers are born aloft on 2 m (6 ft) stems, which bend to a wind like steel wire, their season being from late June to September.

Coreopsis

Coreopsis verticillata has a dainty grace which might persuade a first acquaintance into thinking it tender or capricious. Nothing could be further from the truth, and it has dealt faithfully and well with all that the clay here can offer. The whole habit of the plant is attractive, a dainty little bush of bright green foliage which is starred with yellow flowers from late June until September. On moderate soil the plants reach 60 cm (2 ft) and so far as I can see the only things they positively dislike, in common with lots of humans, are starvation and drought. For several years now I have searched diligently to find some marked difference between the two cultivars of *C. verticillata,* namely 'Grandiflora' and 'Golden Shower' but both in the strong yellow flowers and needle-like leaves the plants to me are identical. Unless, of course, my plants are wrongly named, but they both came from an authority on herbaceous gardening. Increase is effected by division in spring, and as I discovered last year they have no strong objection to being pulled into quite small pieces, provided one makes suitable apology by providing some good soil when replanting.

Dicentra

Dicentra spectabilis, Lyre Flower, Dutchman's Breeches, Bleeding Heart, Ladies' Pendant, Girl in a Boat: perhaps a plant's popularity can be accurately assessed by the number of names it has been given by generations of gardeners. I would agree with Farrer that 'every garden knows' the most bleeding of all hearts'.

They need good soil and a sheltered position, which is one reason why the best groups are usually seen growing amongst the riotous profusion of cottage gardens. Propagation is not easy; careful lifting and division of the crowns, then potting the offsets until re-established, is the safest method. I make no apology for including this in a tough-plant list, because when suited it will ramble and sprawl in the most carefree manner.

Those with any doubt as to the generosity of the hospitality they can provide would be well advised to plant the tougher species from America, *D. eximia.* I use it as ground cover under azaleas, and the moist humus-rich conditions are just those which are desired. The fern-like foliage, glaucous-grey in the early stages, is topped in May and June with rose-coloured flowers on 38 cm (15 in) stems. They have not, I admit, the surpassing loveliness of their Chinese brother with unique flowers of red and white, but for all that this is far from being the ugly sister to the lyre flower's Cinderella.

Digitalis

Digitalis purpurea is the Foxglove of open woodland and hedges of which Parkinson wrote, 'The common purple kind that groweth abroad in the fields, I leave to his wilde habitation'. They look lovely amongst rhododendrons and silver birch for those who can provide such a siting, and often appear uninvited. There are perennial species which warrant inclusion in the garden of tough plants.

Digitalis ambigua, 60 cm to 1 m (2 to 3 ft) high, has yellowish flowers netted with brown in August. Grown with white and blue hydrangeas it will pay a full quota for ground rent. *D. lutea* is rather smaller, only 45 cm (18 in) high with pale cream flowers. Again a proper association is essential for the flowers to show full beauty; *Gentiana septemfida* is a fitting neighbour, the blue flowers offering just the contrast needed.

Doronicum

Doronicums have long been derided by the plant purists as common, preferring as they do the moping miffishness of more demanding yet less constant charmers. Most species have the advantage of flowering early, and this to me outweighs just the hint of coarseness in their character. *Doronicum carpetanum* has heart-shaped leaves with yellow daisy flowers 5 to 8 cm (2 to 3 in) across in May. The plant I have growing on the edge of a gravel path is somewhat dwarfed by the rigours of existence, and it is only 45 cm (18 in) high. In better conditions the stems go up to 60 to 76 cm (2 to 2½ft).

The earliest to flower with me is a plant I have as *D.* 'Miss Mason'. This is such an excellent early cut flower that it warrants inclusion for that reason alone. The flowers, on stems 60 cm (2 ft) high, are pale yellow and appear in April and May. Propagation is simply effected by division.

Echinops

Echinops are somewhat awe-inspiring in their robust enthusiasm for life, and certainly qualify for a 'very tough' classification. Some are just a shade ebullient for the small garden. *Echinops humilis* 'Taplow Blue' is especially desirable. The cobweb-covered leaves and soft blue flower heads are a flower arranger's delight, and anything less like a composite it would be hard to imagine. The height is not extreme, only 1 to 1.2 m (3 to 4 ft) and with a foreground planting of *Lilium* 'Bright Star', will bring character and beauty to the borders. Running the above a close second for a place in my affections is *E. ritro* 'Veitch's Blue' and my solution is to grow both. This plant has even more downy foliage with flower heads of good bright blue on 1 m (3 ft) stems. They are easily increased by seed sown in March.

Eryngium

Eryngiums were much prized in the gardens of the Elizabethan era, and rightly so in my opinion. The roots of the wild *Eryngium maritimum* were claimed as a cure for scrophula and adder bite. *E. alpinum* belies its alpine name by growing 45 to 60 cm (18 to 24 in) high, too grand for all except the large rock garden. Both the flower heads and stems are coloured silver-blue, bringing an unusual character to the borders in July and August. This species is particularly tolerant of a clay soil.

Eryngium amethystinum is an attractive plant with deeply cut leaves and amethyst-blue involucre, slightly taller than *E. alpinum* at 60 to 76 cm (24 to 30 in).

Euphorbia

Euphorbias are at last coming in for a share of the appreciation they deserve, not only for their adaptability, but also for the colourful and unusual interest they bring to the garden. The flower parts are very much reduced, and in most cases it is the bracts which surround them which are coloured. The milky juice of certain species produces a drug, while the milky latex in *Euphorbia heptagona* formed a deadly poison used by the natives of Cape Province to poison arrowheads. *E. epithymoides* (*E. polychroma*) is, however, a low-growing European only 45 cm (18 in) high. In April the yellow leaves surrounding the flowers rival the narcissus in the brilliance of their yellow. I find this species is better in full sun and grow it with tradescantia.

Euphorbia griffithii I have had only five years, but so completely settled has it become that the original five plants have furnished material to start new colonies in a dozen different beds. In the informal setting of the shrub border the bright orange heads make an instant appeal. A good grouping consists of a glaucous leaved juniper, a bold group of *E. griffithii*, and a generous mixture

Eryngium alpinum is not a dwarf species as the name suggests

of ferns and candelabra primulas. A taller but less invasive species can be found in *E. sikkimensis.* In spring the young shoots carry bracts of brilliant red, and eventually the stems grow to almost 1.2 m (4 ft) which rather spoils the plant for a small garden.

Propagation offers no problem; indeed, with *E. griffithii* the plant soon gets out of control unless the suckers are chopped back at intervals. For the others I advise division in spring just as growth commences.

Gentiana

Gentians have a magic appeal which few can resist, and for 20 years my garden has never been without at least three representatives of this beautiful genus. Now it amounts to a positive collecting mania. Gentians have a romantic history, and the root when dried has been widely used for centuries, both as a tonic and antiseptic. *Gentiana asclepiadea* is an extremely variable, yet easy-to-please perennial. I have grown something like a dozen different forms of this plant, all of them beautiful. The graceful arching stems are crowned in July and August with blue trumpets, in some varieties azure, in another purple striped with lighter bands. The dwarf form, *G. asclepiadea nana,* only grows 25 cm (10 in) high with me. The ideal company for the gentian is *Kirengeshoma palmata,* a native of Japan, whose yellow flowers in August and September form a perfect contrast to the robust blue. *G. lutea,* not surprisingly as its native home is in the Alpine meadows of Europe, is a worthy candidate for the difficult garden. The oldest plant here is growing in one of the most exposed beds; after 10 years and three uprootings it shows no sign of senility, and its shape and bearing is most attractive. The pale yellow striped flowers are born in whorls around the strong upright stem. I have seen plants in more favoured localities 1.5 m (5 ft) high, but 1 m (3 ft) is the average.

Were I restricted to one gentian, unless it was certain that my gardening would be confined to acid soil, *G.*

Opposite: Gentiana septemfida is very adaptable concerning soil and situation

septemfida in the best form available would be my choice. This plant grows as well on lime as it does on clay, is equally at home in sun or shade. The stems are 20 to 30 cm (8 to 12 in) high, and the deep blue flowers are carried in terminal clusters from June to August.

I have purposely not included my other loves – *G. acaulis, G. sino-ornata,* and *G.* 'Inverleith' – because they are selective about soil and refuse to flower or even grow in extreme cases. The propagation of all the species described is by seed or division in spring.

Geranium

Geraniums are so outstandingly good that to leave them out of the garden is something akin to cutting off one's left hand. I remember my first sight of *Geranium sanguineum lancastriense* on Walney Island. The purpose of the visit was to see the birds, but all that was forgotten in the beauty of this handsome native. Since that day I have been a devotee of this and other members of the large and lovely genus. *G. grandiflorum* is a good border plant, a shade too good when the creeping roots find a soil to their liking, which they invariably do. The erect stems grow to 38 cm (15 in) the flowers, which appear in July, being a deep blue with a purple eye. *G. ibericum* is much dwarfer and not so invasive. The heart-shaped leaves are so thickly covered with wool as to appear grey. In June and July the rich violet flowers are produced in open panicles with great profusion. *G. macrorrhizum* 'Ingwersen' seeds itself around the shrub border with a reckless abandon which would almost warrant the appellation of weed, were not the flowers so attractive. Any plants which seed out of bounds will find a ready welcome in friends' gardens. The 30 to 38 cm (12 to 15 in) high stems are woody and gnarled at the base, and carry attractive pink-veined flowers from June to August.

The Meadow Cranesbill, *G. pratense,* I prefer to see in its natural habitat, but the double-flowered forms in both light and dark blue can be a pleasant addition to the border, although the season is short. Growing some 1 to 1.2 m (3 to 4 ft) high they need room to develop. In this garden they tend to flop about when exposed to wind, which means providing an unsightly support.

Geranium psilostemon (G. armenum) has flowers of magenta-red which either appeal to or repel the beholder; there is no in-between. The leaves are five-lobed, and the flower stems which appear in July reach only 60 cm (2 ft) which does not make them so prone to wind damage. For *G. renardii* I have nothing but praise, as it is neat and compact in all its parts, being only 25 cm (10 in) in height; the grey-green hairy leaves would be reason enough for growing this attractive Caucasian. In due season, usually early summer, come the large silver-lavender flowers, but for a few brief weeks only. *G. sanguineum,* the Bloody Cranesbill, has much to recommend it, not least the crimson flowers. Where space is limited, however, I would unhesitatingly choose the varietal form *lancastriense,* already mentioned. This has flesh-coloured flowers veined purple, and makes a spreading bush some 30 cm (12 in) high. Propagation of all species is by seed or division in spring.

Helleborus

In astrology the hellebore is the herb of Saturn, used by the ancients to drive away evil spirits, a plant of great virtue in fact. Unfortunately not all this noble family prove amenable to cultivation, but some are undoubtedly capable of putting up with far-from ideal situations. *Helleborus atrorubens* has over many years shared garden company with me. The flowers are interesting rather than beautiful, being dull purple on the outside and greenish within. *H. corsicus* (now *H. lividus corsicus*) is an evergreen shrubby plant, and can always be relied on to carry the interest through the winter. The greenish-yellow flowers on stems 45 cm (18 in) high appear in February, March and April. This is one of the flowers which devotees of floral art dub as interesting, and is an obvious choice for arrangements of spring flowers. Strong stock can be increased by division, but these are often difficult to re-establish. Seed sown immediately it is ripe is a slower but surer method. *H. orientalis* and cultivars with flowers in shades of white, pink and dark purple, must be given the top marks for all-round adaptability. 'Snow White' and 'Winter Cheer', pink and maroon, are forms to look out for. Flowers are in evidence each year in February.

Hemerocallis

Thanks to the efforts of the hybridist, Day Lilies are at last attracting the attention of the gardening public. The light green iris-like leaves offer a foliage contrast to the general run of herbaceous plants. I have had no trouble with Day Lilies, no matter what conditions I have inflicted upon them; from the bog of the stream side, to the arid ground in the neighbourhood of a large horse chestnut, they have given and continue to give a good return of flowers. The name, derived from *hemera,* a day, and *kallos,* beauty, indicates the short life of individual blooms, but as one dies so others come to take its place over several months. The species have been somewhat overshadowed by improved garden cultivars, and the choice depends on personal taste.

'Hyperion' is one which is absolutely reliable. The flowers are canary-yellow, of considerable size, and the height of the plant varies according to soil from 50 cm to 1 m (20 to 36 in). 'Stafford', deep red, and 'Golden Chimes', dwarf with golden-yellow petals, can also be recommended.

Hosta

I have always considered hostas to be plants for the moister areas of the garden, but reading a diary kept by a Gloucestershire gardener I was surprised to read that in his garden they withstood a summer of extreme drought better than most of the other inhabitants of the herbaceous border. Their great enemies are the slugs which eat holes in the leaves, and as these are the plants' greatest attraction, slug damage is to be avoided at any cost, even if it means dwarfing the plants by growing them under drier conditions than they really like. A woodland setting is to me the ideal background against which to grow this beautiful genus. Grouped with astilbe, primula and ferns in moist soil, under the shade of light-foliage trees, hostas contribute in no small measure to the association of leaf and flower. The play of patterned sunlight through the leaves of the trees lends additional beauty to the colony. Though the flowers are in themselves pleasantly pretty, it is the foliage that is the supreme contribution which hostas make to our gardens.

The increased popularity of the genus has resulted in a flood of new varieties and cultivars with a plethora of names for those which even after close inspection seem, to me at any rate, virtually identical. Even the species are not immune from interference.

Hosta fortunei and the various garden forms derived from it are excellent foliage plants for the moister, shadier parts of the garden. Under these conditions the leaves develop to perfection, 20 cm (8 in) long by 15 cm (6 in) wide, with a glaucous sheen. The pale lilac flowers appear in July on 76 cm (30 in) stems. The blue-green leaves of *Hosta sieboldiana* 'Elegans' make this the most attractive member of a lovely genus. The leaves are almost twice the size of *H. fortunei,* and the flower stems taller, bearing in early July pale lilac funnel-shaped blossoms. If it has a fault, it is that the flowers are not carried high enough in some cases to clear the leaves.

Hosta undulata has a pale green leaf splashed with white, and is in this garden the dwarfest of the three. In addition the leaves are waved at the margin, which has gained for the plant a mighty following from the ranks of the flower arrangers. At 50 to 60 cm (20 to 24 in) in height *H. undulata* is a pleasant enough plant for the front of the border, but not to be compared with the species previously mentioned. Propagation is best by division, using a sharp edging iron just as growth breaks in spring.

There are various garden forms of *Hosta fortunei*

Inula

Inula hookeri may not be everyone's idea of a herbaceous plant, but I like the grey-green leaves and dull yellow, slightly scented flowers, plus the care-free way it holds a place in the corner. Without advertising its charms with blatant colour, *I. hookeri* will carry finely-rayed blooms from July until September.

Iris

I believe it was Mr Bowles who said if he was restricted to growing only one genus of plants he would unhesitatingly choose iris. I would not agree with him to that extent, but wherever possible no garden should be entirely without them. The sword-shaped leaves bring foliage variation to the borders, there are species which can tolerate a wide range of soils, and they are not particularly prone to pests or diseases.

The tall bearded iris I would exclude from any garden which could not offer a hot sun-baked position, shelter from the wind, and a free-draining soil. On this heavy clay they are very poor value indeed. Not so the hardy species like *I. douglasiana,* which is extremely variable in regard to flower colour. I like to raise stock plants from seed to get as wide a range of colour as possible, and then plant them out in bold groups at the front of the border. The ultimate height varies but is never more than 30 to 38 cm (12 to 15 in).

Iris innominata is even dwarfer, only 15 to 20 cm (6 to 8 in) high, but just as accommodating. The flowers are golden-yellow veined with brown. Here again I prefer to grow a mixed colony from seed and take what the gods offer in regard to colour. *I. sibirica* flowers best when suitably moist soil can be provided. On a dry soil the flowering season is much shorter and less prolific. Recently the *sibirica* irises have been receiving attention from the hybridist, and many self-coloured cultivars have resulted, 'Perry's Blue' and 'Snow Queen' being two which attract my attention. The ultimate height depends on the moisture content of the soil, ranging from 60 cm to 1.2 m (2 to 4 ft).

Kentranthus

Kentranthus ruber (now *centranthus*), Red Valerian, may not be everyone's idea of a garden plant, but as an individualist with unique ability to take care of itself it has few equals, with the possible exception of that other lovely plant, the dandelion. One example of its adaptability can be found in an old vicarage garden near Darlington, where it has firmly established itself in the cracks of and along the top of a 4.5 m (15 ft) high wall. Here the glaucous leaves and bright red flowers are seen to advantage against the grey of the stone. There are both white and pink forms, and a handful of seed scattered in any barren or dry place difficult to furnish with anything else, is all that is needed to start a colony. From then onwards self-sown seedlings will ensure no further lack of stock.

Kirengeshoma

Kirengeshoma palmata advertises its Japanese ancestry immediately the blooms open. The pale yellow flowers appear in late August, and need a dark background to show their full beauty. On a suitably moist, humus-rich soil growth will reach 1.2 m (4 ft). Propagation is effected by seed or division, but seed ripens sufficiently only in exceptional summers in this garden, for usually a mid-September frost kills the stems before their work can be fully completed.

Kniphofia

Red Hot Pokers are not generally regarded as easy plants, and I agree that the vast majority have a dislike of cold, wet soils. The main trouble seems to be moisture gathering in the crown of the plant during winter.

The Red Hot Pokers show a distinct preference for a well drained, modestly fertile soil and a south-facing border, though there are some which albeit reluctantly will accept a partially shaded site. Certainly in my experience planting is best carried out in spring as the soil begins to warm up. In my last garden a stock of *Kniphofia tuckii* seedlings belied their South African origins by actually flourishing in the mixture of yellow clay and topsoil which was left after laying an electricity supply to the greenhouse. The yellow tinged scarlet flowers on 1.2 m (4 ft) high stems are a feature in July and August. *K. uvaria* is another survivor in adversity, and the first Red Hot Poker to be introduced to this country early in the 18th century. Of the hybrids, 'Atlanta', scarlet and yellow torch flowers in June, and 'Royal Standard', of a similar shade in July, are of note.

Liatris

Liatris spicata I again grew from seed, having some doubts as to its reaction to our northern climate. The doubts proved unfounded, and from strong 60 cm (2 ft) high rosettes of leaves come, in July to September, stiff spikes of mauve-lilac flowers. The unusual habit the plants have of opening their flowers from top to bottom of the spike led me to believe they must have Yorkshire blood in their ancestry; this is not the case, hailing as they do from moist waterways in eastern and southern U.S.A. They have so far forgotten their predilection for moisture in their native habitat as positively to enjoy the much drier soil of the ordinary herbaceous border.

Lysimachia

Lysimachia punctata is an alien which has naturalized itself in various parts of the country. I use it in a part of the garden which had proved difficult to furnish, but now, with a background of hydrangea and the lysimachia in the foreground, the bed is well filled with colour. In a rich soil it is a land hog, and only complete banishment will cure the plant's invasive properties. The flowers appear on stiff spikes 76 cm to 1 m (30 in to 3 ft) high from June to September, and are a good clean bright yellow. Propagation offers no problems; in fact, there is always a surplus of plants for presentation to friends who admire the starry yellow flowers. *L. vulgaris* will rejoice in the moister parts of the garden, but having seen the rapid spread in districts where it is really happy, I hesitate to introduce it to any but the roughest parts of the bog garden. Where suitable space can be spared, Yellow Loosestrife, with erect branching spikes of yellow flowers, spotted orange, makes a warm patch of colour during July and August. A few dry sprigs burned in a room are said to clear away the flies.

Lythrum

Lythrums are excellent plants for the water-side, flowering as they do when the full beauty of astilbe and primula has passed. They will endure the less moist conditions of the normal herbaceous border, but do not give of their best in a dry season. Rainy weather will ensure a good display.

The type plant, *Lythrum salicaria*, is a native of the British Isles, and is better known by the common name of Purple Loosestrife. On St John's Day the witches of Russia are said to be fully occupied in searching for and destroying the roots of this herb, as a plant bitterly hostile to all their dark machinations. The garden cultivars are more desirable for general cultivation, of these 'The Beacon' at 1 m (3 ft) has bright rose-red flowers, and 'Lady Sackville' has deep magenta, and they are the best I have tried. The spikes are bushy, and well filled with flowers which appear in late July to early September. Propagation of named cultivars is effected by division of the crowns in early spring.

Macleaya

Macleaya cordata is a handsome herbaceous perennial of stately growth, sculptured glaucous or greyish lobed leaves, and feathery panicles of cream-coloured flowers in July and August. Some years ago I planted a group of this Plume Poppy with three plants of the tall pampas grass as a bold isolated bed in a lawn against a sombre background of yew. Here the elegance of growth could be enjoyed and was especially lovely when lit from the side by the westering sun. They are said not to enjoy heavy soils, but so far the only complaint I have against them is not of weakness but of excessive virility: in five years they have taken rather more than their fair share of the herbaceous border.

Propagation is by division of the roots in spring, or by cuttings made of the cauliflower-like shoots which grow around the base of mature stems. These will root readily in a sandy compost in June or July. Seeds when obtainable germinate easily from a spring sowing – the plants here do not produce seed with any freedom.

Meconopsis

Poppies of the genus *Meconopsis* can never be classed as plants for any garden or soil, but here they have proved themselves over the years to be first class, and are much admired when in bloom. Some are thought to be monocarpic, though there is some doubt on this point, but they set seeds so freely that there is no problem in assuring a continuity. However, the perennial species do make a permanent contribution and thus fall within the scope of this book *M. betonicifolia* from upper Burma, Tibet, and Yunnan is a plant of variable character. Over the years I have had strains which proved truly perennial, others which were stubbornly biennial. The colour of the flowers also varies between a beautiful clear sky blue, and a rather magenta-lavender. The best method of acquiring a healthy colony with the right coloured flowers is to raise them from seed, or by seeing plants in flower before buying. I prefer the former method and rigorously rogue all those which do not come up to standard. In this way a true-breeding strain is eventually evolved, and will give endless pleasure over the years. Give the young plants a humus-rich soil. I work the land with deep litter from chicken houses the winter before a spring planting, and in due season the 1.2 m (4 ft) stems appear with flowers on long stalks from the upper leaf axils.

The right setting is essential. Planted in drifts in open woodland, or with ferns and lilies in a shady part of the garden, they will make a picture breathtaking in beauty.

Meconopsis cambrica is the only member of the genus native to this country. I once in all innocence planted it in the rock garden here, and since then I have waged total war unto the tenth generation; each year, though progress is made, I succeed only in reducing the numbers to manageable proportions. The double-flowered form can be welcomed for the well-behaved plant it is. The leaves are grey-green, deeply cut, and the flowers vary in shades of orange or yellow on 45 to 60 cm (18 to 24 in) stems. By some trick of nature, the double forms do on occasions set seed but the resultant offspring may be single flowered and should be expelled on sight.

Meconopsis grandis is a true perennial and can be propagated either by seed or by cuttings of sideshoots in early summer. A soil well laced with peat or well-rotted compost will ensure adequate moisture during the growing season. Flowers are carried on 1 m (3 ft stems in June-July, and in the best strains are a deep, almost metallic blue. All plants from Nepal, Sikkim, and Tibet have a particular attraction, especially if one reads the plant hunters' descriptions of them growing by the acre in their natural habitat.

Where possible I like to grow *M. grandis* with candelabra primula in bays amongst rhododendrons, for it is in the company of such plants of the Himalayas that it looks truly at home.

Meconopsis quintuplinervia is another native of Tibet and Western China, but compared to the other species mentioned, a veritable pygmy, growing only 38 cm (15 in) high. The best setting, of course, is in the moister parts of the rock garden with gentians and ferns. The nodding blue stems are not produced with profligate freedom, but for all that are well worth the trouble of cultivation. When suited, growth is rapid and spreading, making division in the spring the best means of increase. Seed sown fresh is an alternative method, with the added excitement that the flowers might be of deeper colouring. This plant is always linked in my mind with that father of rock gardening, Reginald Farrer, whose descriptions of flowers in the wild have given me endless pleasure.

Mimulus

I first remember seeing *Mimulus luteus* as a wild plant on the edge of a moorland stream in Baldersdale. Whether a garden escape or no I could not be certain, but it looked so lovely I went back later in the year to collect seed to sow on the banks of the stream which runs through the rock garden. The result was a positive jungle of yellow flowers, carried on 45 cm (18 in) stems over a solid carpet of hard green leaves. After a few seasons equilibrium has been reached, and now the plant is just pleasantly noticeable without being possessive. *M. cupreus* is very like *luteus* but dwarfer in habit, reaching only 30 cm (12 in). Certainly it will stand much drier conditions. In my childhood it grew in a solid mass along the dry border in front of our neighbour's house. Ten years after leaving the district I wrote and asked for seed, but was sent instead a large box full of healthy seedlings. These are safely installed and flourishing with equal vigour in the rock garden here. The flowers are a deep velvet crimson, yellow in the throat. Propagation is easy once the colony is established, by simple division.

I am always on the lookout for plants of this sort which have grown in cottage gardens for years. The owners are usually eager to talk about their treasures, and many a story can be woven round the ones cultivated for generations on a single plot.

Myosotis

Myosotis alpestris, the plant now commonly known as Forget-me-not, has a dozen different legends, romantic and otherwise, woven round the name. In the sixteenth century when a countryman spoke of the Forget-me-not he referred to the Ground Pine or ajuga. Anyone who wonders why, should do as I did. On advice from a botanist friend I tasted the leaves; the flavour still lingers after 15 years. The name myosotis leaves no room for confusion between the genera, which is justification enough for the botanical name as opposed to the popular or anglicised variety.

This is an extremely variable plant, but all the forms have beauty, except in my opinion those with flowers of pale magenta. My most pleasant memory of Forget-me-nots is of seeing them making a misty blue haze in an old orchard near Richmond, and planted in bold drifts through them were the lovely pheasants-eye narcissus. The whole picture was incomparably lovely: grey stems of apple trees, each twig covered in pink blossom, carpeted beneath with azure blue and white. A quiet place to spend a spring day, fortunately growing more beautiful with each passing year. The species in this case was possibly *alpestris*, but as the original seed came from a seedsman and was not collected, it would be impossible to be certain.

When a new colony is required in my garden I just scatter a handful of seeds on to the soil raked down to a fine tilth, then await my pleasure the following May.

Nepeta

Popularly known as Catmint, nepeta has passed into malodour of recent years, but really the blame should be laid only at the door of *N. mussinii*, for it is this species which seeds with gay abandonment around the garden. *N.* × *faassenii* is quite sterile, and in the arduous conditions of the windswept herbaceous border here is anything but the rampant weed it is reported to be on lighter soils. I like to see large quantities amongst the old shrub roses, where the silver-grey leaves and pale lavender flowers associate so well the various pink shades of the roses.

Oenothera

Everyone has a favourite time for walking around the garden; I have two, dawn and dusk, but if a choice between them were forced on me then it would be sundown I should take. To get the maximum enjoyment some plantings would have to be specially made of those flowers which rely on the night-flowering insects to accomplish fertilization, opening their blossoms as the light fades. *Oenothera missouriensis* does give colour during the day, but it is in the half light that I enjoy this plant the most, when the lemon flowers shine with a strangely attractive luminosity. The stems spread close to the ground, so it is better at the front of the border or in the rock garden. Individual flowers are large, some measured were 10 cm (4 in) across. The season varies, but there is usually colour from June until August. I have had one group for several years in a rather unkind clay patch in the rock garden, but there is no doubt that given a well-drained bed in full sun this Evening Primrose responds with an even greater profusion of bloom.

Division in spring, or cuttings inserted in a sandy soil, offer fairly ready means of increase, but where seed is obtainable this is the method I should choose as the most reliable.

Osmunda

Ferns are an essential part of the garden landscape, for they bring lightness and grace to the picture, as well as possessing the additional merit of fronds which colour yellow and bronze in the autumn. Were it not for the fact that the Royal Fern, *Osmunda regalis,* puts up with the rough and tumble of the woodland garden, both here and in several other gardens I have visited recently, without giving ground, I would hesitate to include it in a book

Opposite: Herbaceous peonies and bearded irises are the very essence of an English garden in early summer

of this sort. The plant's elegance is completely belied by its toughness, a fact I am grateful for. A soil constantly moist is essential to their well-being, and they grow with the candelabra primula and astilbe in the wetter parts of the woodland. The fronds in this garden do not develop to the majestic 2 m (6 ft) that they reach in more southern climates: 1 to 1.2 m (3 to 4 ft) would be a fair average. The fertile pinnules develop into a curious panicle late in the season, dark brown in colour in contrast to the yellow of the fronds.

Division in spring has proved a method of increasing colonies, and this is best carried out just as the 'swan necks' of the young growths break the crowns. They take some years to recover after transplanting, and rather than risk losses it is advisable for the less experienced gardener to buy in when extending the plantings.

Pachysandra

Pachysandras have only one virtue in the garden and that is the ability to colonize positions of almost complete shade under trees. They have bright shiny evergreen leaves and are easily propagated by splitting up established plants in spring.

Paeonia

The history of the genus *Paeonia* alone would fill a book, should anyone find the time to accumulate the wealth of legend and romance which has been woven around it. Pliny even goes as far as to call it the oldest of all plants, but on what authority I do not know. In my garden there is a young plant taken as a layer from a patriarchal specimen in a garden near Pickering, known to be at least 108 years old. The plant is said to be possessed of great healing properties, and indeed, takes its name from Paeon, first physician to the gods.

Paeonia lactiflora, introduced in 1784 by a Russian and then in 1805 by Banks, has given rise, so the authorities on the subject write, to many beautiful garden forms introduced from China from the early part of the 19th century. Since then, of course, the European hybrid-

ists have worked hard to improve on the original varieties available, with considerable success. A glance through any specialist's catalogue will show what a great number there are to choose from. 'Sarah Bernhardt', clear pink; 'Kelway's Glorious' white and fragrant; 'Bowl of Beauty', cherry red with a cream central boss of stamens; and 'Karl Rosenfield', wine red, are all excellent.

Seed is the easy way to increase stocks of the species, but it should be taken only from parents selected for the quality of their flowers. Named forms are increased by division.

Of all this beautiful genus, *Paeonia mlokosewitschii* is my particular favourite. Not only is it first to flower in this garden, but from the glaucous-green leaves to the primrose yellow flowers, 13 to 15 cm (5 to 6 in) across, it is a breathtaking sight when in full bloom. Compared to the species already described this is a dwarf, only 38 to 45 cm (15 to 18 in) high. The flowers appear in May, rather later than in other more sheltered gardens. Propagation, as with other species, is by seed. A word of warning when sowing seed of any peony; make certain the mice cannot gain access to them or nothing will be left but the empty husks.

Paeonia veitchii woodwardii is an even dwarfer plant than *P. mlokosewitschii*. The habit is so neat, the leaves so finely and deeply cut, that I like to grow my plants amongst the dwarf shrubs on the outskirts of the rock garden. The ultimate height is only a modest 30 cm (12 in) and the flowers are a fine, soft rose-pink. There are certain plants which once seen can never be forgotten, and this has certainly been the case with the white-flowered form of *woodwardii* which I saw for the first and last time in a famous Northumberland garden. Should any reader have the good fortune to be offered a dainty, white-flowered peony with a central boss of scarlet stamens, do not enquire into its parentage. Take the parcel carefully, and with suitable reverence plant it in a place of honour, then ever afterwards pay homage at the shrine.

Seed offers a means of increase, but whether the bees were to blame or not, some of my seedlings had flowers of a rather unpleasant magenta. Fortunately those which lost caste in such a light-hearted manner can always be given to less popular garden visitors.

Papaver

Papaver alpinum completely captivated me when I saw it growing in a scree some four thousand feet up on a mountain-side in France. I spent a fruitless 90 minutes waiting to take a picture, but so lightly are the petals poised on the delicate stem that the slightest breeze set them in motion. Eventually I arose at 4.30 a.m., on a glorious June morning, and my sacrifice was rewarded with one good and two mediocre slides. The flowers are said to be either yellow or white, but I have seen orange and pale pink colouring in places where it would be difficult for them to have formed an alliance with any of its Icelandic brethren.

The easiest way to start a colony is to sow a pinch of seed in any sunny position, provided the soil is well drained. Once established the seedlings look after themselves. Sow a pinch of *Linaria alpina* at the same time; the two belong together.

So much is said about special composts, that were gardeners to carry out all the instructions they would get nothing done but mixing soil. I always assume the plant has a catholic taste in this matter, coupled with a firm determination to live at all costs, and this, plus an occasional word of encouragement from me, is all the permanent plantings in this garden seem to need.

Papaver orientale and its many varieties have languished in the horticultural shadows during recent years. Possibly my affection for these brilliant flowers is partly coloured by sentiment; my memories of a double herbaceous border between a row of flowering cherries in a Yorkshire Dales garden, where so much artistry was given to provide a proper setting to the many plants which grew. Be that as it may, I enjoy Oriental Poppies, which have only a brief moment of glory, but how gay they are in that short while!

They need a soil with reasonable drainage, but apart from that make no special demands. In this garden the groups are planted in bays in the shrub borders, and do not require sticks to hold them erect. Of the cultivars I have grown, 'Allegro' with large bright orange-scarlet flowers, 'Sultana', pink, and 'Marcus Perry', an orange-scarlet, are all good perennials. Propagation offers no problems, rather the reverse when the plants are happy, for every piece of cut root will grow.

Phlomis

Phlomis samia has powers of recuperation which are quite remarkable. I had occasion to move some plants from one part of the garden, which was being used as a nursery, to make way for an extension to the rock garden. The phlomis were dug out and put out of the way under some lilac bushes to await their turn to be planted. In the rush of work they were overlooked and stayed unplanted right through the following summer – a shocking piece of mismanagement. The oversight was rectified in October, and the following spring all grew away as if nothing had happened. This shows how extremely tough this plant is.

With the increasing demand for unusual shapes to use in flower arrangement, *Phlomis samia* has regained a lost popularity. The heart-shaped leaves and candelabra type flower spike, greenish-cream, arranged in whorls at intervals up the stem, make a pleasing, albeit unusual picture. In an average season the overall height is somewhere in the region of 1 m (3 ft), the flowers appearing in June. As with other flowers carrying a hint of green in their composition, the right background is important to get the best result. In this instance one of the red-leaved berberis or Japanese maples have proved adequate to the task.

Seeds sown in October out of doors or division of the plants in spring enables the stock to be increased at a fairly rapid rate.

Phlox

From the rock garden through to the herbaceous and annual border the genus *Phlox* plays an important part. Who, seeing a bed of *Phlox paniculata* hybrids in full glory of colour, could doubt the wisdom of Theophrastus when he chose the name for them which so aptly describes the flame flowers?

Some of the alpine species require careful handling to survive, and are better left to the enthusiastic gardener who enjoys the challenge to his skill in cultivation. There are, however, members of this very beautiful family which ask only the bare necessities to make a brave contribution to the summer garden of flowers.

Phlox douglasii, a native of Western North America, is a dwarf of the race, only reaching a modest 15 cm (6 in) in height. Both the type plant and the varied forms of it are excellent for the windswept parts of the garden, provided a well-drained soil can be made available. The dwarf stature in no way inhibits either the quality or quantity of the flowers which come from late May right through to early August. A choice can be made from *Phlox douglasii* 'Boothman' with mauve flowers; *rosea,* pink; 'May Snow' with dazzling white blossom; or 'Margery' with lavender-blue flowers.

Compared with the peonies, *Phlox paniculata* is a plant of relatively recent introduction; a mere 234 years or so. In spite of its youth it would be difficult to imagine a herbaceous border without the brilliant flowers and sweet scent, so pronounced in the evening. The range of colours to choose from has been vastly extended over recent years, and includes salmon, red, pink, violet, and blue-grey. I have no doubt in due course it will be extended to include a true yellow and a blue which are not yet available.

When I asked a famous breeder's advice on growing phlox some 12 years ago, he answered with the question of whether I had my potato land ready, if so to plant them there; a humus-rich soil retentive of moisture is the thing to aim at. Failing farmyard manure, peat

makes an excellent substitute, creating that puffy soil texture these plants thrive on.

There is one great snag to growing phlox, and that is their susceptibility to infestation by the stem eelworm. The presence of this pest is indicated by the leaves becoming narrow and twisted, swelling and then turning yellow; the stems are stunted and split. Only by lifting in winter and making cuttings of the thicker roots about 8 cm (3 in) long can this pest be circumvented. They are inserted in a compost of loam, peat and sand, and then covered with a further layer of the same material. Young plants raised in this way provide clean, pest-free stock which can be planted in a different part of the garden. Some cultivars are much less susceptible to eelworm than others, and the following have proved themselves resistant in this garden: 'Balmoral', light clear pink, 60 to 75 cm (24 to 30 in), 'Border Gem', purple, 75 cm (30 in); 'Hampton Court', heliotrope, 60 cm (24 in); 'Pastorale', pink, 75 cm (30 in); 'Windsor', carmine, 75 cm (30 in); and 'Starfire', deep red, 75 cm (30 in). No border would be complete without phlox, but they will not stand a dry soil and care should be taken to ensure adequate moisture. Planted in bays down a shrub border, and well mulched, they will go four or five years without division.

Phlox subulata and all the cultivars listed from it must again be named a dwarf amongst giants, only growing 10 to 15 cm (4 to 6 in) in height. For the top of a low wall or in any position which guarantees good drainage, no matter how exposed, this handsome species will give colour for several weeks. When a suitable place is provided, the plants rapidly fill in to cover the space allocated to them. Three reliable cultivars to make a beginning with are: 'G. F. Wilson,' bright blue; 'Temiscaming', a warm carmine-red; and 'Vivid', a good pink. Propagation is effected by nodal cuttings, or pull-offs, taken with a heel of old stem in July or early August. These root readily in a cold frame.

Phlox subulata, ideal for the top of a low wall

Phormium

Phormium cookianum (P. colensoi) is a New Zealander which at first I thought would be a problem on this heavy clay. For 10 years it has grown with quiet contentment in a wet cold corner of the herbaceous border, but this acceptance of a northern garden is not complete for as yet it has made no attempt to flower. The evergreen, tough, leathery leaves are attractive enough to warrant at least a trial planting, especially near a stream or pond against a background of astilbe or primula. A rich, loamy, moist soil is essential.

Propagation can be achieved by seed sown in a frame in spring, but this must be of the previous autumn's harvesting, because old seed loses viability rapidly. Well-furnished plants can be divided in spring before growth begins; new roots are soon formed if a little compost is worked round the base at planting time.

Physalis

I once made the mistake of planting *Physalis alkekengi* in a sheltered border close to a bed specially prepared for violets. The next three years were spent in fighting a losing battle to stop the plant taking over the whole border. Eventually I won the war by using a flame gun on the bed at fortnightly intervals. This plant is particularly interesting to the flower arranger, and as such warrants a small corner to itself.

Opposite: Oriental poppies, *Papaver orientale*, have only a brief moment of glory but make a brilliant display in a mixed border

During the summer the bed will present a rather bedraggled appearance, but as the foliage dies down the highly ornamental fruit make a bright patch in the garden. As the fruit ripens the inflated calyx turns bright orange and assumes the characteristic lantern shape from which the plant derives the popular name of Chinese Lantern. Left in the open these eventually become skeletonized, but if cut and dried in an airy shed, they make interesting material for winter flower arrangements. The fruit was at one time valued for its supposed medicinal qualities, being thought especially useful for those unfortunates who suffered from gout.

Cultivation and increase offer no problems, rather the reverse. Seed will germinate readily, or appreciation expressed to a friend who already has the plant usually results in several roots being pressed into the hand at the time of departure.

Polemonium

The genus *Polemonium* is again beginning to command attention, judging by the number of enquiries when the plants are in flower. Some of the species are not very long lived, but can be relied on to shed enough seed around them during their lives to ensure perpetuation of the species. Sometimes these chance seedlings turn up in the most unusual places, hundreds of yards away from the parent.

Polemonium caeruleum is a rather variable species which may be anything from 20 to 75 cm (8 to 30 in) tall, according to the soil. The bell-shaped flowers can be a pale milky blue or a deeper shade of the same colour. They bloom in early summer, usually late May to June and into July. Several varieties exist and can be used to extend the flowering season. *P. c. tanguticum* is a slender graceful plant which looks well with the glaucous-leaved veronica on the outskirts of the rock garden. *P. richardsonii* is the name of one late blossomer which I was given by a nurseryman acquaintance. The parent plant lived only three years, but in that time produced much seed.

In the seven years since is was acquired *P. pauciflorum* has coloured, in the most dignified manner, all corners of a fairly extensive rock garden. The 38 to 45 cm (15 to 18 in) stem carries solitary pale yellow flowers, and its fern-like leaves, too, are attractive. A free-draining soil seems to be the only requirement, while seed offers a ready means of increase.

Polemonium reptans 'Blue Pearl' is a good creeping plant which has made itself at home amongst the bulbs on the edge of the heather garden. Mulched every second year this cultivar is a more reliable perennial than the rest of the genus. The flowering season is from May to June and the bright blue contrasts well with a background of the yellow-flowered Spanish Gorse. Even in a fairly rich loam the overall height is never more than 30 cm (12 in).

Polygonum

These are usually classified as incorrigible bandits because of the bad reputation acquired by some of the more rampant species. There are three which I would certainly include in any garden where there was room to accommodate them. *Polygonum affine* is a mat-forming perennial about 23 cm (9 in) in height, and makes first-class ground cover either at the front of the herbaceous border, or amongst shrubs in an open sunny position. The dark green, leathery, spear-shaped leaves take on a bronzy hue in winter. The rosy-red flowers are carried on stiff 23 cm (9 in) spikes during late August and September.

Propagation is usually by division, or just cutting off and transplanting the spreading shoots when they venture beyond prescribed limits.

Polygonum campanulatum first reached me as a bonus in a wagon load of soil bought in to make up some terrace work. I noticed the grey-green leaves breaking through with the grass seed, and not recognizing them lifted them out for planting in the shrub border. From that one clump, in a matter of 10 years there are now three healthy colonies in the shrub borders and 14 in the woodland. I think it is amongst the light shade and grey stems of the silver birch that I like best to see the deep pink flowers. They are carried in clusters right through summer into autumn, but this is no plant for the small garden, being quite capable of holding its own against even strong-growing grass. The roots run only on the surface and are quite easy to chop out in mats. Ultimately *P. campanulatum* will make a rounded bush of 1.2 m (4 ft) in height, quite lovely when carrying a full complement of flowers.

A handsome little bandit from the Himalayas, *P. vaccinifolium*, is prostrate in habit. Reaching only 15 to 23 cm (6 to 9 in) high it is an excellent perennial for covering a sunny bank. The leaves are long and narrow at both ends, the flowers, produced in short spikes, are bright rose in the best forms, and appear in great profusion in September and October. Again propagation is by simple division in spring.

Polypodium

As I have mentioned before, ferns are, in my opinion, an essential to the garden scheme, and this genus and its varieties are excellent when planted in a cool, shady position. Those fortunate enough to possess a piece of open woodland have the ideal site; there the graceful evergreen fronds will brighten up the dull days of winter, especially in association with bamboos or rhododendrons.

Propagation is usually by division in spring, the individual portions being replanted in a moist, leafy soil. Shady corners in the garden can be made not only interesting, but truly beautiful, when forms of *Polypodium vulgare* are used with bulbs drifted amongst them. Snowdrops, bluebells, daffodils, Glory of the Snow, and crocus all gain added grace against a background of ferns.

Potentilla

The name potentilla is derived from the Latin *potens*, powerful, from the alleged medicinal properties of all parts of the plant. A herb of the sun, according to Culpeper the root seems possessed of the greatest virtue. It is a large genus which offers a wide selection of colourful varieties for use in gardens, and most of the family have a preference for a poor soil rather than a rich loam.

Potentilla atrosanguinea used to be listed as a variety of *P. argyrophylla*, but now by one of those inexplicable whims of the botanists, who rule the ultimate designation of all botanical names, it is given specific character in its own right. Whatever the name, this plant of loose sprawling habit looks charming in the front of a herbaceous border. The leaves are silvered, against which the blood red flowers, 4 cm (1½in) in diameter, look extremely well. The long-stalked palmate leaves reach 60 to 75 cm (2 to 2½ft) high.

One of the genus which has proved itself remarkably easy-going in the wilder parts of the rock garden is *P. fragiformis*. The three-lobed leaves are covered in silvery, silken hairs. Reputed to be rather parsimonious with its flowers, the strain here has either not been told about this characteristic of the race, or is so well contented that it has decided to ignore it, for there is no dearth of yellow flowers up to 4 cm (1½in) in diameter.

Seed is the best method of increase. I let the plants perform this natural operation for themselves, then collect the result of their labours when needed. Division is not a good idea as the large crowns do not readily form roots. Of compact habit, the overall height is rarely more than 20 to 30 cm (8 to 12 in).

Potentilla × tonguei is a plant of intriguing presence, the flowers being a pleasing combination of two colours: yellow, stained glowing crimson at the base. The individual blossoms are small, but make up in quantity what they lack in size. Allowed to sprawl on a dry bank or over a low wall it will attract attention through July to September.

As with so many other garden hybrids it would be a wise potentilla which knew its own father, or mother for that matter. The list of hybrid potentillas is fairly extensive, some very good garden value, provided a pedigree is not required, although the blood of *P. argyrophylla* can be seen in some of the red-flowered offspring. A choice can be made from 'Gibson's Scarlet' with fine red single flowers from June to August; 'Mons. Rouillard' with large deep red velvet flowers or, and this for me is the pick of the bunch, 'William Rollison' with flowers of vermilion-red, striped yellow.

Propagation is by crown cuttings in June or by division.

Primula

Well named *primus*, first in all respects, the primulas are a fascinating and lovely race. Within their ranks can be found temperamental species calling on all the skill a gardener can muster, but there are, too, easy-going varieties which have been well-loved garden inhabitants for centuries. I once became involved in the study of popular plant names, tracing them back through history wherever documentary evidence could be found; the Cowslip was one which gave me considerable interest. Few authorities give a definite definition, but suggest the Anglo Saxon Cúslyppe, for the plant was supposed to spring up round the patches of dung. Only the most easy going of the race warrant inclusion, and only those which have grown well in a wide variety of soils and situations.

Primula altaica or, as I believe it should now be called, *P. amoena*, and its cultivar 'Lingwood Beauty', has marked passage with me over years of gardening, and my hope is they will continue to do so. This plant has flowers of lavender-blue on 15 cm (6 in) stems, the leaves being typical primrose but rather spoon shaped. 'Lingwood Beauty' is identical except that the flowers are deep magenta.

Propagation is by division which should be carried out every three to four years, or the crowns deteriorate.

Primula auricula, for edging a shady border, or in any position where the soil is not excessively baked, is hard to beat. My father could properly be termed a primula enthusiast, and collected together a very representative collection of auriculas in pursuit of this interest, and I grew up, so to speak, not under a gooseberry bush but in the middle of a primula garden. The auriculas grew along a path edge which led from the tool shed to the herbaceous border and their colour and fragrance is still fresh in my memory after 20-odd years. The soil as I remember it was well prepared with well-rotted compost, then dressed each year with a mixture of the same material and peat.

The best way to start a collection is to sow a packet of mixed seed. I always liken this method to getting married, for one is never sure how the experiment is going to turn out, but, unlike taking a wife, if one does not like the result it can be consigned to the compost heap, or given away to a friend.

For those who prefer named cultivars 'Old Yellow Dusty Miller' has yellow scented flowers and the leaves are dusted with a meal-like substance called 'farina' in primulas. 'Blue Velvet' is well named and the blue is relieved by the white central eye. 'Jean Walker' is mauve and fragrant. 'W. Cook' is a cultivar I struggle with, but it does well in a friend's garden, and has red flowers. These named cultivars must be increased by cuttings to get young plants true to colour. Cuttings are made from leaf rosettes with a length of stalk attached, and rooted around the edge of a 13 cm (5 in) pot filled with sand.

The true *P. auricula* is an alpine, and hybridizing between this and several other species has resulted in some handsome, trouble-free cultivars which will be found, for want of a better place to put them, under the heading of *P. pubescens*.

Primula beesiana and *P. bulleyana* are moisture-loving species, but where a suitable soil can be provided, will rapidly colonize a wide area around the parent group. Some years ago I had occasion to plough up a large grass tract in rough woodland. As I am a firm believer in a rich soil for this type of primula, the land was heavily dressed with compost, and then planted with groups of species candelabra, more popularly called bog primulas. In the unplanted areas there is now a rich herbage of grass, but as the primulas colonize all available space, it is being rapidly reduced each year. These species at least are capable of looking after number one in the best modern tradition. *P. beesiana* has rosy carmine flowers on 60 cm (24 in) high stems, while *P. bulleyana* has deep orange flowers in June and July. Let due warning be given that one may plant true species in an excess of purist enthusiasm, but the first year's seedling will produce a very mixed, though altogether glorious band of hybrids.

Primula denticulata, with pompon globose flower heads, is a harbinger of spring which everyone seems to love. One of the best collections of the many colour forms of this plant I have ever seen were grown by an old lady in a narrow border along the front of her cottage, with no water nearer than the tap in her kitchen. She loved each one of the hundreds of plants, and this probably explains the vigour with which everything from peonies to primulas grew in that pleasant domain. They like a moisture-retentive soil and without it the flowers tend to be small, those of the type being pale purple with a yellow eye.

Again a mixed packet of seed is a good way to begin a collection, and from this will come a wide variety of colours from pale lavender through to rich glowing crimson. On a suitable soil the stems reach 20 to 30 cm (8 to 12 in), but as the seed ripens the stalk goes on elongating, to 60 cm (24 in), in some cases, so if seed is not required the heads should be removed. Selected colour forms are propagated by division after flowering.

Primula florindae is for me a plant of the waterside, even seeding down to grow in the actual stream bed. Most people will recognize it better by the popular name of Giant Cowslip, since the nodding yellow flowers on 1 m (3 ft) stems certainly bear a strong resemblance to those well-known herbs of English meadows. The flowers themselves are sweetly scented; an added enjoyment to a walk by the water on a July evening. They are easily grown from seed sown in February or immediately it is ripe.

Another easily grown candelabra is *P. japonica* with large cabbage-like leaves. Given a moist, rich, loamy soil it will successfully deal with any weeds which attempt to encroach on its territory. The species has purplish-red flowers on sturdy scapes 45 cm (18 in) high, but many forms with white, rose or purple flowers are available. This to me is one of the least desirable of the candelabras, as some of the colours have a washed-out look which is distinctly unpleasant under strong sunlight.

On the other hand, *P. pulverulenta* is a species of considerable character which has given rise to many fine hybrids. A bold group of mixed seedlings growing in moist, well-prepared loam in open woodland is a sight for any gardener to behold. The scapes have a slender grace not possessed by *P. japonica,* reaching 1 m (3 ft) in height. Flower colours vary from the deep red of the true species through all the colours one would associate with progeny resulting from a union between this and *P. bulleyana* or *P. beesiana.* Cross-pollination between the candelabras mentioned is usual when the species are grown in close proximity.

Division of the clumps, or seed sown in February, are the two methods of building up a large collection of healthy youngsters.

Primula rosea is not a plant for any situation, but so well does it grow on pond or stream side, and so lovely are the bright rose flowers in early spring, that no garden which can provide this kind of accommodation should be without it. A little bed on the edge of a stream, gay with double marsh marigolds, *P. denticulata* and *P. rosea* under an April sky, is a sight to lift the spirits. There is a freshness about this picture, which recurs annually on the streamside in this garden and which encourages me to waste valuable hours each spring-

A waterside planting of candelabra primulas and *Iris pseudacorus*

time. However, of what use is a garden of flowers, if no time can be spent in contemplation of their beauty? Had we to spend all our days hoe in hand, eyes to the earth, with no thought for the beauty around, then we should be at one with the slugs which made a meal of petal or bud, and see no more than a means of assuaging the pangs of an empty belly.

Seed sown when fresh germinates readily. or the plants may be divided after flowering, when they re-establish themselves very quickly. For the connoisseur the hybrid 'Delight', with brilliant carmine-red flowers, is especially desirable and can usually be obtained from specialist nurseries.

Our own native Primrose, *Primula vulgaris,* is the best loved of a genus rich in beautiful flowers. Strange that a plant which grows in riotous profusion in so many woodland glades should prove difficult when brought into the confines of the garden! So far as I am concerned this only adds to the attraction of this little moon flower, and is an excuse to visit the woodlands where it really is happy. The places which seem most acceptable to it are tall hazel groves just on the limestone belt. The soil when I tested samples just bordered on neutral. The coloured forms are less intolerant of the hand of the gardener, and, coming readily from seed as they do, play an important part in the spring scene. White flowering cherries, carpeted underneath with coloured primroses and spring bulbs, give excuse enough to lean idly on a fork in quiet contemplation. After all, one must enjoy the garden to the full.

Pulmonaria

Pulmonaria angustifolia is an easy-going species in any moist soil, and remains just as good natured when grown in shade. When first open the flowers are pink, and then as they mature become bright blue. My particular favourite is the variety 'Munstead Blue' which begins to flower in early April and continues through May. The blossom is a deep but very bright blue, a useful colour amongst the yellow of spring bulbs. It varies in height from 20 to 45 cm (8 to 18 in) depending on the soil. Propagation is easily effected by division of the clumps in early spring.

Introduced from Northern Europe, *P. officinalis* – Lungwort or Jerusalem Cowslip – has naturalized itself in some districts of Southern England. Linnaeus, the father of botany, christened the plant 12 divinities, supposedly because of the 12 reversed pink flowers. Certainly the Lungwort has long been grown in gardens where the white spotted leaves gave rise to the fallacy that it was a remedy for diseased lungs. In shade the spotted character of the leaves loses some of its brilliance, and there is less freedom of flowering. Rather coarser in habit than *P. angustifolia,* it is some 45 to 50 cm (18 to 20 in) in height, with the flowers a rather insipid pink at first, turning blue later. Propagation is again easily accomplished by division of established plants.

Pulsatilla

Pulsatilla vulgaris, the Pasque Flower, is an absolute treasure, and fortunate are those who have seen the plant, alas now increasingly rare, growing wild in the hills of Oxfordshire and Cambridge. This plant is lovely in all its parts, the delicate grey-green, deeply cut leaves cupping the deep purple chalices of the flower which open to show the golden crown of stamens within. When all this loveliness is thought to be ended for another year, come the long silver silken tassels of the seed-head to bring beauty in maturity. The flowers are at their best in April and May, the height ranging from 25 to 45 cm (10 to 18 in).

Pulsatilla vulgaris is lovely in all its parts

A well-drained soil, but not liable to dry out excessively during drought, is ideal and as the plants strongly resent being disturbed, care should be taken to ensure they have enough room to live. The best method of increase is by means of seed sown immediately it is ripe.

Of the many good forms available the strongest I have found are 'Red Clock', the colour heightened by the rich gold of the stamens, and *rubra,* whose stamens lack the newly minted colour of the former, thus lessening the picture. *Pulsatilla vulgaris* 'Budapest' I cannot quite have suited, probably because a select place was chosen for it away from its companions. The blue colouring of the petals is exquisitely delicate, and, as I have seen strong healthy specimens in other gardens close at hand, venture to include it here. I shall replant it close to its relatives, not in splendid isolation with preferential treatment.

Pulsatilla alpina sulphurea is now *P. alpina apiifolia,* a victim of the fashion of name changing. It has rather cup-shaped flowers 5 cm (2 in) across, in the best forms a deep, almost golden-yellow. Seedlings should be pot-grown for intolerance of root disturbance increases with age.

Ranunculus

Ranunculus aconitifolius I include because in this soil no trouble has so far been experienced in persuading it to flourish; indeed, persuade is hardly the right word. Usually it takes two years to prepare a bed for planting in our woodland. The first year after digging

Rodgersia aesculifolia associates well with ornamental grasses

the whole area stands in water, and time must elapse for the soil structure to reach some sort of stability. One such bed in the open part of the woodland was planted with astilbe, bamboo, and the ranunculus, and these settled in so well that in the course of years they have provided material to establish other colonies with equal success. In this garden they need a moist soil at all times, and where possible light shade to develop full beauty.

The name Fair Maids of France is probably an association with the Huguenot refugees who supposedly introduced the first plants to this country in the early 17th century. In cottage gardens, where it grew with great freedom and vigour, the popular name, indeed the only name I knew it by for many years, was White Bachelor's Buttons. In towns the pure whiteness of the flowers is lost under grime, and in many cases the resentment of pollution is such that death results. The height varies from 25 to 60 cm (10 to 24 in), and the leaves are deeply lobed, the branching flower stems being covered in May with double, round, button flowers each 1 to 2 cm (½ to ¾ in) across. It is remarkable that a plant once so popular is rarely listed by nurserymen. Once acquired, stock can be increased by division of the roots in early spring, or failing this after flowering. Make sure the roots are not allowed to dry out when lifting and dividing the plants.

Rheum

Few people realized, until the increasing interest in flower arranging created a demand for plants with unusual leaves, just how effective this member of the rhubarb family could be both in the herbaceous border and at the waterside. The rounded leaves are deeply lobed, especially in *Rheum palmatum tanguticum,* and in good soils plants reach 1.5 m (5 ft) in height, creating amongst primula and astilbe that change in leaf character essential in any well-planned landscape. The deep red flowers are carried in large panicles, and excite considerable comment in late June and early July.

When it is desired to start another colony, take up the parent plant and cut it up so that each piece has a crown bud, precisely as one would treat the culinary rhubarb.

Rodgersia

Rodgersias are best on the waterside or in moist woodland and will thrive only when sheltered from high winds. Given this shelter and a moist soil they will hold their own against grass, nettles, and most other weeds. As the name implies *Rodgersia aesculifolia* has leaves very like a larger edition of the horse chestnut, and will make from 1 to 1.5 m (3 to 5 ft) depending on the situation. In June to July the white flowers are carried in clusters on tall stems. *R. pinnata* is smaller, only 60 cm to 1.2 m (2 to 4 ft) in height, with pinnate leaves, the individual leaflets being 15 to 20 cm (6 to 8 in) long. A variable species, but those in this garden have flowers which are red outside and white within, and they make an attractive picture when in full bloom, usually in mid-July.

Propagation is by seed or division.

Rudbeckia

Rudbeckias, natives of North America, do not appeal to everyone, but as they are easy to grow in most garden soils which do not dry out readily, they are worthy of inclusion. *Rudbeckia fulgida* ranges in height from 30 cm to 1 m (1 to 3 ft) or more. It has slightly spoon-shaped leaves, and the flowers which appear in July are rather thin petalled, orange-yellow, with a central disc of dark purple. Possibly the best known of the family is *R. speciosa,* with its coarsely-toothed lower leaves and long narrow upper ones. Then in August come the deep orange flowers with an attractive central boss of purple-black stamens.

My favourite of this not very exciting family is *R.* 'Goldsturm'. It has much larger flowers than any of the others mentioned; they are deep rich orange and appear from mid-July to October. I had this plant as *Rudbeckia sullivantii* 'Goldsturm', and on moist soil it makes a modest 60 to 75 cm (2 to 2½ft). Propagation is by seed for the species, by division for the cultivar last described.

Herbaceous Plants:
Salvia to Veronica

———————❀———————

Salvias, from the Latin *salveo,* to heal, have long been cultivated in the gardens of this country. I have a great affection for the shrubby as well as the herbaceous species, each making a particular contribution to the interest of the borders. Unfortunately, some are only short-lived perennials, others need the protection of a heated greenhouse to survive, and only two have proved their easy-going nature to my satisfaction.

Of fairly recent introduction, *Salvia superba* is a true perennial. Possessed of the grey-green aromatic foliage characteristic of the better known shrubby members of the genus, it does well in any soil of reasonable quality. In July and August the flowers bloom on erect branching spikes. The individual flowers are small, violet coloured with just a hint of red, but are carried in such profusion as to give the plant a well-furnished appearance. The height varies appreciably, but is usually between 50 and 75 cm (20 and 30 in).

Under the same heading must be grouped two more excellent herbaceous sages. *S. s.* 'East Friesland' is a smaller edition of the parent, but with brighter flowers and greyer leaves. To get the best from the delicate colouring a background of variegated foliage is essential. I use *Scrophularia nodosa* 'Variegata', whose cream-coloured leaves are just the right shade to complement those of the salvia. Of all the sages my choice is *S. s.* 'Lubeca', inheriting all the grace of the parent with bluer flowers. In the late summer the dead florets take on a chestnut colouring, in itself quietly pleasing. This habit of certain herbaceous plants of donning autumn livery, albeit subdued in tone, is often overlooked, or lost completely, if the gardener makes a fetish of neatness by clipping the borders over too early.

Those people who enjoy arranging flowers are well aware of the beauty of the sage in autumn, and use the dead flower heads with more vivid leaves from the shrub borders.

There are other excellent garden plants within the ranks of the sages, but these I have found are either short-lived on a cold soil, or naturally biennial in character and so must be left out of any list of tough characters.

Sanguisorba
The name sanguisorba is derived from *sanguis,* blood, though it is not derived from any colouring of the sap, but from its styptic qualities, as the latter part of the name explains; *sorbere* – soaking up or absorbing. These are plants for the moister parts of the garden, and compete well with the coarse grasses of the open woodland. *S. obtusa* has pink, fluffy, bottle-brush heads of flowers from late June through to mid-August, and there is a white form. Planted amongst ferns or grass the arching 1 m (3 ft) stems look most handsome.

The native *S. officinalis* adapts itself readily to garden conditions. With only 60 cm (2 ft) stems, the brownish-red flower heads are not of a shade which makes immediate appeal. However, where room permits a few roots may be included. Stock can be increased by division or by seed sown in early spring.

Saponaria
The juice of the leaves of *Saponaria officinalis* forms a lather with water, and like the soap from which the name is taken, has the power to dissolve grease. Helvetius, in the *Doctrine of Plant Signatures*, lists it under the hands and nerves, which seems fair enough at all events.

Some of the double forms are plea-

Opposite: The stately verbascums look really at home in cottage gardens

A scree is needed for *Saxifraga burseriana*

sant, but even these tend to be too invasive. In case of soap rationing, and just to have a plant with the common name of Bouncing Bet, a place should be found for one or two of the double-flowered forms. The other common name, Goodbye to Summer, is something of a slur on the plant's character, for the flowers are in evidence from July to September. The height varies from 30 cm to 1 m (12 to 36 in) depending on the soil, but it will be a very brave man indeed who gives Bouncing Bet her head in rich loam.

Satureia

This, the herb supposedly of the satyrs, and to be avoided by expectant mothers, was nevertheless much esteemed by the Romans as a flavouring for sauces. The Summer Savory, *Satureia hortensis,* is an annual, and as such must take second place to *S. montana,* the Winter Savory. There are some plants that we grow in our gardens not possessed of the fiery, opulent, sometimes oppressive, beauty which characterises the more popular denizens of the border, which over the years quietly win a firm place in the affection of the people who grow them, and so it is with Winter Savory. Were someone to ask why I treasured my small colony, it would be extremely difficult to give a logical reason. Maybe it is the neat semi-evergreen habit, or the richly aromatic leaves, or the slender panicles of pale purple flowers which come each year in August. I think it is a combination of all these virtues, linked with a good tempered, easy-going disposition which endears *S. montana* to me. Shrubby in character, in truth it should be included in another part of the book, but a plant of such modesty might be lost in the shrub section. Reaching only 30 cm (12 in) in height, it is easy in any freely drained soil.

Saxifraga

The rock breakers, as saxifrage literally means, offer little to the seeker after self-sufficiency, for excellent though so many are in the rock garden, they could hardly be classed as easy plants for difficult places. For the treasures like *Saxifraga burseriana* and *S. hostii,* screes must be built or rock crevices provided for their delight, as otherwise they will sit in a sullen discontent dreaming, no doubt, of windswept mountains. The same may be said of the two most lovely of all this wonderful genus, namely *S. oppositifolia* and *S. retusa;* the rock garden with tender solicitude must, unfortunately, be their chosen lot.

Two saxifrages are capable of standing on their own vigour. *S. fortunei* has large leathery leaves, glossy green above, reddish-brown beneath, with loose panicles of creamy-white flowers on 45 cm (18 in) stems. A cool shady position with ferns and dwarf astilbes suits them very well, and the flowers take on an elfin charm when surrounded by the more formidable blue trumpets of *Gentiana sino-ornata*. As I said before, the latter demands an acid soil, but not so *S. fortunei*. Increase is effected by division of the plants in September, the pieces being potted in a peaty compost for planting out in the open ground in spring.

Better known as London Pride or None-so-pretty, *S.* × *urbium* grows wild in parts of Yorkshire, proof enough of its ability to look after number one. The rosettes of leaves are evergreen, and the dainty sprays of pale pinkish-red flowers on 38 to 50 cm (15 to 20 in) stems lighten the darker corners of the garden, for the plant grows best in shade. This, I think, is one of the least appreciated members of the genus, but given a little attention and a dressing of compost or leafmould, the reward will be a myriad of handsome plumes in early summer.

Division after flowering, or seed, are suitable methods of propagation.

Scabiosa

Scabiosa is the name given to the genus because of the virtue some members are said to possess of being able to cure certain types of skin diseases. Unfortunately this family, so rich in popular names, useful both in the border and as a cut flower, has a marked dislike for heavy soils. In addition, unless young plants are constantly available for division, the stock deteriorates after several years, and begins to die out. Bearing in mind all these defects it is still impossible to ignore the beauty contained within the genus, and certainly none of the difficulties attendant on the successful cultivation require anything more than a very minor effort to surmount. A free-draining site can usually be provided in even the worst of heavy soils, and a proportion of the plants can be divided, or used to supply cuttings each spring to ensure a continual supply of vigorous young stock. Seed of *Scabiosa caucasica* sown in spring will germinate readily, but the flower colour does vary, so culling of the poorer forms has to be resorted to. In company with a goodly number of other gardeners I tend to think all my seedling geese are swans, and my culling is never ruthless enough.

It is best to plant in spring as the soil warms up, the selected site having been dressed with chalk or lime rubble a month or six weeks previously. Of the many cultivars introduced over the years, none has so far surpassed in popularity or beauty the well-known 'Clive Greaves'. Like the species it will grow to some 45 to 50 cm (18 to 20 in) in height, and the pincushion flowers, so typical of the genus, are a rich shade of blue. Strangely enough, the white cultivar 'Miss Willmott' has proved reasonably content on this clay soil, a fact which has surprised me, as by reputation and past experience there is a certain doubt about the strength of its constitution.

Scrophularia

Scrophularia nodosa 'Variegata' came to me like so many other plants in the herbaceous border, from Bressingham Gardens, Norfolk. I have a built-in suspicion of most plants with variegated leaves; affection either comes with acquaintance or dies still-born, and in this instance the former turned out to be the case. I now treasure this plant with the dark green leaves, richly laced with yellow using their colouring as a foil for the sages. In good soil it will grow to 1 m (3 ft) but I keep the plants from flowering by giving them an occasional clip over with the shears during the season. Division is the usual means of increase, just as growth breaks in the spring.

Sedum

Sedums are richer than most in popular names, the native Stonecrop is a prime example. Jack of the Buttery, Welcome-home-husband-though-never-so-drunk or Wall Pepper, disclose the country folks' turn of phrase, and the language of flowers is the richer for it.

Most members of this family are happier growing in crevices of the rock garden, on walls, or even roofs of old cottages, but there are some which make a valuable contribution to the open garden. The loveliest of all is *Sedum cauticolum*, a plant for which I would go to any trouble to ensure that it had all the essentials for happy, contented growth. From the time when the glaucous-grey leaves first show in spring, until the glorious deep rose-red flowers unfold in late August and September, this is to me a thing of beauty. Though it will grow and blossom on an acid soil, this is but a pale shadow of what the plant can really do when dressed with chalk to provide the calcium it seems to love. A well-drained soil and a position in full sun is a further requisite. Propagation is by cuttings in spring, or by seed. The height varies according to soil between 10 and 20 cm (4 and 8 in).

Above: A cool shady
position suits *Saxifraga
fortunei*. This is
'Wada's Variety'

Right: *Senecio przewalskii* is an
excellent plant in any part of the
border where adequate moisture
at the root can be assured

Right: For the front of a border, *Sedum spectabile*

Sedum maximum 'Atropurpureum' is a strong-growing perennial, whose principal attraction lies in the dull bronze-purple of the stems and leaves. I must confess that I have not found a soil to really suit this plant, but in many gardens it grows with great freedom and resolve up to 60 cm (24 in) in height. The fault is either mine or the garden's, and in no way a reflection on the vigour of the species. A sunny position and a well-drained soil are essential; perhaps I should be spurred to greater endeavour were the flower heads, which appear in August, a little less repulsive a shade of pink.

In spring the young growths of *Sedum rosea*, Roseroot, have a peculiar beauty, and for clothing a retaining wall or dry bank they have much to recommend them, but later in the season they are not the tidiest of plants. The unbranched, leafy stems grow up to 30 cm (12 in) in length, surmounted in May by the greenish-yellow flowers. Many colour forms are available, even a purple-leaved variety, so should the taste run to more brightly coloured flowers these can be found in *linifolium*, with narrow leaves and deep rose blossoms.

Sedum spectabile provides us with a trio of cultivars all of which are fit to grace the most select herbaceous border. Ranging in height from 25 to 45 cm (10 to 18 in) the glaucous grey-green leaves make a perfect foil to the flowers, which peak in September to October, when the autumn light brings out the best of colour in any shade of red. Additional interest is furnished by the butterflies which flock to drink the nectar almost as eagerly as they greet the buddleia. Of the varieties available 'Brilliant', with very large flat heads of deep rose, is 45 cm (18 in) in height, while 'September Ruby' is deep rose pink. Finally, the pick of the trio is 'Meteor', whose flat corymb of blossom is glowing vermilion red; a treasure of a plant. Division in spring is the safest way of ensuring progeneration of the varieties.

At only 10 cm (4 in) high, *Sedum spurium* 'Glow' might seem a trifle

small to be allowed outside the confines of the rock garden, but as an edging plant along the herbaceous border this cultivar has the strength and vigour to make a place for itself. I particularly like the deep red foliage and rose-red flowers in association with dwarf ferns, situated where the evening sun strikes it, for it is under this light that the colour shows to advantage. Another small sedum which has done well planted in the front of the herbaceous border is the cultivar 'Weinstephener Gold'. I feel this is a cultivar of *floriferum* and not *spurium* at all; however, the two are much alike in habit though not in parentage or flower colour, those of 'Weinstephener Gold', as the name implies, being copper-yellow.

Of the many good plants sent to me by Mr Alan Bloom, *Sedum telephium* 'Autumn Joy' is one of my special favourites. In habit slightly taller than *S. spectabile,* the only vice in an otherwise virtuous plant is that in a wet season the flower stems bend over in a most untidy manner. The flowers open a brilliant, almost shrimp pink, then in graceful old age assume a delightful copper-bronze shade, which fits in very well with the changing hues of autumn in the plants around. As the growth breaks in spring division is easily effected, the pieces being replanted in well-prepared soil and re-establishing rapidly.

Senecio

Senecios, the venerable gentleman of gardens, have never really made any appeal to me, largely because of the endless battle over the years with those invasive members of the clan – groundsel and ragwort. Efficacious though these may be as a cure for sunstroke, I feel the only chance of suffering from a surfeit of sun in this climate would be in pulling the endless legions out of the garden.

There is one member of the family which has no resemblance at all to its less worthy cousins except in name; *Senecio przewalskii* (*Ligularia przewalskii*) is an excellent plant in any part of the border where adequate moisture at the root can be assured. Unfortunately at the first sign of drought, or anything approaching drought, the leaves droop and the whole aspect of the plant becomes depressing in the extreme. Properly suited, the tall, deep brown-purple stems reach 1.5 cm (5 ft) or more, starred in July and August with orange plumes of spider-like flowers. The deeply-divided, shiny leaves have a purple tinge too, which contributes much to the overall value.

Seed, or division in spring are simple methods of increasing the colony.

I include *Senecio tanguticus* rather by chance, for it was by chance only that a seedling sowed itself into the most perfect position behind a group of *Lilium speciosum* 'Painted Lady'. The greeny-yellow flowers formed just the right indefinite background needed for the splendid red-white bloom of the lily. This senecio is a hardy rampant grower, the stems soaring to a majestic 2.1 m (7 ft) in most seasons, but provided a careful watch is kept to see it does not transgress, no harm can come from just a modest group.

Serratula

Serratula tinctoria had at one time some economic value in that the foliage yielded a yellow dye; horticulturally, however, its value is nil. Not so *Serratula shawii* which is worthy of a place for the lilac-purple flowers it carries late in the autumn. The stems are stiff, erect, 23 to 30 cm (9 to 12 in) in height, and I like to grow one or two as specimens amongst the low-growing sedums previously described. A position in full sun, on any well-drained soil, is all that is asked or required. Seed or division with a sharp knife in spring will serve to increase the stock of this handsome little plant.

Sidalcea

Sidalceas have been improved considerably over the years since the war, which, no doubt accounts for their popularity. The old cultivars had the ungainly habit of opening their flowers intermittently, which meant that some were already dying back to a virulent magenta shade before the others had fully developed, spoiling the whole appearance of the plant. This has been largely overcome now, and no border is complete without at least one representative of the genus to add charm and character.

The fashion of dividing sidalceas every three or four years was one I followed slavishly until I started planting them amongst shrubs. When after six or seven years there was no sign of a decline in the masses of spikes or their quality, I discontinued the practice in the rest of the garden as well. 'Rose Queen' with clear rose-pink flowers at 1.2 m (4 ft) and 'Mrs Alderson' at the same height with much larger flowers, though paler pink, are my favourites. Other choice cultivars grown here are 'Mrs Galloway', pink flowers, 1 to 1.06 m (3 to 3½ft); 'Wensleydale' (at least this was the name I had the plant under), 1.06 m (3½ft) deep red; and 'Wm. Smith', the most compact of all at 75 cm (2½ft) with orange-red flowers. Any moist position in full sun will suit the sidalceas, though the moisture must not be stagnant. Division, when seen to be necessary, should be carried out in spring, taking only the young vigorous pieces from the outside edges of the clumps.

Solidago

Solidago once was greatly prized as the basis of a cooling draught for healing wounds. In fact, the Latin *solidare,* to unite, gives the plant its name. I have no doubt the solidago which grew so luxuriantly in the herbaceous border at home 25 years ago were the coarse invasive type, but I cherish a memory of the golden-yellow of the solidago and the blue of Michaelmas Daisies. Like so many of the popular garden border flowers, the Golden Rods have been improved enormously over the years, not only in the quality of the flowers but in beauty of foliage as well.

There are so many excellent hybrids to choose from that the species are best left out of the garden proper, with the exception of *Solidago canadensis* which looks very well in the rougher parts. The stems reach 1.5 m (5 ft) in good soil and the flowers carried in a one-sided panicle are yellow-green. Given the choice, however, I would plant 'Golden Wings', a hybrid with all the vigour of the parent, but larger flowers. Of the other hybrids, 'Goldenmosa' is the best here, with well-filled heads of flowers and handsome leaves in August and September. Of the dwarfer varieties, 'Golden Thumb' (syn. 'Queenie'), at only 30 cm (12 in) with golden-yellow flowers, looks lovely planted with autumn-flowering gentians. All the others differ only slightly in shape or colour of the spikes. 'Golden Falls' and 'Golden Gates' are 1 m (3 ft) high; 'Lemore' has more distinction with blooms of palest primrose yellow; while 'Mimosa' has the softest flowers on arching graceful stems.

I feel that these plants lack the essential distinction of character to gain them a high place in the gardener's affection, but nevertheless they are indispensable for the autumn border. Division of the roots in spring is extremely simple when extra plants are needed.

Stachys

Stachys lanata, the Lambs Lugs of my childhood, in its better forms is excellent for the front of the border, where the white, felted leaves can be seen to full advantage. I have grown this plant in the driest, poorest soil, and in the wet pug of the Harrogate clay; in both it manages to preserve the prim contented silver of the leaves. The 38 cm (15 in) spikes of pink-purple flowers in July are quite attractive, but it is the leaves which give the stachys such value especially when planted with cottage-garden pinks. Increase is by seed or division in spring.

Symphytum

Symphytum peregrinum has a novelty rather than a garden value, the flowers opening a brilliant blue, then turning pink with age. They are carried on 1 to 1.5 m (3 to 5 ft) stems for several months, but in the border the habit is untidy, and planting is better confined to the wilder outskirts of the garden. I grow several bold groups in open woodland with asiatic primulas and astilbes, and get good ground rent in return.

Great care should be taken that the plants offered are true to name, as some confusion exists in this respect; the Prickly Comfrey, *S. asperum,* often sold as *S. peregrinum,* is a much more invasive proposition, and needs careful watching or it will quickly establish itself where not wanted.

Thermopsis

Thermopsis montana must hide its light under a bushel in some districts. Having read in several books it needed careful handling and well-drained soil, I put the first rootlets in here with a good bed of sand. Any illusions I had have long since been shattered, as the plants have spread far beyond the space allotted, smothering a lot of less vigorous neighbours in the process. The glaucous leaves and bright yellow flowers on 60 cm (24 in) stems brighten the border in May and June, especially if a few plants of the blue-flowered Jacob's Ladder, polemonium, are scattered amongst them.

Stock can be increased by division.

Tiarella

Tiarella trifoliata is the pick of the

Above: Stachys lanata is a silvery leaved ground-cover plant

Opposite: *Trillium grandiflorum*, the Wood Lily of Canada, is not difficult to cultivate and needs no special attention when well suited in regard to soils

For ground cover under shrubs, *Tolmiea menziesii*

genus, and makes a useful ground cover in the shade of shrubs where the soil is sufficiently moist. The lobed leaves are coarsely toothed, and the 30 cm (12 in) sprays of creamy-white flowers are carried from May to August, I use this frequently in association with dicentra, *Cornus canadensis* and geraniums as ground planting in shady borders.

Pieces can usually be forked from the edge of the clumps whenever a few plants are needed.

Tolmiea

Tolmiea menziesii is usually grown as a house plant, but like the tiarella it gives good value when used as ground cover under shrubs. One pot planted out in the open garden four years ago under a group of three *Rhododendron* 'Praecox' has carpeted several yards of ground. The name Pickaback Plant comes from its habit of producing tiny plantlets in the centre of the leaves. The flowers are greenish-cream. Propagation is by division or leaf cuttings.

Tradescantia

Tradescantia virginiana (*T.* × *andersoniana*) was named after John Tradescant, one of the truly great men of gardening, both in the collecting and growing of plants. Few men have deserved or been honoured by a more lovely memorial, for the tradescantias are amongst the longest-flowered of herbaceous perennials. The long list of common names is an indication, not only of the popularity of the genus, but of its antiquity, for they were one of the early introductions from America. Spiderwort, Moses-in-the-bulrushes and Wedon's Tears, are just a few of the names which have been applied to the plant in common usage.

The habit of growth is strongly reminiscent of a rather soft-leaved iris. The three-petalled flowers are carried in clustered heads, and can be procured in a wide range of colours. Any good, moist soil suits them. I have grown cultivars of the species with equal success on heavy clay and light sand, in sun or partial shade, and it seems to make no difference to their benign good temper. Most of them grow to around 50 cm (20 in).

I enjoy growing many cultivars of the species, but have one particular favourite and this is of fairly recent introduction, with large Oxford blue flowers, named 'Isis'. The pure white form, *alba,* unlike some albinos, is no weaker than the others. *Rubra,* with deep-red flowers, was the first tradescantia I ever grew, and it still has a sure place in my borders. 'Iris Prichard' has white flowers stained blue. 'Purple Dome' has slightly larger flowers than 'Isis', coloured rich velvet purple. There is also 'Osprey' whose white blossoms are accentuated by blue stamens.

They need dividing every four or five years, and this is best done in early April, as the soil begins to warm up, at least this is so in a cold, exposed situation. In a sheltered garden mid-March might be possible. The plants can be grown from seed, but like marriage this is a gamble, for something very good might come up but on the other hand the reverse could be the case.

Trillium

Trillium grandiflorum, the Wood Lily of Canada, has not yet attained the popularity that it so richly deserves, for this is a truly beautiful plant. It is not difficult to cultivate, and no special attention must be constantly paid to its well being, at least not in my experience of growing it in three gardens in various parts of the North. There are two strong colonies which have coped quite adequately with the rough and tumble of the heath garden for 10 years, and it is one of the most beautiful of the spring-flowering plants which make their home here.

The name is taken from *trilix,* meaning woven from a triple leash, the parts of leaves and flowers being in threes. The leaves are three-whorled, the flowers are carried single, framed in the greenery, rather like a six-pointed star in effect. A moist yet well-drained peat or leafsoil suits them, and they look uncommonly pretty with rhododendrons.

Division of the roots is one method of increase, but not to be recommended as it spoils the look of the established planting. Seed germinates readily, and I have had seedlings flower in three years from sowing.

Trillium sessile has variegated leaves and purple flowers but is not so easy as *T. grandiflorum*, and it would be as well to confine the plantings to the latter in the initial stages.

Trollius

Trollius europaeus, the Globe Flower, is a native of the British Isles, and in particular of Northern districts; indeed, I have seen meadows in Teesdale yellow with the abundant flowers in spring. They demand a soil which will not dry out, and where there is any doubt about the soil's ability to hold water a good mulch of peat or compost will act as an insurance. I grow them in all their rich variety with other moisture-loving flowers such as primulas and iris. The flowering season is May to June, and division of the plants, either as growth breaks in spring, or immediately after flowering if the weather is wet, ensures healthy stock with rapid increase.

The average height is in the region of 60 to 75 cm (24 to 30 in). Cultivars include 'Canary Bird' light yellow; 'Commander in Chief', very large deep orange; 'Earliest of All', yellow globes in late spring; and 'Golden Queen', one of the latest to flower and the tallest. Some of these are now lumped for ease of classification under *T. × cultorum*.

The latest of the Globe Flowers to blossom is *T. yunnanensis*. The colony is strong and robust in spite of growing in rather poor soil. A form I grew for years as *T. yunnanensis stenopetala* now goes under the name of 'Wargrave', and is larger-flowered than the type. In both, the flowers are golden, opening to fully 5 cm (2 in) wide. The height is 60 cm (24 in). Propagation is as for *europaeus*.

Verbascum

Verbascums have much to recommend them as anyone who has seen them in cottage gardens will realise. Though some are biennial, and only a few are long-lived, they are so easy in most soils. When they die they usually leave a few self-sown seedlings to carry on the line, so it is a pity to deprive oneself of their company for that reason.

The fleshy-rooted kinds, if perennial, come readily from root cuttings taken into a sandy soil in late winter, and I have had a proportion root in autumn. *Verbascum nigrum*, *V. chaixii* and *V. phoeniceum* will stand division in spring. *V. chaixii*, the Nettle-leaved Mullein, is a jewel of a perennial with me, and reaching only 1 m (3 ft) stands a windswept position better than most. The yellow flowers with purple stamens are carried in branching spikes from June to early August.

For its large rosettes of grey-felted leaves alone *V. olympicum* would be worth growing, looking especially pleasing in the crevices of York paving. Do not be misled into thinking this a dwarf of the race, for the spikes of golden-yellow flowers reach up to a noble 2 m (6 ft). I have had individual plants live for five years, but seed germinates so freely wherever it is sown that lack of perenniality need be no drawback.

I first had seed of *V. phoeniceum* from the Moscow Botanic Gardens; the resulting plants lived for four years, and produced such a rare mixture of flowers that I thought they could not be the true species. Apparantly the colour is typically violet or deep purple, but this can vary from pink to lilac, rose, purple and white. This species is a short-lived perennial and in some garden seeds so freely as to become a nuisance, but so well did it solve one problem spot in my garden that I would find a corner for it in any case. All gardeners have these problem spots where nothing will grow, and this particular spot was under a venerable hawthorn on a steep bank which sloped down to the stream. I must have tried a dozen different plants, all with a reputation for adaptability, from polygonum to *Allium moly*, but without success. Then the blind goddess saw to it that at 5.10 p.m. I was passing this spot with a half-empty box of Purple Mullein seedlings; as tea was calling I popped them in the arid plot of ground, and from that day onwards the desert has blossomed. The 60 cm to 1 m (2 to 3 ft) slightly branching spikes appear from June to late August, and so far the self-sown seedlings have not spread beyond their prescribed limits.

Verbascum thapsiforme (*V. densiflorum*) may be monocarpic in some gardens, but some of my plants have flowered for three years in succession. I think this is the most graceful of all the mulleins, in spite of the large wrinkled leaves and erect 1.5 m (5 ft) branching spikes, which are thickly set with brilliant yellow flowers from June onwards. I usually grow this species with blue delphiniums and *Rosa alba* 'Celestial', and it may be that by contrast with the heavier spikes of the delphiniums the verbascum does take on a lighter quality. The three colours blend beautifully. Seed will germinate freely, but strangely enough does not seem to do so in the open garden, as does that of some other species. As with most other genera of horticultural merit the verbascums have received attention at the hands of the hybridist. I have grown several, but few are perennial, or indeed anything more than biennial with me. 'Cotswold Beauty', with copper-coloured flowers and lilac anthers; 'Cotswold Queen' buff and purple; and 'Gainsborough' with felted leaves and soft yellow flowers, are worth growing, even if their life is but an evening one. 'Maud Pugsley' is a dwarf of 38 cm (15 in) which I have had only for one year, but a good crop of rosettes formed the first autumn, which indicates a degree of perenniality at least. Do not leave old flower spikes too long after the blooms fade; cut them hard back as soon as possible.

Veronica

Veronica was known in olden times as Forget-me-not, the Bird's Eye or Cat's Eye. The petals fall almost immediately the flowers are picked, and from this unfortunate habit comes the best known of all the many names given to this plant, namely Speedwell. Several species are used in Europe as a substitute for tea, but I have not yet plucked

Opposite: Traditionally herbaceous plants can be grown in their own special borders but the trend now is to grow them with shrubs and other plants

up enough courage to test its ability in this direction. From this large family have come several valuable additions to the illustrious line of border plants.

The common Bird's Eye, *Veronica chamaedrys*, though charming and lovely, and beloved by young and old alike, is apt to get a little above itself when brought into the garden by rampaging over the territory allotted to other plants. I like to grow it in the bottom of the boundary hedge in company with foxgloves and other native beauties.

A great favourite in the borders here is *V. exaltata*, but for some strange reason one rarely sees it offered in nursery lists. I got my plants from St Nicholas, a well known Yorkshire garden near Richmond, and look for the flowers each year in August with undiminished interest. The blue flowers are borne aloft on 1.2 to 1.5 m (4 to 5 ft) spikes which curl slightly at the tips, an individualistic touch which adds grace to the picture. Almost any soil meets the approval of this species, and it goes well with *Lythrum virgatum* 'The Rocket', and *Lilium regale* hybrids. The root system is strong and easily divided in autumn and spring.

Veronica gentianoides I chose by name from a botanical list, being immediately attracted to anything with the word gentian attached to it. The plant comes readily from seed, and in an erroneous conception of its vigour I planted a dozen where three would have been enough. In May and June came the lovely pale blue flowers on 60 cm (2 ft) spikes above the neat rosettes of oblong leaves. In due season these set seed, and this is where the mistake was made. The clumps should have been clipped hard over after flowering and then they would have given a second crop in late summer. Left unshorn they get very untidy and seed themselves in a most un-gentian-like manner. A full understanding of plants only comes from growing them and, unlike the rose, a gentian by any other name does not behave the same. However, this is a brave beautiful veronica, only asking for a moderately

well-drained soil to do well in the garden. Roots should be divided every five years, but I prefer to start again from seed.

With grey leaves and the most brilliant blue flowers, *Veronica incana glauca* is of special value in the border in July. This plant came to me in a paper bag in company with a dozen other treasures of similar quality, and no labels on any of them: very much a lucky dip. Division of the root is a sure way of perpetuating the variety true to type, but seedlings are worthwhile and give some interesting variations. Try 'Saraband', grey leaves and spikes of violet-blue, or 'Wendy', lavender-blue.

I used to get *V. longifolia* inextricably mixed with *V. spicata*, and on occasions still have moments of serious doubt. The height varies from 60 cm to 1.2 m (2 to 4 ft), and the flowering season is July to September. When the leaves are in whorls as in the variety *rosea* there is no problem in identification, but even this characteristic is not constant, and they can just as easily be opposite only. The flowers come in dense terminal racemes, in the type plant, lilac; in the variety *albiflora*, white; in *rosea*, pink; and in *hendersonii nana*, deep blue. A word of warning, *hendersonii* has proved a mope, and is, I suspect of a tenderer constitution than the others, or it could be our clay soil. With *V. spicata*, I grow the cultivars in preference to the species. The best of these is 'Blue Fox', with bright lavender-blue blossoms on 45 cm (18 in) stems. 'Minuet' is only 38 cm (15 in) high with pink flowers. Most flower from late June to August, and the surface-rooting mats need dividing every four or five years for they die out quickly from the centre. A well-drained soil is essential, as this is far from being the best natured of the species.

A thoroughly easy-going plant on almost any soil is *Veronica teucrium*. Even in light shade amongst shrubs it will continue to produce profusely its brilliant blue bird's-eye flowers. Neither the type plant or its cultivars have grown over 45 cm (18 in) in this soil, but I am told there are some which reach 1 m (3 ft). All are first class perennials and have gone 10 years without division in the borders here. The leaves are linear, toothed and the flowers are large, deep blue, in axillery racemes. The number of cultivars which exist is quite surprising, but I have seen nothing to surpass or equal 'Crater Lake Blue', which wanders around *Potentilla* 'Moonlight', whose pale yellow blossoms contrast so pleasantly with the blue. 'Shirley Blue', rather smaller at 30 cm (12 in) is an excellent front-of-the-border cultivar. 'Trehane' I have to cherish a little, but it is worth the extra trouble, for the leaves are yellowy-green, and the flowers are deep blue. All flower during June, and the only fault to be found with these charming plants is that their blossoming is so fugacious.

Veronica virginica, and the white form *alba,* are slender graceful plants up to 1.2 m (4 ft) tall which can hardly be said to run riot in the border, but for all their slow growth are thoroughly reliable. The flowers are pale, almost misty, in effect, set very close on the spike, and appear late in the summer.

General Remarks

These are the herbaceous perennials that I have found to be good in far from ideal conditions. I make no claim that this is a complete list, containing only those plants which have proved themselves to my personal satisfaction. There are, of course, many, many more than I have described existing quite contentedly in the corners and borders; but though happy here doubts have been expressed as to their character elsewhere by gardeners I have talked with over the years. Where any doubt existed, I have left them to further prove their sterling character.

Trees and Shrubs:
Acer to Fuchsia

⎯⎯⎯⎯◈⎯⎯⎯⎯

Herbaceous plants provide the changing patterns of the garden; they are easily moved from one bed to another, and even a small collection is capable of endless permutation to create different designs. These, then, are the colours in the painter's palette, but a garden composed entirely of herbaceous plants is an impermanent thing, a boneless body in winter, lacking landscape and interest. To provide an air of permanence shrubs must be included, and if herbaceous plants are the colours in the palette, then shrubs are the flat wash which provides the undertones, changes in level, and above all depth to the garden. This does not mean that shrubs are dull, since anyone who has seen forsythia mounded in yellow on a sunlit April day, or *Rhododendron thomsonii* hung with scarlet against a background of silver birch, would soon give the lie to that.

A herbaceous border needs considerable thought to achieve a balanced, pleasing design, but, should any part fail to attain the required standard, the fault is easily rectified. A shrub border needs even more understanding, and an intimate knowledge of what each species or cultivar included in the pattern looks like, not only in full glory of blossom, but also in the depth of winter when shapes, twig tracery, and foliage colour bring their own special interest. I look across from my house on the west to the open moors, but on the south-west to a farmhouse planted close about with trees, running into a hedge which leads the eye along to a spruce and larch plantation. This view is pleasant at all times, but on a frosty winter night with trees outlined against the red of the setting sun, the scene takes on an added beauty which never fails to delight me. Gardeners are

subject to a continually accelerating bombardment of new ideas, new methods, and introductions of new cultivars which, excellent though they may all be in cutting out the more laborious tasks attendant on the cultivation of plants, tend to bring confusion and doubt, especially in the matter of choosing shrubs for furnishing the borders. With annuals, herbaceous, or alpine plants, faulty judgement results only in the loss of pence, but with shrubs the expense could run into pounds and several years wasted work. Experience is the best teacher, I have no doubt, but with the present price of shrubs the school fees can be extremely heavy. I should not be stupid enough to desire a halt to the development of new cultivars, but only permission to suggest that some of the swans might be rather disappointing geese, at least under northern conditions. The shrubs described in the following pages have all proved their worth on a difficult site.

I have my favourites amongst them, and this list will be added to as the years pass. Each season sees some additions to the borders, and it would be ridiculous even to suggest that the following pages include all the cultivars which will grow in a northern garden. It is, however, as complete as my experience to date can make it. I omit conifers here, treating them later in a separate chapter (pp. 141 to 149).

Acer
This genus contains some of the best, and, unfortunately, the worst of trees for the garden. The Sycamore, *Acer pseudoplatanus,* is a bad gardener, and unless, like past barons of West Scotland, one is in need of a 'dool tree' for hanging refractory servants, better left in the hedgerow or mixed woodland. *A.*

Opposite: Japanese maples, cultivars of *Acer palmatum,* need shelter from strong cold winds

capillipes makes a small tree; its beautiful white-striped bark is a pleasing picture right through the winter, and in the autumn the leaves colour up in a most spectacular manner. *A. hersii* (*grosseri hersii*) has bark marked with whitish stripes, the young shoots are yellow. Planted in a very exposed position the leaves turn a most glorious scarlet in the autumn. Ultimately it will make a tree 7.6 to 9 m (25 to 30 ft) high.

Acer griseum, the Paper Bark Maple, is so distinctive that a special corner will not be wasted on it. Though this native of Central China is better pleased with a southern climate, it grows with modest vigour in Yorkshire and further north still be the soil acid or alkaline. The bark peels in long strips to reveal the cinnamon-coloured bole beneath, then when the leaves turn scarlet in autumn the Paper Bark Maple returns with interest the capital invested on its purchase price. In winter sunlight through the flaking bark catches the warmth of a gentler season to make it one of the most gracious of small trees.

Acer japonicum 'Aureum' is a very slow-growing maple. The leaves are a soft yellow, edged with red in the early spring. In autumn the yellow intensifies in a most remarkable way. *A. j.* 'Vitifolium' is anything but slow growing compared with its yellow-leaved counterpart, but does make an extremely handsome small tree, with large vine-like leaves which take on the most brilliant autumn colours. I once tried to describe the myriad colours contained in one leaf and finished up by taking a colour slide and sending that instead. A mixture of scarlet, yellow, and soft pink would be a very bald description.

Acer negundo 'Variegatum' is valuable because of the silver-white variegation of its leaves, and a good-humoured adaptability to the most unpromising situations. The least salubrious place I can imagine would be a stiff, uncompromising clay soil soaked after rain by water from a tarmacadam road, and exposed to the full blast of the south-westerly wind. Not being enamoured of variegated leaves at the time, I planted it in such a place with little ceremony, then watched the results. In cold, windy springs the leaves get browned, but apart from that in eight years growth has been steady, if not luxuriant. A further point in favour of the Variegated Maple is the comparative ease with which it strikes from cuttings, made in October and inserted in a sand-peat compost in the propagating frame.

Acer palmatum has given rise to some of the loveliest of small trees, collectively known as Japanese Maples. Unfortunately, they object most strongly to being exposed to strong winds which damage the leaves, and in extreme cases the trees present the appearance of having been scorched by fire. Given a sheltered position they make a picture of graceful beauty it would be hard to equal. In winter there is the delicate twig tracery, in summer the attractive deeply-cut leafage, then in October the crowning glory of brilliant autumn colour. This leaf tenderness seems to grow less with age, for trees here have grown beyond the sheltering shrubs, and have to face the full blast of the westerly wind which now seems to do no permanent harm. So handsome are the several cultivars of *A. palmatum* that it is worth providing a little protection for the first few years, and the best way to do this is with the more robust infants of cotoneaster and berberis. The type plant grows quicker than the cultivars, with the possible exception of *coreanum* and 'Heptalobum Osakazuki', which seem to have a similar rate of extension, eventually making a small wide-spreading, yet graceful tree 9 m (30 ft) high. *A. p.* 'Atropurpureum' is the best of all the colour forms, the leaves maintaining a rich bronze-purple throughout the summer. I like to plant so that the leaves can be seen with the sun behind from as many viewpoints as possible. A plant so placed, flanked on one side with a cream-flowered *Potentilla fruticosa,* and on the other by a glaucous-leaved juniper, never fails to give one the keenest pleasure from bud burst until the last leaf falls in November. Of the various forms of *A.*

p. 'Dissectum' I can only say that in my experience they require the most sheltered, and best-drained spot the garden can provide. When happy they are worthy of the highest honour.

Coupled with a similar rate of growth, *A. p. coreanum* has all the grace of the type plant. In autumn the leaves turn brilliant vermilion-red, seen at its best against the sombre dark green background of the yew. Most brilliant of all in autumn is 'Heptalobum Osaka-zuki', a superb plant when associated with the silver pampas grass. So many of the ideal plant associations come about merely by chance, and this was the case when for want of a more suitable site I chose *Cortaderia selloana* and this maple to plant round a specimen birch in one corner of a large lawn. Over the years this group has grown into a mature beauty which leaves nothing lacking except sunlit autumn days to bring out the colour.

Acer platanoides, Norway Maple, will, in maturity, make a very large tree indeed. Not surprisingly because it has been so long in cultivation there are numerous cultivars bred from the species which offer an alternative to the plain green leaf. 'Crimson King' is one with leaves of crimson-purple where space can be offered to a forest tree.

Having damned Sycamore at the outset, a form of *A. pseudoplatanus,* 'Brilliantissum', craves consideration, a very slow growing mushroom headed tree whose young leaves open in spring, shrimp pink, lime green, and finally the more usual dull green of the parent. An under planting of Forget-me-not will add to the charm of this composition.

Aesculus

The genus *Aesculus* includes in its many species the well known Horse Chestnut. Trying to acquire the fruits of this plant once seemed to be my one aim in life during the month of September, and small boys have changed their ambitions very little, if my own son is an example. The taller growing species are of little use in the smaller gardens, for a big, canopied tree of this type permits little to be grown underneath and occupies far more space than its beauty warrants. There are, however, two species of shrubby character which do not require half the garden for their domain. *Aesculus parviflora* makes a stiff, erect, rather spreading shrub which in August produces 30 cm (12 in) panicles of white flowers with red anthers. Like most of the family this shrub moves relatively easily up to quite a large size, and is very contented in the most exposed places. In autumn the leaves turn a deep golden-yellow.

Aesculus pavia, or Red Buckeye, has a grace which distinguishes it immediately from the no less handsome but more geometric sturdiness of *A. parviflora,* sometimes unkindly called the Bottle-brush Buckeye. The first specimen I had flowered when only 1.2 m (4 ft) high, and has continued to produce erect panicles of bright red flowers each June in the years since then. Ultimately it will grow into a shrub 3.7 m (12 ft) high, a worthy addition to the ornamental garden without its outgrowing the welcome it so richly deserved. A cultivar planted three years ago under the name of 'Atrosanguinea' has deep red flowers, and in my opinion is even more desirable then the type. Increase of the species is ususally effected by seed sown in October, but grafting or budding must be resorted to when a particular colour-form is desired.

The Indian Horse Chestnut, *A. indica,* will eventually make a broad spreading tree, though growing so slowly it presents a long-term problem which will need no solution in my life time. The flowers, white flashed pink, open in July and are produced on very young trees. A 14 year old specimen had reached only 2.7 m (9 ft) high, and yet had flowered nine years prior to that.

Amelanchier

For the June Berry or, as they are better known in this country, the Snowy Mespilus, I have the greatest affection. A more easy-going tolerant, yet withal handsome shrub I have yet to meet.

Amelanchier canadensis, or Shad-bush, will make a tree of 6 m (20 ft), but it takes a long time thinking about it. I have transplanted specimens 2.7 m (9 ft) high from one part of the garden to another, without their showing any great resentment. The white flowers open in April, burying the bush under a snowy blanket, but it is in autumn when I appreciate this shrub the most, since the leaves turn first yellow and then red-bronze. Seeds germinate with reasonable alacrity if sown in a cold frame immediately they are ripe.

I first met *A. lamarckii* (*A.* × *grandiflora*) growing in a clearing amongst silver birches with a ground planting of pink-flowered azaleas. The whole bush was covered with the beautiful white flowers, which, no doubt, gained additional lustre by contrast with the pink of the azaleas and glistening of the silver of the birch. Then in the autumn came the frost to bring out the rich scarlet in the dying leaves, lovely against the yellow of the birch's own autumn array.

Cuttings of all amelanchiers show a stubborn reluctance to root, the callus in most cases splitting and then rotting. Those taken in September into a peat-sand compost gave best results with a 20 per cent. strike.

Aralia

The Japanese Angelica Tree, *Aralia elata,* is a shrub to love and hate at the same time. I have a bold group planted in a very damp, windy corner of the garden and after 14 years the tallest has reached 3 m (10 ft) in height. In winter the group does not make a striking picture, just straight, very thorny stems, but when the 1 m (3 ft) long compound leaves open in late spring, topped in August by the enormous panicles of white flowers, the effect is quite different. Framed as they are against a view of the Pennines, with a well-wooded valley between, I can think of no other shrub which could be used to such advantage. The hate comes when suckers appear in the most inaccessible places, and have to be removed at the expense of a good deal of torn skin. They may be increased by these

suckers, which are so freely produced that I have never had to recourse to the more arduous methods of sowing seed or taking root cuttings in March or April.

Arbutus

Arbutus unedo, Killarney Strawberry Tree, though a native of the Mediterranean region and the moist gentle climate which the West of Ireland is blessed with, still qualifies as an easy plant. Growth is much slower in the cooler climate of central England, though I suspect this is as much the fault of a niggardly 60 cm (24 in) of rain a year rather than lack of hardiness on the tree's part. The dark, shiny evergreen leaves and the plant's habit of producing a fresh crop of white flowers just as the strawberry-like fruits from the previous year are ripening, is a commendable piece of enterprise. In 20 years, with absolutely no more encouragement than an annual mulch of compost, growth has progressed from 81 cm (32 in) at the time of planting to 1.8 m (73 in) – a rate of progress which can only be described as tortoise like.

Aucuba

The family which includes the well known spotted laurel, *Aucuba japonica* 'Variegata', so frequently seen in churchyards, would not have been so widely planted if they had been less readily adaptable to most soils and situations. They will make well-furnished evergreen shrubs 2 m (6 ft) or more in height, extremely good to look on when well grown. When first introduced the male and female forms were cherished as pot plants, and the flowers being hand pollinated, produced enormous crops of scarlet berries. Indeed, one would almost be prepared to agree with Fortune that his journey to Japan in 1861 to obtain a plant was fully justified. All the forms of *A. japonica* are extremely tolerant, not only of shade, but also of drip from overhanging trees, and this leads people to all sorts of planting indiscretions. The worst I have ever seen was a dense planting of *A. j.* 'Variegata' under sycamores, on a dripping day in November. The variegated leaves, all plastered with the dirt and grime which had washed down from the trees above, made a most depressing picture. Given a decent chance in life, all the forms of *A. japonica* make attractive plants.

Aucuba japonica 'Crassifolia', with thick evergreen leaves; 'Variegata', the most commonly grown variegated-leaved form; and the compact 'Nana Rotundifolia', with beautiful leaves and a profusion of berries, are all easily propagated by cuttings taken in late summer.

Berberis

The barberries are a large and complex company; some are superb garden plants, others (and these unfortunately include most of the European species) are undistinguished. In Italy the Common Barberry is looked on as the Holy Thorn, because the spines grow in sets of three. Both fruits and leaves were used until comparatively recent times for flavouring sauces and jelly. Both the deciduous and evergreen species are easy to cultivate, showing no particular dislike as to soil, unless it is a dripping bog. From the vast number of species available, and the hybrids which are so freely produced, it is difficult to make a selection. *Berberis × carminea* 'Buccaneer', and 'Pirate King' are in the top rank of deciduous varieties. They will grow in the most windswept places, and in the poorest soil, into a densely furnished bush 1.2 to 1.5 m (4 to 5 ft) high. The flowers are paniculate, followed in autumn by masses of scarlet berries. The birds hardly ever touch them, unless driven to it by extremely hard weather. The foliage colours in October to make a brilliant background to the scarlet fruits. The evergreen barberries have a special merit, bringing, as they do, colour to the garden in winter. *B. darwinii* is one of the best known, and the rich orange flowers brighten many a shrub border in early May. Later in the season, the dark green makes a lovely background to the delicate soft pink flowers of *Rosa alba* 'Celestial'.

Under moderate soil conditions it will make a shrub 2.5 m (8 ft) high, the only fault lies in the base of the stem, which tends to become bare, and in arctic winters the top growth is killed back to soil level, but it breaks away from the roots in spring.

B. candidula is an evergreen species which has provided an alternative to dwarf conifers in so many planting schemes that I feel we now enjoy a special relationsip, as politicians term it. Eventually this species will make a dome-shaped bush, the shiny evergreen leaves, silvered below, form a suitable backcloth to the single yellow flowers which open in May. Indeed, there are several species of similar character in this group, all of them worth investigation, particularly *B. hookeri*. All of them make tough, durable shrubs up to 1 m (3 ft) high.

Of the hybrids listed under *B. × stenophylla,* 'Coccinea', a dwarf bush with coral red flowers, and 'Corallina', with yellow flowers, are good value. Probably the most brilliant flowers produced by any of the genus are to be found on *B. linearifolia,* the earliest to bloom here. They are deep orange, darkening with age to rich red, in perfect contrast with the glossy green of the leaves. The height is recorded as 2 m (6 ft), but after 14 years my plants have only managed 1.2 m (4 ft), albeit in a rather exposed position on clay soil.

Berberis × stenophylla is to me the pick of the genus, though there are three or four others which press it very hard. No matter where I have planted this fine evergreen it has made a determined effort to settle in and grow. In well tilled borders, or on the western edge of the woodland in rough coarse grass, each May the arching branches are wreathed in a multitude of sweetly scented bright yellow flowers. For the garden with room to spare the quickly-spreading branches will make a superb hedge, which clipped once after flowering and then allowed to make flowering wood for the next year, will make a wonderful spectacle when in full bloom. The dimensions on this soil are 2.5 m (8 ft) high and 2.5 m wide.

Berberis darwinii, one of the best-known evergreen barberries

Propagation is easy because of the plant's habit of suckering at the root.

Berberis thunbergii is superb in the glory of its yellow flowers, but in the autumn all previous admiration is rendered as nothing by the brilliance of the autumn colour and the scarlet berries. The growth is more compact than that of *B. × stenophylla,* namely 1.2 to 1.5 m (4 to 5 ft). This parent has given rise to a hybrid with reddish-purple leaves, invaluable for foliage effect when planted with dark green conifers.

The name is *atropurpurea,* and no doubt stimulated by the enthusiastic reception given to it by gardeners, has duly obliged by producing a whole series of variations on the original purple-leaved theme. 'Atropurpurea Nana' is a dwarf form which is a most excellent candidate for inclusion in the rock garden or dwarf shrub border. 'Erecta' and 'Red Pillar' are both very upright growing which automatically qualifies them as useful hedging shrubs.

Were it not for the unfortunate habit of some nurseries of grafting *Berberis verruculosa* on to a rootstock whose leaves bear a certain resemblance, but completely lack the quality of the scion, I would hold this species in greater esteem. Most gardeners have no time to make a critical examination of each individual in a large shrub border throughout the year, and it is not unusual for the rootstock to gain dominance before the danger is realised. Where one is prepared to take the risk, this species with small glossy leaves, which are white beneath, makes a neat, compact shrub for the front of the border.

Berberis vulgaris is thought to be, if not a true native, at least a plant of very early introduction to this country. Indeed, until comparatively recent times it was extensively cultivated as a fruit bearing bush, as Culpeper has it, 'they get a man a good stomach for his victuals'; but I have never tested the veracity of this statement, having found that a couple of hours' exercise with a spade creates a sufficiently sharp appetite. Whatever the plant's virtues may be in the culinary or medicinal field, no one seeing the Common Barberry in fruit or flower could possibly doubt its value as an ornamental garden plant, but only where room can be permitted for its full stature to be developed. Several cultivars exist, and the best of these, 'Atropurpurea', has developed purple leaves in most striking contrast to the hanging racemes of yellow flowers. Another excellent cultivar can be found in 'Macrocarpa', with rich scarlet berries appreciably larger than those of the species.

All these barberries make shrubs of 2.5 to 3 m (8 to 10 ft) and are quite readily increased by seed sown immediately it is ripe. Germination takes place quickly, and the resulting seedlings show immense variation, so cuttings must be preferred where trueness to type is desired. These may be taken in September, of current season's wood, with or without a heel, and inserted in sand in a frame, or in a sheltered bed outdoors.

Betula

No one who has visited any of the windswept areas of the northern counties, and seen the Silver Birch growing under almost impossible conditions of exposure, could possibly doubt its exceptional hardiness. This genus includes amongst its members some of the most handsome trees, possessed of a graceful elegance which is completely at variance with their adaptability. For a specimen in the long sweep of a lawn, few trees can equal the Western Chinese form of *Betula platyphylla szechuanica.* In nature it is reputed to reach 18 to 25 m (60 to 80 ft) but the largest I have seen was in Lancashire, and was only 13 m (42 ft). The beautiful white bark of the stem and the spreading branches make a singularly pleasing picture, especially in spring with the young green of the leaves just breaking through.

Betula costata is, compared to some of those described, a recent acquisition. In the nine years since planting a specimen in the garden I have wondered on several occasions why we have not met before, for this is a lovely species. The bark is creamy white and the rich yellow of the leaves in autumn is better than any other birch I grow. Another quality is that approximately every three years it produces a prodigious quantity of seed. When sown in February the resulting saplings are 38 to 45 cm (15 to 18 in) high by the following autumn. The temptation to keep sowing a proportion of the bounty is irresistable.

B. jacquemontii with the whitest stem of all paused only briefly in the garden on its way to the bonfire, leaving such an illusion of beauty I will certainly plant another, this time well away from giraffe-necked horses who destroyed the last one.

None of the birches I have seen or grown can equal the best forms of our own Lady of the Woods, *Betula pendula,* and one garden I visit regularly is singularly fortunate in that the part of the woodland consisting of indigenous birch contains a large proportion of trees with thoroughly white stems. In spring, when the rhododendrons are in bloom between the groves of white stems, with a haze of daffodils all around, the woodland is a scene full of beauty which defies superlatives. Where space is limited and does not permit the planting of even the light-canopied Common Silver Birch, a useful alternative will be found in the cultivar, 'Tristis', which makes a much narrower head, but whose branches have the same graceful sweep to the earth. Finally there is the beautiful pendulous Young's Weeping Birch, 'Youngii', which has been used to such good advantage in the suburban gardens of Birmingham. This never makes a large tree, but has all the grace of the type plant together with an extremely pendulous habit.

Buddleia

Buddleia is a widely distributed genus, ranging in habitat from America to China, and as a result has provided several valuable additions to the gardens of this country. Most of them adapt themselves readily to the conditions which prevail in a particular locality. The only thing I have found is that they will not tolerate a badly drained soil, but otherwise they show remarkably good temper, and revel in full sunshine.

Buddleia alternifolia is a rather large plant, but where space can be made available it will grow long arching branches, glaucous-leaved, covered in June to July with bright lavender flowers which are exquisitely fragrant. The height here is 4.5 m (14 ft) but in more favoured localities may be up to 6 m (20 ft). Propagation is by means of half-ripened shoots taken in July, or seed sown in late February in a frame.

Buddleia davidii is the best loved of all and the most widely grown. As a small boy I had to pass a garden which boasted a collection of these shrubs, two of which overhung the footpath. I spent many pleasant hours watching the butterflies which congregated on the flowers in late summer. Indeed, sometimes I feel the harvest of butterflies is more attractive than the flowers; certainly they are so far as children are concerned. The list of hybrids available grows longer each year; of the reddish-purple cultivars I find 'Royal Red' the most satisfactory, and 'White Cloud' is a good white. 'Black Knight' with very dark flowers excites comment from visitors, and looks most attractive when planted round with Golden Ray Lilies. 'Fascination' is the best of the pinks. Hard pruning is essential; the one-year wood should be cut back to within two or three buds of the old wood in March. I do a small amount of bud rubbing to space the remaining branches to best effect.

Cuttings taken as semi-ripened wood in July root readily in a sand frame, as will hard-wood shoots inserted in a nursery border in October.

Buddleia globosa grew for many years in a corner of my garden but I never found the gaunt, ill-furnished habit other than overpowering. I hasten to add that most of my friends hold different views, and consider this a first class shrub. The orange globular flowers are carried on short stalks in July, and are sweetly scented. They require no

Buddleia alternifolia has a graceful arching habit of growth

pruning, apart from a general thinning of the older wood in April. The hybrid between *B. davidii* and *B. globosa,* known as *B.* × *weyerana* 'Sungold', attracts me even less than *B. globosa,* but again I find myself in the minority. Certainly the plant grows with vigour, even on heavy clay soil. The globular flowers, which are developed on young wood in July and August, are a mixture of colours, with pink and orange predominating. One day someone will bring forth the yellow colouring of *B. globosa* on a shrub with the habit of *B. davidii,* an event I await with great interest.

Buxus

The box is one of those adaptable shrubs which will grow equally well either in sun or partial shade. The common species, *Buxus sempervirens,* has been widely used as a hedging plant and for topiary work. In common with several other evergreens, it was closely associated with certain religious ceremonies in olden times, and until recently the leaves yielded an extract which was used as a sedative. *Buxus sempervirens* makes a creditable dwarf hedge in those gardens where hedge clipping is considered a pleasure rather than a penance, and does not make any demands regarding soil.

The golden and silver-leaved cultivars 'Aureovariegata' and 'Elegantissima' respectively make attractive additions to the shrub border, and the bright leaves add interest to the winter landscape.

Cuttings of side shoots taken with a heel of old wood in September will root readily in sandy compost in a sand frame.

Calluna

In any garden with suitably acid soil it would be advantageous to include at least a small selection of the many cultivars of our native Ling, *Calluna vulgaris.* In the space available it would be impossible to include all the cultivars, but two or three are outstanding and thoroughly reliable. The first, *Calluna vulgaris* 'H. E. Beale', makes a brilliant display of rose-pink double

Opposite: A tasteful grouping of shrubs – *Cornus alba* 'Spaethii', *Cotinus coggygria* 'Royal Purple', and *Picea pungens* 'Erich Frahm'

flowers from August to November. The flower spikes are long, well formed, and reach approximately 75 cm (30 in). I keep the plants trimmed hard back each year after flowering to preserve the rounded, bushy habit. 'Alportii' has dark crimson flowers, and an almost military appearance with its stiff, erect habit.

For those who cherish white heather for the legendary good fortune it brings, then 'Mair's Variety', with long spikes, is excellent for cutting and presentation to those about to embark on the sea of matrimony. In spite of the fact that these plants grow well anywhere in this area, I still prefer to work the soil before planting with a dressing of peat, and lime-free sand. Every three years they get a further dressing of peat or well-rotted compost. Clip them over every year after flowering.

Cuttings of semi-ripe side shoots, taken in August, root readily in a compost of peat and sand. Alternatively the terminal cluster of shoots can be removed; this gives a quicker return, but fewer cuttings, unless there are a large number of stock plants from which selection can be made. To get the best results, fill an ordinary seed tray level to the brim with sand-peat compost, insert the cuttings, then place a piece of glass over them so that each shoot is pressed flat on the rooting medium.

There are few more attractive features than a well-laid-out heather garden, planted here and there with dwarf conifers to provide change in height as well as foliage contrast.

Caragana

At first sight *Caragana arborescens* appears much too delicate for the really exposed garden, and a clay soil. This was the impression I laboured under until forced, through lack of other suitable material, to use it in a bed of sticky clay at the top of the garden. Here it surprised me by outgrowing cotoneasters, and *Prunus cerasifera* 'Pissardii' ('Atropurpurea'). Eventually the caragana or Pea Tree makes a tall shrub, around 4.5 m (15 ft), with delicate compound leaves which colour a soft

yellow in early autumn. The blossoming period is in early summer, and the yellow flowers are carried one to four in number on short slender stalks. The named cultivars of *C. arborescens* require more shelter to do well, so it would be better to restrict the inital planting to the type. A light sandy soil in full sun would be eminently suited to their needs.

Propagation is by seed gathered in the autumn, immediately it is ripe, and then stored overwinter for sowing in February. Soak the seed for two or three hours in water before sowing, using a well-firmed John Innes seed compost. Cuttings of half-mature side shoots taken in August can also be tried. These should be 8 to 10 cm (3 to 4 in) long, and taken with a slight heel of old wood.

Carpinus

For me trees are the very essence of gardening, yet few private gardens offer sufficient scope for indulgence in planting them. The hornbeam, *Carpinus betulus*, rivals the beech in its quality as a hedging plant, and is well worth growing for its beauty as a specimen tree. Unlike beech, when grown as a hedge it will not retain its leaves through the winter, unless clipping is delayed until July. Eventually the hornbeam will make a tree some 15 m (50 ft) high, and will grow reasonably well on most soils. The finest trees have strongly ribbed stems, and the branch arrangement gives an impression of rugged strength not noticeable in the smooth trunk and pendulous habit of the beech.

Carpinus betulus 'Fastigiata' is one of the most beautifully formed fastigiate trees available, and because of its erect habit is useful for gardens of small dimensions. I take great care to keep them to a single leader in the formative years, so that the clean outline is preserved. The most attractive period is when they are carrying their fruiting catkins. 'Columnaris' is even slower growing, upright in growth as a young tree, becoming broadly cone shaped with age.

Ceanothus

Ceanothus is such a well-favoured genus that though in the open ground they are liable to be killed outright in very severe weather, given the shelter of a wall they will survive and flourish. The most desirable are those with blue flowers which are carried in such numbers, that a bush in full bloom is a sight to rejoice the gardener's eye.

Though suspect as to hardiness, most grow so quickly from cuttings taken in mid-summer as to make up for any deficiences in this respect.

C. × delilianus forms a convenient heading under which to include the cross between *C. americanus,* New Jersey Tea, from the United States, and the Mexican *C. coeruleus* which is very susceptible to even a slight frost. 'Gloire de Versailles' is the cultivar most widely grown with large trusses of powder-blue flowers in late summer. Surprisingly the lilac-pink 'Ceres' has survived on a south-facing wall in one garden I visit which is situated nearly 300 m (1000 ft) above sea level.

Ceanothus dentatus is a most attractive evergreen and most likely to achieve mellow maturity. The bright blue flowers are a feature in May. 'Autumn Blue', also evergreen and reliable, will carry the season on by opening blooms of darker blue in autumn. 'Cascade' covered a 3 m (10 ft) high, south-facing wall with dark green foliage in my last garden. The powder-blue panicles of flowers against the pale fawn stone and dark green leaves were a part of May in the garden.

Chaenomeles

Few shrubs have suffered as many name changes as the Japanese Quince, familiarly known as Japonica. It makes a dwarf spreading shrub of only 1 m (3 ft), and the bright orange flowers are carried in clusters on the previous season's shoots. The fruits, which seem enormous in comparison to the size of the bush, are a dull grey-green, but can be made into a most delicious jelly. I always keep a few of these unappetising looking fruits in a bowl on my desk, because they have a bouquet which is

unique. It is a combination of all the scents of autumn, which carries the mind back to that golden time, even in the depths of winter. *Chaenomeles speciosa,* often catalogued as *C. lagenaria,* includes amongst its hybrids some of the most gorgeously coloured spring-flowering shrubs. I am convinced that in the north of England they need a wall to get a thorough baking from the sun, which is neccessary to exploit their full floral abilities. Given a wall and judicious pruning, I have had specimens up to 2.7 m (9 ft) in height, but the average on an open planting is not more than 2 m (6 ft). Let it not be thought for one minute that because I mention wall cultivation the plant is in any way tender, for in my experience it is almost indestructible, the only need being sun. The shrub and I are very much akin in this respect, but often suffer disappointment.

There are hybrids enough to choose from. 'Nivalis' is the best white so far introduced. 'Phyllis Moore', pink, semi-double, and 'Simonii', blood red, are good value for ground occupied.

A cross pollination between two species, *C. japonica* and *C. speciosa,* resulted in hybrids of modest size, yet strong constitution. 'Boule de Feu', orange-red, 'Crimson and Gold' whose golden anthers contrast so vigorously with the blood-red petals, and 'Knap Hill Scarlet', with the longest flowering season of all, are the pick of a very heavy crop.

Correct pruning is important or the flowers tend to be hidden. Shorten back shoots of the current season's growth to five or six buds in September.

Chimonanthus

Of the chimonanthus I can only speak with respect as one does of the departed, for this shrub has so far utterly refused to have anything to do with the hospitality offered by any garden in my care. In due course, with more shelter, the pale yellow, sweetly scented flowers may be persuaded to make redolent with fragrance the winter air. As a shrub to plant in a rough place, no, a thousand times no!

Cistus

I am tempted to speak in a similar vein of cistus, that lovely race of plants whose fragile flowers make the dusty aridity of a journey in Greece or Spain endurable. Yet I do the Rock Rose an injustice, for two species are capable of surviving even quite severe winters.

Cistus × corbariensis which, for eight years, until someone pointed out the mistake, I grew as *C. × cyprius*. A neat evergreen 1 m (3 ft) high which in June opens pure white petals. *C. laurifolius* grows a little taller, up to 1.5 m (5 ft) and has dark green leathery leaves. The white flowers stained yellow at the base appear during late June-July.

Clethra

Clethra alnifolia, with white fragrant flowers, offers a solace to the departed summer, the blossoms appearing in September and October in this part of Yorkshire. They positively demand a soil devoid of any lime. In the open woodland six plants have formed strong open bushes, 2.1 m (7 ft) high in 11 years. One group suffered from the attention of a Highland bullock which broke into the garden, and spent a night sampling all the vegetable delicacies, eventually settling on the clethra as a main course. In spite of being debilitated, this plant has now developed into a wide spreading specimen; a glorious sight in pale September sunshine. One result of this ruthless pruning was a good crop of young branches ideally placed for layering. These were pegged down in early spring, and rooted 100 per cent. Alternatively, cuttings taken into a sun frame in mid-July will give 50 to 60 per cent. rooted material the following spring.

The cultivar 'Rosea' has proved by no means as tractable, the habit being rather lank, and the flowers an unprepossessing muddy pink.

Cornus

The genus *Cornus* contains an extensive, diverse range of species, much underrated as ornamental plants until recently. I remember a woodland on the Skipton to Clitheroe road,

For a lime-free soil, *Clethra alnifolia*

fringed with a dense planting of *Cornus alba*, whose shoots, wet with a passing shower, glowed under the morning sun as if the bushes themselves would burst into flame. Never until that February morning had I fully appreciated how truly beautiful this easily-grown plant could be.

The cultivar *C. a.* 'Sibirica' has even more scarlet shoots, but without the vigorous uncomplaining health of the type plant, needing care in cultivation or it sickens in a most disheartening manner. Not so the lovely *C. a.* 'Spaethii', whose golden-variegated leaves warm the dankest days of October. As with the type plant it will eventually make a bush 3 m (10 ft) high, and again like the parent every branch where it touches the ground will root. This is a pleasing habit, for all who see desire to own a plant. Cubits are added to the gardener's stature if, like the benevolent genie, he can conjure from under the bush a well-rooted plantlet all ready to be wrapped and carried away.

Of all the dogwoods, *C. canadensis* has long been my first love, though it hardly warrants the name of shrub, as the stems spring annually from a perennial rootstock. Anyone who cares for a charming wanderer which each year sends up a carpet of 15 cm (6 in) shoots, tipped in June with pure white bracts almost 2.5 cm (1 in) across, followed in due season by scarlet berries, will never regret the small sum demanded in exchange for this North American. A moist, peaty soil suits it to perfection; allow it to wander amongst groups of deciduous rhododendrons, in company with *Anemone apennina*, and that corner of the garden will henceforth need little further attention, apart from a word of approbation during the flowering season. Division forms the easiest means of increase, late April or early May being a suitable time.

Cornus kousa is praised by the poets of the south for the beauty and longevity of its large, pure white bracts, but in the north, except after exceptionally hot, dry summers, it only vouchsafes a meagre indication of the glory. Never have I seen them – as some describe the horizontal branches – completely hidden by the erect flowers. Rather, after painstaking search, a few sear blossoms might be found sheltering under the leaves. Nor is the habit sufficiently attractive to warrant the shrub's inclusion in a select border. However, if a warm, sunbaked corner can be given, the more optimistic will probably find reward in a riot of blossom, for if nothing else *Cornus kousa* is bone hardy and willing to grow. As with *C. alba*, layering is the most certain way of increasing stock. I have never secured one seed to try the alternative more natural process.

I believe *Cornus mas* was the first foreign representative of the family to be introduced, and with Gerard I would agree that here is a rare and dainty plant. Its constitution, like the wood, is iron hard, for it needs a fair degree of determination to stand the full blast of winter gales at the top of this garden, and then flower in February or March. Each year without fail or lack of prodigality, before any leaves appear, the naked branches are studded with yellow, pompon like umbels. It is best planted so that they can be viewed against the open sky.

A form of the species, 'Variegata', has, as the name implies, leaves which are broadly margined with white. Though somewhat slower growing this is a most handsome shrub. Of the other variant, 'Elegantissima', I harboured doubts until, two years ago, discovered a place for it in the shade of *Malus* 'Profusion'. There, protected from too much sun, the attractive green, pink and pale yellow of the leaves remained pristine. That the youngster flowered as well pleased me even more.

Cuttings taken in July of half-mature sideshoots offer an alternative method of increase to layering, but be satisfied with only 30 to 40 per cent. rooting unless bottom heat can be given.

Corylus

Corylus avellana, our native hazel, is almost worthy of inclusion for the joyful hope of spring it brings when flaunting yellow lamb's-tail catkins in February.

A hazel underplanted with snowdrops and yellow primroses is an encapsulation of April. Instead, practising a degree of selectivity, I grow only the Corkscrew Hazel, *C. avellana* 'Contorta', whose twisted branches look even more outrageous when in catkin. Snowdrops and primroses then add an elfin quality to the shrub's Quasimodo character.

Cotinus

Cotinus coggygria, Venetian Sumach, makes such a contribution to the autumn fiesta it is worth growing on that account. Indeed, it is more of a bonfire with the smoke grey flowers rising from the scarlet and gold of the leaves, especially in the form appropriately called 'Flame'.

'Foliis Purpureis' offers foliage interest from early spring in the rich plum-purple leaves to October when they colour to shades of red. A group of orange-red *Crocosmia* 'Firebird' adds to the Sumach flames. Provide well-drained reasonably fertile soil and, to enjoy all the beauty of foliage, light patterned shade. To produce fresh stock I just remove shoots from the parent plant with roots attached, using a sharp knife.

Cotoneaster

A better name would be Legion, for in truth they are many. The genus includes some of the finest of all winter-berrying shrubs, the only problem being to select from the wealth of talent available one or two of the best when garden space is limited. The choice offered by the species is wide enough, but once two or three are planted in close proximity cross-pollination results in hybrids, which the gardener must harden his heart against, and cut off in their prime. Unfortunately, I have not enough moral fibre, and the result is that the garden is dotted with unnamed hybrids. Some are very good, the majority are no improvement of the species.

I use *Cotoneaster adpressus* for covering up poor workmanship, caused by lack of stone in the rock garden. It will grow with equal facility on a hot

The Corkscrew Hazel, *Corylus avellana* 'Contorta'

bank, low wall, or across a manhole cover. In this garden it does not berry well, neither is the autumn colour anything to rejoice over. Instead I would choose the variety *praecox,* which is taller in habit with glossy foliage and attractively contoured branches. I grow this on a raised bed in the path of the west wind, and even there it has condescended to grow a sample of the large orange-red berries, which is more than the type species has deigned to do.

Cotoneaster bullatus must be a shrub of iron, since it is planted in pure clay on the windiest corner, yet never fails to flower, and then berry in autumn. I am reliably informed, by those blessed with a more sheltered garden, that the ultimate height is around 3.7 m (12 ft) but here it makes a spreading shrub of only 1.2 m (4 ft) at 15 years old. The berries are red, and the leaves turn a good purple-red in October most years.

In the rock garden where the tight, ground-hugging character can be seen to full advantage, *C. congestus* is a gem of a plant. As with all the genus it accepts almost any soil, acid or alkaline. I like to give it a rock to climb over, even putting an extra stone here and there so that the outline is broken as the branches surmount it. The flowers are small and pinkish, but carried in great profusion, and the berries are dull red and large in proportion.

Until this year I would have classed *C.* 'Cornubia' as indestructible. It had served as a windbreak for 15 years without any sign of damage apart from a slight incline from east to west. A late frost caught the young buds just as they broke, and in consequence most of the main branches were killed. This was something of a tragedy, for the evergreen habit and massive clusters of red berries made the corner of the garden in which the three 6 m (20 ft) high trees grew a place considerable beauty.

Cotoneaster dammeri is a useful, prostrate, evergreen shrublet for clothing steep banks or awkward slopes in the rock garden. The branches root wherever they touch the ground, but the specimens I grow have the unfortu-

nate habit of hiding their coral-red fruits on the undersides of the branches. Where pleasant greenery is all that is required, *C. dammeri* will, with good temper, accept almost any soil or situation.

A graceful deciduous shrub of spreading habit, *C. divaricatus* at 2 m (6 ft) is suitable for a garden of modest dimensions. The oval leaves are a rich glossy green throughout the summer, and in a sunny, dry position will turn scarlet in the autumn. The first specimen, acquired by devious means, was put in an out-of-the-way corner for two or three years, only to be moved into the august company of prunus and acer, planted so the westering sun of October could shine through the colouring leaves. The ground carpet is of colchicum and *Polygonum vacciniifolium,* a place of pilgrimage for those who love good plants.

Cotoneaster henryanus makes a stately shrub of 3 to 3.5 m (10 to 12 ft), and like most members of the genus comes readily from seed. The evergreen leaves have a grey cast, giving them an appearance not unlike certain rhododendrons. The flowers themselves are quite handsome, white with purple anthers, but it is when the rich crimson berries colour in the autumn that the shrub warrants the homage usually reserved for the magnolia or similar exotics. A ground carpet of white heather completes a picture altogether satisfying.

Probably the best known of the genus is *C. horizontalis* with its fan tracery of branches. On the wall of a house, no matter what the aspect, the rich autumn tapestry of scarlet leaf and orange berry never fails to mature however inclement the weather. I like it best planted as a free-growing shrub, where the branches can build up tier on tier into an intricate network.

Sharing one parent, namely *C. frigidus,* though of entirely different character *C.* 'Hybridus Pendulus' is the most versatile of the whole range of species and hybrids this vast genus offers. Whether grown draped over a drystone wall, or as ground cover, it never fails to give an abundant crop of bright red berries. I like it best as a small weeping tree budded onto a 2 m (6 ft) high stem. A green curtain beaded with coral red in autumn – a delight to both gardeners and visiting birds. As the branches touch the ground they develop much larger leaves to become very passable ground cover. I grow one plant in company with glaucous-leaved hostas and Winter Aconite.

Cotoneaster microphyllus thymifolius is one of the most closely habited, ground huggingly prostrate shrublets I grow. As they progress the branches grow roots to form a near weed-proof carpet. The plant I have growing along the terrace gets trimmed with the lawn when out of bounds, which only makes the network of twigs thicker.

Another gem for the autumn is *C. nitens,* which grows 1.5 m (5 ft) here. The glossy dark green leaves change with the shortening days through dull red-purple to scarlet, against which the long purplish-black fruits show to good advantage. I feel sorry for those who spend the glorious autumn days lamenting the approach of winter, the gorgeous colours all around the garden leave no room for regret, only complete and absolute contentment.

With its graceful weeping habit, *C. salicifolius* makes an excellent small specimen tree for a lawn. There are several forms ranging in height from the elegant 5 m (16 ft) of the type species, to the 30 cm (12 in) or so of *C. salicifolius prostratus* which is used to hold the soil on steep roadside verges. Enough of the varieties, *C. salicifolius* needs no retinue of bastards to support its throne in any garden. It has graceful arching shoots, clothed throughout the year in slender pointed leaves, then in autumn the ripe rich red of the fruits.

Cotoneaster simonsii was the first of this genus whose name I knew, simply because it grew as a hedge in the garden of the house where I was born. Passing years add lustre always to childhood memories, and yet even with the increased knowledge which maturity brings I would not deprive myself of the company offered by this attractive shrub. The habit is more erect than in most cotoneasters, a characteristic inherited by most hybrids with *C. simonsii* as a parent. The leaves are a dark glossy green, and in a mild winter are retained. The bright orange-scarlet fruits stud the branches from base to tip. It is on *Cotoneaster simonsii* that I look for the waxwings each year. They, unfortunately, enjoy the berries as much as I do though for less aesthetic reasons, but the pleasure of watching the birds compensates for the havoc they work amongst the fruit.

An evergreen hybrid, though of doubtful parentage, *C. × watereri* should be given a place of honour, so that the charm of spreading branches and brilliant berries can be enjoyed free of the clutter of subsidiary vegetation. Its branches are loaded with scarlet fruit each autumn with never-failing prodigality.

Propagation of the species is effected by means of seed gathered when ripe, then sown in sandy soil. After a winter's exposure to frost a good proportion will germinate the following spring. The dwarf species like *C. dammeri, C. horizontalis, C. congestus,* etc., root from cuttings made of the current season's wood in November.

Crataegus

The hawthorns include some species which seem well-nigh indestructible. From the mountains of Scotland to the windswept Cornish coast, even in towns notorious for atmospheric pollution, the ubiquitous thorn can always be relied on to give a good account of itself. In Ireland the thorn was thought to be a trysting place of fairies, by the Greeks a defence against sorcery or witchcraft. Chaucer propounds the legend of the man in the moon carrying a thorn bush on his back. Legend upon legend has been woven around the hawthorn, while I, as a child, unaware of the shrub's less mundane virtues, joined with other children in eating the young breaking buds, calling them 'bread and cheese'.

From the many species, only two and their cultivars need concern the gardener in search of tough, adaptable shrubs. *Crataegus monogyna,* more frequently a tree up to 9 m (30 ft), spreads a film of white over the hedgerows in May, and then in the autumn supplements the sun with its reflected scarlet. A walk along the hedgerows will reveal a wide variety in form and quality of the berry. One specimen growing on a piece of scrubland here makes a perfect umbrella of scarlet, the berries three times the size of those on the surrounding bushes.

Crateagus monogyna aurea is a yellow-berried form, slightly less vigorous, and to me not quite so pretty as the type, but interesting as a contrast where space is available.

Crataegus monogyna 'Pendula Rosea' makes a graceful weeping tree, with each slender shoot wreathed in deep pink flowers. On the specimen I have these are sterile, and I never see the same branches clothed with scarlet berries.

Crataegus oxyacantha occurs less frequently wild than *C. monogyna* in Yorkshire, but provides rather more garden-worthy cultivars. Probably the best known is the double crimson, which in spite of frequent repetition I still think looks very well with laburnum. It is slightly dwarfer in habit than the previous species, 4.5 to 6 m (15 to 20 ft) being the average height, and flowers in June.

Other hybrids include 'Pendula Rosea'; 'Plena', double white; and 'Rosea Flore Pleno', a pleasant full double pink. Propagation of cultivars is effected by means of budding or grafting on to seedling stock of *monogyna.* Pruning presents little difficulty, as can be seen in the neatly trimmed farm hedges. Hawthorns are very tolerant of the knife, and can be kept more or less to any shape or dimension desired. Heavy cutting is best carried out in November.

Cytisus

Cytisus are short-lived plants, requiring careful pruning to keep them in shape and full beauty. There are so many hybrids that unless a special colour is needed to fit into the garden scheme, greater interest can be gained by raising one's own stock from seed. I have seen beautiful mixed hedges of seedling broom, and, having planted several dozen in rough grassland to good effect, can vouch for their adaptability. They must be trimmed over after flowering to keep the bushes from becoming bare and leggy. With a pair of hedge shears remove two-thirds of the flowering shoots as the blossoms fade.

Of all the brooms, *Cytisus multiflorus,* the White Spanish Broom, is my favourite. Growing 2.5 m (8 ft) high and almost as wide, it is a mass of pure white flowers in late May and early June. When a particularly fierce gale finally laid it low, a self-sown seedling took over the position, and at first flowering proved to possess all the qualities of the parent.

Cytisus × beanii is an excellent dwarf yellow-flowered broom for the rock garden, and grows with as much aplomb on peat as it does in the better drained slope. Again, however, it is short lived, eight years being most I have come to expect.

A *C. multiflorus* seedling of considerable merit is the procumbent *Cytisus × kewensis,* just 30 cm (12 in) high. With a mass of creamy-yellow flowers in May, it is excellent for covering dry sunny banks.

Cytisus purpureus 'Atropurpureus', though dwarf in stature at 30 cm (12 in) bids fair to become the veritable patriarch of the race. This is easily the best dwarf purple broom and well worth a choice place.

Cytisus × praecox, the Warminster Broom, another *multiflorus* hybrid, is the most popular of all the brooms, and certainly the easiest to accommodate. Soil type, be it heavy clay or blow-away sand, offers no problems to this easy going shrub. In May the 1 to 1.2 m (3 to 4 ft) high framework of branches disappears under a canopy of rich cream flowers.

The Common Yellow Broom, *Cytisus scoparius,* which makes such a blaze of colour on the edge of Thorsgill Beck in Teesdale, has long been superseded by many hybrids. Of these I would choose 'Dragonfly', yellow and crimson, 'Firefly', bronze and crimson, 'Golden Sunlight', rich yellow.

Cuttings of semi-mature side shoots 8 to 10 cm (3 to 4 in) long taken in August, will root in a shaded frame. Alternatively, firm side shoots 10 to 15 cm (4 to 6 in) long, but taken with a heel of old wood so that the pith is not exposed, may be inserted in a cold frame in October.

Daphne

Daphne only just gain admittance on the strength of experience gained over the last nine years. Two species have grown, flowered, and provided self-sown seedlings since I planted them on a windswept plot 243 m (800 ft) above sea level.

Daphne mezereum has pink, sweetly scented flowers which have closed the door on winter and opened it to spring in all the gardens I have known since childhood. Two were planted, a white and a pink; self-sown seedlings in abundance have been given to friends since then and my own stock has increased to six. A well-drained soil, be it chalk or not, will ensure success.

The other species growing nearby is the slow-growing shrublet *D. retusa*. Unlike *D. mezereum* it is evergreen, and the flowers of deep rose-purple nestle close against the foliage to distil their fragrance in May. Propagation in this garden is simply a process of digging up self-sown seedlings – usually available every year.

Deutzia

Deutzias are fairly easy-going natives of China and Japan provided they are given an exposed position. I discovered this more by accident than anything else, for shrubs on a sheltered border, having been encouraged into precocious growth, were caught by frost, while those put in as shelter to nursery beds, and having to face the full blast of north and west winds, remained safely dormant, thus escaping damage.

In a sheltered position *Deutzia* 'Perle Rose' is an elegant 2 m (6 ft) plant, but

here it is only 1 m (3 ft). The pale rose flowers are borne in late June, and look delightful with a carpeting beneath of the white *Viola cornuta alba,* a plant, incidentally, which comes easily from seed. Given a little attention to thinning out of surplus shoots, 'Perle Rose' is a shrub of great charm.

Deutzia scabra in a garden near Clitheroe astonished me by appearing as a giant of 3.7 m (12 ft). Elsewhere, both in open woodland, and fully exposed in the garden, it stubbornly persists at a maximum height of 2 m (6 ft). The flowers in July in the best forms are a clean brilliant white, carried in large clusters 15 cm (6 in) long. A cultivar I grow as 'Pride of Rochester', but listed in some catalogues as 'Plena', has double flowers tinged with rose-purple. When pruning, and this I only do if the bush becomes straggly (which does happen), just remove the old wood, leaving the younger more floriferous previous-season's growth to furnish up.

Seed is set quite freely on some species, and may be sown in spring with hope of success. If a particular varietal characteristic is desired, cuttings should be made from semi-mature wood in July inserted into a sand frame. Alternatively hardwood cuttings in October are satisfactory.

Enkianthus

This is a much neglected race of shrubs for the lime-free garden. Not only are the flowers attractive and unusual, but the autumn colour also is exquisite. Their hardiness is not in question so far as I am concerned, for anything which will take the full brunt of the weather which comes out of the west in this area without complaining has my unstinted admiration. With a thick coat and gloves I still complain most bitterly, but then I do not flower, so even if in the tender class I am also undesirable.

Enkianthus campanulatus has the happy knack of producing its branches in whorls round the main stem. The cup shaped flowers are pale yellow, veined in red, deliciously lovely seen with the evening sun through them. This is a

shrub which really should be grown in association with silver birch; in autumn the scarlet tints of the dying leaves look lovely against the silver stems and soft yellow leaves of the birch. The tallest specimen planted 20 years ago has reached 3 m (10 ft).

Enkianthus cernuus is smaller in all its parts except the flowers, and is possessed of an elfin grace which somehow underlines its Japanese ancestry. I had a specimen which sat quite happily in a 15 cm (6 in) pot for eight years and only grew 45 cm (18 in) high, but in the open ground it will grow to a majestic 1.5 m (5 ft). The flowers on the type plant are creamy-white, but in the variety *rubens* they are a rich red, the colour of port wine with the light behind it.

Seed is set freely, and ripens here in the New Year, and must be kept dry; better still sow immediately in a compost of 2 parts peat to 1 part sand. Keep shaded, but not dark, until the seed germinates and for a full season afterwards. Layering is an alternative method of increase, and I have had a modest success with cuttings - about 20 per cent. strike, but very slow and laborious it is.

Erica

Ericas or heaths are now rich in a wealth of new cultivars, enjoying a popularity they thoroughly deserve. It would be impossible in a book of this sort to mention them all, but ground cover is important in the interest of weed control, and for this purpose heaths are excellent.

Erica herbacea (*E. carnea*) is the versatile species accepting a lime soil with unshakable equanimity, whereas most of the other species abhor even a trace. I have grown this on north-facing banks, under cherry trees and even silver birch, and it never fails to pay full token of ground rent. Suitable cultivars are 'King George' with deep pink flowers from January to April; 'Myretoun Ruby' is easily the first choice, the dark green foliage setting off ruby-red flowers in a way which commands admiration; 'Praecox Rubra' is deep red; and the best white is 'Springwood White'. Where good foliage is considered important, a point often overlooked, 'Foxhollow', which is yellow in summer, then pink tinted in winter, is a prime cultivar. *E. herbacea* has the happy habit of layering shoots as it spreads, so propagation is self-inflicted, rooted offshoots being detached as required.

Another of the genus which accepts lime is *E. terminalis;* fortunately the flowers come in late summer, and I delude myself that on the acid clay here the colour is a richer pink. The habit is bushy and erect up to 1 m (3 ft). Cuttings of short sideshoots, taken with a heel, root readily in a sand and peat compost.

Erica vagans is of such robust character that for several years it competed on equal terms with the native Blaeberry. This is one of the lime haters which if well mulched each year with peat or pulverized bark will succeed.

Cultivars to try are 'Lyonesse', with pure white flowers made even more attractive by the protruding brown stamens; 'Mrs D. F. Maxwell' deep cerise, which is one of my special favourites; and *rubra* is a cheerful rosy-red. Cuttings of sideshoots taken in August and September root with almost vulgar alacrity.

Escallonia

It seems somehow remarkable, in the light of my own experience, that this genus was once considered quite unsuitable for northern gardens. Admittedly not all are hardy, but others are now used to shelter tender shrubs. In a hard winter they become deciduous, but soon recover with the flush of spring. The two hybrids I would unhesitatingly recommend are *Escallonia* 'Edinensis' which is neat and bushy, up to 2 m (6 ft) in height, with bright pink flowers from late May and early June onwards. Indeed, I can pick an armful of well-flowered sprays from bushes in the garden in late October, and have done the same each summer. The other is *E.* 'Langleyensis' which has deeper flowers of rosy-crimson, and longer, more

Opposite: Daphne retusa is a slow-growing shrublet

Erica herbacea (E. carnea) accepts a lime soil

arching branches up to 2.1 m (7 ft) in height.

After growing the Donard cultivars for nine years I would include 'Donard Radiance' with rose-red flowers, and 'Slieve Donard', a pink blossomed hybrid, as contenders in the field of tough shrubs.

Escallonias are extremely tolerant of clipping and make good informal windbreaks. Cuttings of semi-ripened shoots taken in July and August will root in a sand frame.

Euonymus

Because of their happy-go-lucky disposition, and ready acceptance of most soils, acid or alkaline, euonymus quite frequently receive only scant praise for their efforts. They are essentially shrubs of the autumn and the scarlet leaves and vivid fruits glow under the light of October sunshine in the most heart-warming manner. *Euonymus alatus* has the curious habit of producing corky wings on the branches, a figuration which has attracted the admiration and attention of those who indulge in flower arranging.

The cattle which invaded the garden, and made a meal of the clethra (p. 82), ate three bunches of the euonymus to the ground with no apparent ill effects, so it is not only the flower arrangers who admire the plants. Growth is rather slow in exposed situations, it has taken the largest specimen eight years to reach 2.1 m (7 ft); a desirable habit for the small garden, but certainly not a shrub for quick effect. The dark green leaves turn rich red in the autumn, usually before the other shrubs begin to colour.

I have not had a great deal of luck in raising this species from seed, so make resort to layering as the method of increasing stock. Cuttings taken with a slight heel in August will root with moderate ease given a compost of 2 parts sand and 1 part peat by volume. Pruning consists of removing surplus shoots of old wood to keep the plant shaped-up.

The well known Spindle, *E. europaeus*, is a native of our own chalk lands. Again this is a shrub for the autumn, the leaf colour exquisite but fleeting when compared with the acers. The seedpods are the prime attraction, the pod being pink and the fruit inside orange; an outrageous combination, yet the effect is far from being offensive. This species shows none of the reluctance displayed by *E. alatus* to germinate from seed, the only problem being to beat the birds to the harvest. I sow immediately they are ripe in sand, let them stand overwinter, then open up the drills 0.5 cm (¼ in) deep in a sheltered bed outside, and sow sand, plus seeds, into these. This is a modified form of stratification which has worked well with me.

Euryops

Euryops acraeus from Basutoland seems a most improbable candidate for election. After 10 years of severe trials it earns, if not a full blue ribbon, at least one only a shade paler than established toughies. A dwarf shrub some 45 cm (18 in) high which makes a silver-grey mushroom of foliage in early summer. The leaves disappear under a mass of canary yellow flowers. Though the plants show signs of age after six or seven years, cuttings root so easily if taken in July. I keep up a succession without difficulty. One essential factor is the drainage must be good and sharp.

Exochorda

The name exochorda gives an impression of exotic tenderness to me, so the first specimens I handled received almost red-carpet treatment. Now, having proved their resilient hardiness, they are used to shelter seedling rhododendrons planted out of frames. Most are too big for a small garden and all are deciduous.

Exochorda giraldii makes a bush 3 m (10 ft) high with white flowers 2.5 to 5 cm (1 to 2 in) across, borne in erect clusters during May. This rather bald description does less than justice to the beautiful picture the flowers make, but I can always find it in me to admire white-flowered shrubs.

Layering offers the readiest means of increase, and often branches will do this

Euryops acraeus is proving to be a tough plant

of their own accord. Prune to keep the plant within bounds, and occasionally remove old worn-out wood.

Exochorda korolkowii is a wide-spreading shrub of 4.5 m (15 ft); here it is not so free with its floral tributes as is *E. giraldii*, but beautiful nevertheless. Again the blossoms are white and appear in May. Propagation is the same as for other species.

Forsythia

Like the cherries, no garden large enough to hold them should be without forsythias, for the golden cascade of colour with which they greet the spring. The genus is named in honour of William Forsyth, and there can be few gardeners who have a more beautiful memorial. *Forsythia × intermedia* 'Spectabilis' in its best forms has no equal, and I hold to this in spite of the bud sport 'Lynwood', having planted one alongside the patriarch of all the forsythias in this garden seven years ago, and having been able to compare the virtues over consecutive years. The bush here has a rather upright habit, just topping 2.5 m (8 ft), the branches arching at the tips, and wreathed from base to tip each April in bright yellow flowers. I prune old wood out only every four or five years when flowering suffers. To cut old wood out each year, as some advocate, results in a shrub which is the picture of gaunt austerity.

In the cultivar 'Lynwood' the individual flowers are larger, but under arduous conditions of soil or climate there is not the same vigour or eagerness to please. However, it is a class shrub in every other respect, and does not show the variability of 'Spectabilis'.

Propagation is easily effected by cuttings which seem to root at almost any time. I once used prunings from forsythias as sticks for early peas, and 75 per cent. of these rooted after lying in a heap for a week before insertion. I like to grow a forsythia against a glaucous juniper or similar cool colour, for it deepens the tone of the flowers and later when out of blossom the gaunt habit of the plant does not impinge on the eye.

Fuchsia

One would suppose a plant so intimately associated with the warmth of a greenhouse to be completely unsuitable for cultivation outdoors in a northern garden. Yet strange as it may seem *Fuchsia magellanica*, and several of the hybrids from it, have proved some of the most tractable shrubs tried here, especially on the heavier soil.

Fuchsia magellanica, the type species, makes a bush 2 m (6 ft) high, covered for many months from midsummer until well into autumn with pendulent flowers of a typical fuchsia combination of purplish-blue and scarlet. There is a white form of similar habit.

Fuchsia magellanica gracilis is more erect in growth, reaching 1.2 m (4 ft), the branches being thinner than in the species, giving a lighter, more fragile appearance to the bush. However, the flowers are still plentiful, and over the same period. I grew this plant for years as 'Corallina', until I acquired *gracilis* and found them to be one and the same.

Fuchsia 'Riccartonii' fully deserves the reputation of being hardiest of the race. Recently I spent a long day in driving rain searching out species heathers amongst the Lochans of Connemara. Returning home in early evening we passed along lanes arched over with 'Riccartonii' in full bloom.

There are numerous fuchsia hybrids with larger flowers which, though herbaceous because all the top growth is frosted in most winters, are reliably perennial. From those cultivars established in the garden I would suggest 'Mrs Popple', scarlet and violet, 'Lena', pink and deep rose, and 'Genii' with yellow-green foliage topped by a profusion of small violet and cerise flowers. 'Lady Thumb', 'Tom Thumb' and 'Phyllis' are three more of the ever lengthening list of cultivars which are hardy enough to survive outdoors in my garden.

Propagation by means of semi-ripe side shoots taken as opportunity offers is easy enough to flatter the gardener's ego. Pruning consists of removing dead wood and thinning out overcrowded shoots.

Trees and Shrubs: Gaultheria to Pyrus

Like many ericaceous plants, gaultherias dislike lime in any shape or form, but otherwise are invaluable, acting as weed suppressors under taller trees or shrubs. The evergreen foliage gives a quiet undertone during the winter. I use them in open woodland, and to clothe steep banks, especially those with a northerly aspect. Nearly all the species spread by means of underground stems. *Gaultheria hookeri* is a native of the Himalayas, and had a rough time in the first three years of our acquaintance. First it was planted in uncleared woodland with some crested ferns, then almost under a beech tree, neither position being conducive to vigorous growth. It survived the vicissitudes of the early years, and is now happily carpeting the ground under a salix in the peat garden. The leaves are fairly large, and the habit a little sparse when compared with the more popular species. In exposed places it will grow to around 60 cm (2 ft) but in more favoured localities will reach 2 m (6 ft). The pinky-white flowers in April are followed by purple berries which the birds enjoy before they ripen.

Introduced from Japan in the late 19th century *G. miqueliana* is an excellent dwarf shrub. Reaching only 30 to 38 cm (12 to 15 in), the ideal combination of this plant is with meconopsis, gentians and ferns. The white flowers open during early June, then in September they are transformed into large, waxy, white berries, faintly flushed with pink. The berries are said to be edible, but I prefer to crush them and inhale the rich acrid fragrance, strongly reminiscent of wintergreen.

Gaultheria shallon was widely planted at one time to give cover for the nesting birds on game preserves, and is therefore the best-known species. In shelter it will grow up to 2 m (6 ft) high, especially in the dense shade of taller trees. On the rather exposed banks where it is used to hold the soil, and be decorative in the winter, the height is rarely more than 60 cm (2 ft). The leaves are broad, leathery in texture, and almost hide the pinkish-white flowers which open in June. A native of Alaska and Western North America, the English climate must be to its liking, judging by the rapid rate of spread.

Propagation is simple. Just remove the runners which spread out around all the species mentioned or take cuttings, in August, rooting them in a sand frame.

Genista

This genus has not supplied any really long-lived species, capable that is of surviving more than eight to ten years on this soil. *Genista hispanica* is usually listed as being first class on sun-baked banks, which tends to mislead the gardener into restricting it to the hottest, poorest parts of the garden. In fact *G. hispanica* has grown happily in some of the stiffest clay, on a very exposed border for 10 years, never failing to smother the whole of its spiny 60 cm (2 ft) frame with yellow flowers in May. This is one of the neatest and most handsome shrubs for the small garden, for even when not in flower, the dense habit, each branch overcast with a faintly grey colouring, is altogether satisfying.

Propagation is effected by means of seeds sown under glass in February, or out of doors in spring. Cuttings of nearly mature sideshoots, taken with a heel, will root with reasonable alacrity in a sandy soil. I find from experience September is the best month to do this.

A first-class plant for clothing dry

Opposite: Magnolia ✕ soulangiana with an underplanting of muscari

banks or covering retaining walls is *G. pilosa,* a native of south-west England. Prostrate in habit, and beautiful in May and June when each shoot is hidden under a myriad of yellow flowers, this shrub will not tolerate the least hint of poor drainage, but it does not mind the bludgeoning and cruelty of a northern winter. Cuttings of semi-ripened side-shoots, or seed sown in spring, are equally effective methods of propagation.

The lovely *G. lydia* has proved rather temperamental on the clay; six or seven years is the longest a specimen can be persuaded to sojourn. A rooted cutting planted eight years ago on the edge of a terrace shows promise of becoming a patriarch. Now 60 cm (24 in) high, in June a cascade of golden-yellow flowers tempts me into rooting more cuttings to establish colonies elsewhere in the garden.

Hamamelis
This name is apparently derived from either an ancient Greek word meaning pear-shaped fruit; or (and to me, a more logical derivation) from *hama,* together with, and *melis* fruit, because in its native home fruit and flowers may in some years be found on the branches at the same time. The shrub is better known by its popular name of witch hazel, and decoctions from the bark are still a useful remedy for inflammation and insect bites. An indication of the futility of using popular names for plants might be noted here, for in Essex the name witch hazel is used to describe hornbeam. No matter, any shrub which has sufficient fortitude to present flowers in mid-winter – for to me and most northern gardeners the black unpredictable weather of February is mid-winter, not spring – is welcome to bed and board in my garden.

Hamamelis japonica makes a shrub of 2.5 to 3 m (8 to 10 ft), and the whole habit indicates its Japanese origin. Gaunt and angular in outline, with the yellow flowers in clusters up the leafless branches in February, it makes a picture to delight the eye. Unusually the month does bring one or two days of soft spring-like gentleness, beguiling plant and gardener alike into the feeling that winter has gone. The witch hazels are content in most soils if the drainage is good, with a little peat or well-rotted manure to hold the essential moisture against a time of drought. Several cultivars of the species can be obtained such as the tall growing 'Arborea' which looks superb in the rough grass of a birch wood, and grows up to 3.7 to 4.5 m (12 to 15 ft), having golden-yellow flowers with contrasting calyces of dark purple. The foliage turns soft yellow streaked with copper in the autumn. Another variety not quite so tall is 'Zuccariniana'.

The Chinese member of the family, *H. mollis* is undoubtedly the finest of all. The flowers are bright golden-yellow, with the same spider-like character of the others, and delightfully fragrant withall. It is strange that this plant has not won the place in my affections that *H. japonica* 'Arborea' occupies, but this is through no fault of its own. I put the first three specimens of *H. mollis* in a bed which appeared perfectly well drained, but unknown to me cherished a spring of evil smelling water, said to be possessed of medicinal properties. The efficaciousness of this liquid was the reverse of any which legend purported it to have on humans. Two of the plants sickened and died before the culprit was discovered. The third was removed to the wood and has since been joined by two more. Released from the bonds of sulphur, this species is proving a most lovely comfortable shrub to live with. Where previously I worried about its pallid limpness, now all that is needed is time to enjoy the beauty when each branch is ringed with fragrant yellow.

Layering is the obvious means of raising new stock where facilities do not exist for grafting, which is the method of commerce. Use strong shoots of the previous season's growth, tongued 20 to 25 cm (8 to 10 in) from the tip. Mound up over the tongue when the layer is pegged to the ground, with a sandy compost to a depth of 15 cm (6 in).

There is a cultivar of *Hamamelis mollis* which has been given the name 'Pallida' which suggests to me a plant just recovering from some malaise. In fact, this is the loveliest of witch hazels. A well-grown shrub with branches wreathed in primrose yellow, sweetly scented flowers has the power to wean even the most reluctant gardener into ungrudging admiration. Growth is slower certainly than on other witch hazels I have grown, but like Jacob, for so lovely a Rebecca the investment of years is a minor inconvenience.

Hebe

Still better known to the gardener as veronicas, coming as most of them do from New Zealand, hebes could hardly be expected to make a major contribution to the exposed garden landscape. There are one or two which make a brave face, only suffering superficial damage in severe winters. *Hebe ochracea (H. armstrongii)* is easily my favourite of the reliably hardy types, but occasionally is offered in a form which grows lank and straggly up to 1.2 m (4 ft). The plant I have is still a compact, close-growing bush of 30 cm (12 in) high after 10 years, with foliage a deep shining gold, strongly reminiscent of a cypress. In July the milky-white flowers cluster at the tips of the branchlets.

Propagation is by sideshoots taken in early September and rooted in a sand frame. So far the heavy soil and several severe winters have not succeeded in removing one cubit from its stature.

Hebe brachysiphon has proved something of an enigma; one or two of the bushes were scorched in the hard winters of the last 12 years, but recovered completely. The soil made no difference, those on the alluvial sand are no better or worse than those on the heavy clay fully exposed to the west. Growing up to 1.2 m (4 ft), the evergreen leaves are a pleasant green, starred in June with white flowers.

It is easy to take cuttings of sideshoots in September, but I wait for a fairly severe winter, then gather up the self-sown seedlings which germinate in abundance the following spring. I believe that in most situations all hebes are granted an extension of life if the soil is reasonably well drained.

Hebe buxifolia is a pleasant evergreen shrub 60 cm (2 ft) high. Compact and well-furnished it is a perfect bun for the front of the border, for even in mid-winter the leaves have that dark lustrous green appearance which gives an impression of good health. The white flowers in June and July are carried in closely-knit spikes. Side shoots taken in August or September will root with reasonable alacrity.

Holodiscus

Holodiscus discolor ariaefolius is a tall-growing, one might almost call it a powerful shrub, from North America. I underestimated the vigour of this plant, and put five bushes much too close together, and the resulting struggle for supremacy could almost be felt. This shrub is very tolerant of pruning, indeed, a cutting back of old wood in February is of considerable benefit. A moisture-retentive soil, not liable to dry out in the summer, is ideal, so a heavy clay is accepted gracefully. The leaves are greyish-green above, covered with grey matted wool underneath, and are seen at their best when teased by the wind, showing first one colour and then the other. Flowers appear in late June or July in large feathery panicles, completing the list of virtues which added together make a very garden-worthy plant. Cuttings of half-matured sideshoots, 13 cm (5 in) long and cut at a node in July, will soon root in a compost of 3 parts sand to 1 of peat by volume.

Hydrangea

Hydrangea arborescens 'Grandiflora' in full bloom against a setting of dark green pines is a sight for the gods. This is how the plant is grown at Parceval Hall in a narrow gully, thickly wooded with rhododendrons and pine trees, against which the large heads of white flowers stand out in bold relief. A hardy shrub, 1.2 to 1.5 m (4 to 5 ft) tall, essentially informal in character, it is an ideal

Hydrangea macrophylla needs shelter

associate for rhododendrons. I grow it on clay with equal success. The only pruning is an occasional thinning out of old wood once every four or five years.

Cuttings of sideshoots or internodal material root in a sandy compost. An alternative would be to peg long shoots of the previous season's growth firmly to the ground and then as the young growths break in spring mound them up at the base with compost. The rooted shoots can be lifted and separated from the parent branch the following spring.

When in flower *H. cinerea* bears a strong resemblance to the last mentioned and though the 10 to 15 cm (4 to 6 in) white flowers are more spreading the height is the same. It blooms about one week earlier. Propagation is by cuttings as for *H. aborescens*.

Hydrangea petiolaris is in reality a climber, but can be utilised pegged down to cover north facing banks. It is best grown on a north wall as a self-clinging climber. I have used it to cover unsightly stumps where it develops a pleasing shrubby habit. The white flowers are borne in July and August, and the picture is rendered even more pleasing if a pale blue clematis of the 'Perle d' Azure' type is so planted as to twine amongst it.

The various forms of *H. macrophylla*, the Common Hydrangea, need shelter from the full blast of winter in the depths of the woodland or border, as otherwise they are purely foliage plants with no beauty.

Hypericum

Hypericum or shrubby St John's Worts, the herb of St John, are plants of many virtues, not all of which are confined to the garden. In Folkard's *Plant Lore* they are listed in some detail as cures for melancholia and insanity, or for deep wounds or poison. Certainly a hypericum in full glory of golden flowers can be guaranteed to lighten the blackest melancholy of an English summer. They thrive in almost any soil, even poorly drained clay, and display their bright golden flowers during late summer and autumn.

A free flowering bush up to 60 cm (24 in), *Hypericum androsaemum* tolerates with equanimity the dense shade of a horse chestnut. Flowering continuously from July into the autumn, quite frequently the early flowers have become red seed-pods before the late blooms have fallen, the yellow and red making a brilliant picture.

Seed sown in spring will germinate, but must be stored in a dry place until the operation takes place; damp seems to reduce the viability.

Hypericum calycinum or Rose of Sharon, when not disciplined like a wilful child, soon becomes a nuisance. On a dry shady border the boskage of 45 cm (18 in) high stems, topped by enormous yellow flowers, lift a fairly inhospitable site in a way that is ample recompence for the scant problem caused when shoots need chopping back within bounds.

A surprisingly tough native of the Canary Isles, *H. elatum* makes a dense bush. Driving through one of the Leeds suburbs which was in process of being demolished, I was astonished to see, in the shattered remains of a garden, a vivid yellow-flowered shrub quite unperturbed by the grime and dust. I stopped to investigate, and discovered it was a hypericum, and as there were none like it in my own garden brought away some cuttings. They have since been identified as *H. elatum*, and are now comfortably established and bloom continuously from July to late October. Cultivation is as for *H. androsaemum*.

Hypericum patulum is a spreading shrub from China, 1 m (3 ft) high with yellow flowers, but has long since been superseded by cultivars developed from it. *H. p.* 'Henryi' is excellent, neater in habit than the species, bearing continuously from July to October the golden-yellow saucer-shaped flowers 5 cm (2 in) across. Provided the drainage is not impeded, any soil seems to suit, though I have a bush underneath a *Prunus* 'Kanzan' which has as neighbours a wide selection of candelabra primulas. It is not wise to take too many liberties with the plant's tolerant good nature.

Opposite: *Hypericum patulum* 'Hidcote' has a flowering season from July to October

Cuttings of firm wood 10 to 15 cm (4 to 6 in) long with a heel, taken in November, will give a fair percentage of rooted material if inserted in a cold frame. Soft-wood cuttings in July are just as reliable, but require a regular watering to keep them from drying out.

'Hidcote' is my favourite and has comfortably the largest flowers of any hypericum grown here. Possessed of the same good nature as the other species described, I have used it as a dwarf hedge to shield less reliably hardy plants from the east or west wind. Once again the flowering season is from July to October. Propagation is the same as for *H. p.* 'Henryi'.

Ilex

Ilex contains that well-loved evergreen in its ranks, the common holly. There can be no more delightful berrying shrub than this, seen against a severe winter landscape with bright red berries and glossy evergreen leaves. In sun or shade, fully exposed on the edge of the moors, or closely sheltered in some well-wooded valley, it brightens the heart of winter, and provides a link with all the festivals of Christmas both past and in the future.

Ilex × altaclarensis gives us the pyramidal 'Camelliifolia', a beautiful almost fastigiate tree which berries two years out of three. When it berries it generally produces very heavy crops of fruits.

The Common English Holly, *Ilex aquifolium*, has given rise to so many cultivars it would be impossible to include them all. Of the golden-leaved ones my choice would be 'Golden King', which by some curious chance happens to be female; 'Golden Queen' which, strange as it may seem, is male, and 'Madame Briot', which in addition to having leaves banded with gold also berries freely.

Propagation is a problem for the amateur, but cuttings taken in late July will root, though only a small proportion, so be prepared for this. Commercially, recourse is made to layering or grafting but mist propagation has offered further possibilities and ensures a high percentage rooting.

Jasminum

In the jasmine family are contained some very desirable shrubs; only two, however, are reliably hardy here. *Jasminum nudiflorum* is undoubtedly the best known, and flowering as it does unprotected right through the long dark winter, deservedly so. Most gardeners cherish a kindly feeling for plants associated with early childhood, and the Winter Jasmine is one which I can always picture as it grew on the side of the house where I spent the first 22 years of my life. Because of the lax, rambling habit, Winter Jasmine should be grown as a wall plant so that the long four-angled shoots can be pulled upright showing the yellow flowers to best advantage. Where a wall is not available, a fence or the shrub border will suffice, the long shoots being shortened back to encourage side buds to break. The leaves are glossy green, and the flowers are carried in the axils of the leaves from November to March or even April, if the winter has been severe enough to inhibit flower production earlier. The fragrance is delicate, and can best be appreciated if the sprays of blossoms are cut and taken into a warm room. Pruning consists of cutting back each flowering shoot as the blossoms fade, to within two or three buds of the base. If the plant is grown as a shrub, it may be necessary to thin out the tangle of older branches to let in light and air. Stock is easily increased by means of cuttings made from half-ripened shoots in August.

Jasminum revolutum would be more correctly listed as a form of *J. humile*. This nearly evergreen shrub which for 11 years has come unscathed through the worst winters, growing in the most unspeakable, poorly drained, yellow clay, just where the west wind sweeps around the corner of the shrub border, shows a remarkable constitution. I hasten to add that there is protection from the east, that black chasm from which the killing winds come in spring. Unlike *J. nudiflorum*, *J. revolutum* flowers in June, July and August. Propagation is, however, effected by the same means. *Jasminum officinale*, the Common White Jasmine, has turned its face stubbornly to the wall so far as I am concerned, all advances on my part to persuade active growth having been rebuffed. Good drainage is one absolute essential, and if this is provided this strong vigorous climber will start to produce its white fragrant flowers in abundance during late June, and continue until September. A cultivar I saw growing recently on a house wall in the upper Dales had larger flowers with just a tinge of pink, and the name given was *J. officinale* 'Affine', but the flowers had that washed-out look, the pink sullying the white rather than relieving it.

Kalmia

Charming, delightful shrubs though they need a lime-free-soil, and, in the case of *Kalmia latifolia* and *K. polifolia,* shelter from strong winds to give of their best. *K. angustifolia* is a narrow-leaved shrub 60 cm (2 ft) high. The type plant, now safely established in the heather garden, was brought to me by a gentleman who found it growing wild on the Yorkshire Moors. How a native of North America managed to transport itself to Yorkshire I do not know, but the fact that it has survived in competition with our native Ling is sufficient proof of a vigorous colonial intent to make the best of the situation.

A moist, peaty soil is most suitable, and then it will spread happily by means of sucker growths from the base, which are a useful means of starting a fresh colony, as they make good 'Irishmen's cuttings'. The flowers open in June, densely packed in clusters on the previous year's growth. The colour in the best forms is a rich rosy-red. The cultivar 'Rubra' flowers more profusely and the red is deeper, but, apart from the darker green leaves, other characters are identical with the type.

Kalmia latifolia will grow in full exposure, but presents a rather unhappy appearance with gaunt stems and brown edges to the leaves. Given modest shelter the glossy leaves and bright pink flowers in June make this a very beautiful shrub. In full exposure it will grow to 1.2 m (4 ft), in the woodland up to 2.5 m (8 ft).

Kerria

This is a monotypic genus. Only one there may be, but *Kerria japonica* is of great merit. Originally the double form was cultivated under stove conditions, but once hardiness was established, ease of propagation soon assured the spread of kerrias into gardens all over the country. This ease of cultivation is one reason, no doubt, for the lack of popularity, gardeners seem to resent anything which grows so easily as to present no challenge to their skill. A deciduous shrub 1.2 to 2.5 m (4 to 8 ft) in height, with glossy slender shoots, it has yellow flowers in April and May. I have seen kerrias flourishing on alkaline clays, on sand, and here on the heavy acid clay of this district. The long arching branches reach up to 2 m (6 ft) and give shelter to tender rhododendrons planted behind. I know of many plants of considerable merit which receive slavish devotion, and then manage only a travesty of flowers. In an exposed garden such as this I prefer reliability to miffish indifference. The double-flowered form is entirely different in character, sparse, much stouter branched than the type, with flowers a mass of bright yellow petals, like the pompons on a child's slipper. In the garden of the school-teacher's house in Barningham it grew up to 3 m (10 ft), and trained on a wall it was very becoming against the grey stone. Propagation is effected by division, or if preferred (though I could hardly see any reason) by cutting or layers.

Laburnocytisus and Laburnum

Laburnocytisus adamii is a graft hybrid between a laburnum and a cytisus. So far as I am concerned it is an object of curiosity rather than a thing of beauty, but visitors express admiration, and the specimen here has grown with vigour in the most exposed situation so it is only fair to include it.

At first glance it has the look of laburnum, then one notices the cytisus leaves mixed up with those of the

Kalmia latifolia needs lime-free soil and shelter

laburnum. In the flower the confusion grows, some racemes yellow, some pink, and some a mixture of the two, resulting in a coppery-pink shade. All that is required is a well-drained soil, and where possible a position in full sun. Cuttings taken in late November and December of the current season's growth, 23 to 30 cm (9 to 12 in) long with a heel, are the safest means of increasing stock.

Laburnum anagyroides 'Vossii' is an excellent long-racemed free-flowering hybrid, but on heavy soils the roots do not develop sufficiently to hold the tree upright in the face of the sort of gales inflicted on long-suffering gardeners by the weather gods of the west. On well-drained soils it shows no such inclination to a prostrate habit, and a well-grown specimen, such as one sees at Newby Hall, is a truly remarkable sight against the intense blue of a June sky. The ultimate height is 6 to 9 m (20 to 30 ft).

Ligustrum

The common name privet is usually ejaculated with a disdainful curl of the lip by well-informed gardeners; the very word reeks of contempt, which is a great pity. They are useful, fast growing shrubs with no particular preference as to soil, and a remarkable tolerance of shady places. *Ligustrum ovalifolium* is a good hedge plant, tolerating the atmosphere in towns without any signs of displeasure. The golden-leaved form, 'Aureum', is equally good tempered as a hedge plant, but I like to see it growing in the shrub border. Foliage plants of this calibre have an important part to play, for most flowers are fugitive, but the foliage is there throughout the season.

Cuttings of semi-mature shoots will root in a sand frame.

With softly glaucous-green leaves, *L. sinense* has quite lovely sprays of white flowers in July. In this garden the height is some 3 m (10 ft) after 12 years, and the only fault I can find is that it spreads out under heavy snow. In mild winters some of the leaves are retained, but usually it is deciduous.

Lonicera

Shrubby loniceras are also usually only thought of as hedging plants, a role they are quite unsuited for in an exposed garden where labour is at a premium. The shrubby species, as opposed to the climbing honeysuckles, enjoy moist soil but, to give of their floriferous best, demand all the sunlight our usually dank summers can afford.

Used almost exclusively as a hedging plant, *Lonicera nitida* needs cutting too frequently for my taste, and has a nasty habit of dying back in patches. A hard frost blackens the leaves, but a hedge here, 15 years old, has shown no permanent ill effects. So those who want a quick screen or shelter could safely plant *Lonicera nitida*, unless they are allergic to hedge clipping, for of that there will be enough and to spare.

Cuttings root at almost any time of the year. I have seen clippings around the rubbish heap root.

Lonicera rupicola is a deciduous shrub, making an impenetrable tangle of branches on which appear pink fragrant flowers in May and June.

The lilac, sweet-smelling flowers of *L. syringantha* look dainty against the sea-green leaves. Unless carefully watched it tends to be a ground hog. For instance, a plant here 1.2 m (4 ft) high spread to 3.7 m (12 ft) across, no mean feat when one's next door neighbours are *Berberis wilsoniae* and *Hypericum patulum*. The main crop of flowers open in May and June, but continues intermittently until September.

Propagation is fairly easy. Often there are enough rooted layers about to keep any but the Fagins content.

Magnolia

Magnolias are not planted as frequently as they should be, and though some species may take 20 years to flower or prove tender unless grown on a wall, there are others which grow and flower well in far from sheltered positions. All they ask is a well-drained, loamy soil, and the absolute minimum of root disturbance.

Magnolia denudata exhibits its pure white, cup-shaped fragrant flowers in

Opposite: Laburnum anagyroides 'Vossii' and *Rhododendron* 'Pink Pearl' – both well-loved and easy cultivars

April, a precocity often rewarded by severe frosting, but otherwise it has survived the rigours of the garden in perfect contentment. Eventually it may be 6 m (20 ft) tall, but after 14 years has reached only 2.7 m (9 ft).

Of all the members of this lovely genus *M. sieboldii* is my favourite. The alacrity with which it grows from seed, the vigour with which it grew unsheltered on the west side of the woodland, and the pure loveliness of the white, cup-shaped flowers with the glowing central boss of scarlet stamens, are enough to excite the most reluctant heart. In seed it has a second season of beauty, since the capsules turn pink and then open to show orange pips. Virtue heaped on virtue, the flowers are perfumed and carried in succession from May until August.

One word of warning; choose your plant in flower, for in one the flowers may be only 5 cm (2 in) across with dull brown stamens, while in the best forms individual blooms run to 15 cm (6 in) across with glowing scarlet eyes.

The result of a happy union between *M. denudata* and *M. liliiflora, M. × soulangiana* is the most widely grown of all magnolias with the possible exception of *M. stellata,* a species which contrary to my expectation does need shelter from cold winds to do really well. With *M. × soulangiana,* however, there is so far as I can see, little need for cosseting from the elements. One plant growing in an absolute wind tunnel on the outskirts of Harrogate is a joy to behold each year in late April and May. It grows to a small tree up to 3 m (10 ft) high in the north and as much in width. The angular branch formation is something I find particularly attractive when seen against a frosty winter sky. The white flowers are stained purple at the base, the purple in some forms spreading up to the tips of the petals. Given no root disturbance, and a mulch of peat or well-rotted manure, this is a comfortable shrub to have in the garden.

Mahonia

Mahonia, once listed under *Berberis,*

The blooms of *Mahonia japonica* have a delicate fragrance

and closely allied to it, is distinguished to the gardener's eye by its lack of thorns and unusual leaves. *Mahonia aquifolium* is a useful shrub for use as ground cover with, for instance, kalmias or acers, especially the latter. Against the dark evergreen leaves of the mahonia, the rich autumn colour of the acer gains added brilliance. In the best forms the flowers are carried in massive clusters, in colour a pleasantly rich yellow. It is tolerant of shade, but if too dense, flowering is inhibited. When further plantings are contemplated, a search round an established shrub usually reveals a self-layered branch. If not, the habit can be encouraged by pegging a stem down and mounding it up with soil.

Flowering in February in a fairly exposed situation, *M. bealei* is now 1.5 m (5 ft) high at 15 years old. The pale yellow, sweetly scented flowers grow in short stiffly erect racemes. During the winter some of the leaves turn dark red, while the majority remain green. These virtues would lift *M. bealei* into the front rank of winter-flowering plants, were it not for the fact that in *Mahonia japonica* all these virtues are intensified in larger pinnate shiny leaves, and clusters of racemose pendulous primrose-yellow flowers. The delicate fragrance of the blossoms when smelt for the first time is something no gardener ever forgets, and certainly the plant draws me back two or three times a day when in flower, so that not an atom of beauty is wasted. In late summer the flowers are replaced by blue-black shiny berries, as indeed are all those of the species previously described. They grow here amongst the heathers, and seem well content with their lot.

Malus

It would be impossible to list the many kinds of crab apple available. All flower from April to May, but not all are possessed of sufficient floral merit to warrant inclusion in any but a large garden. The best forms are amongst the finest of flowering trees, and some of these will be found listed below. *Malus*

× *aldenhamensis* has deep red flowers, dull green-purple leaves, and is as hardy as a mountain ash on a windswept hill-side. 'John Downie' is remarkable for its bright yellow and red fruits. I used to visit a tree, in what was once a garden but long since overgrown, and gather basketfuls of the delectable fruit. The tree, a veritable patriarch, was growing forgotten there, amongst the elder, wild raspberry and nettles, but still full of abundant health.

Another crab of outstanding virility is *M.* 'Lemoinei'. In the early days these crabs were some of the first trees to be planted as the framework of a garden, and took the full blast of the wind, in ill-prepared soil. Apart from a slight lean west to east, they have flowered unperturbed. The leaves are a pleasing purple, the flowers a deep wine-red.

A beautiful bush up to 4.5 m (15 ft) high, and equally handsome as a hedge, is *Malus* 'Profusion'. When young the leaves are a deep crimson shot with bronze and the flowers deep red and sweetly fragrant.

Malus × *purpurea* is undoubtedly the most widely planted, and deservedly popular crab. For town planting or in windswept situations or indifferent soils, this must be the first choice for beauty and reliability. The flowers are rose-crimson against young leaves which open a mixture of green-bronze and purple.

Malus 'Simcoe' is a wide spreading tree 6 m (20 ft) high. The flowers, which wreath the naked branches in deep rose pink during April, make of a rough grass field, for a short season at least, a garden. Now, with such an incentive, the grass field is being planted with choice shrubs to match the perfection of the lovely malus. I am told, however, that *M.* 'Simcoe' is something of a mope in certain situations, but this I can never believe, for wet clay and full exposure are no encouragement to any plant; yet it miffs not nor mopes here.

Malus tschonoskii gets profuse apologies from me each time I pass, for this is a tree which possessed virtues unsuspected. In flower it might almost be termed insignificant, although the upright pyramidal habit is attractive. For two years I suffered the flowers, and then to make way for a catalpa moved it to the furthest corner of the garden. Never have I regretted anything more, for now it means walking a considerable distance to enjoy the brilliance of *M. tschonoskii* in full autumn regalia. The combination of scarlet and gold is perfection in its subtle blend of colour, and right willingly do I pay the homage of that walk to feast my eyes on its beauty.

New hybrids are presented for evaluation each year to be compared with established favourites like 'Golden Hornet' whose branches each autumn are bowed down under a burden of bright yellow fruit. 'Wisley' with apple sized dark purple fruits earns a corner because the wine and jelly prepared from the autumn crop is so very well received.

Myrica

Myrica gale is a shrub which is quite common on certain moors in the British Isles. This is not a plant to occupy pride of place in the garden, for certainly it has not the striking beauty to uphold such a position. However, where a moist corner of acid soil can be found the Gale Myrtle makes a quietly pleasant home for itself. The catkins in spring are undoubtedly handsome, especially when lit with warm spring sunshine, but it is for the resinous scent I grow it, acrid, yet somehow oddly reminiscent of verbena, it brings to memory the moors of Autalon or Long Green. Propagation is easy by cuttings or seed. The ultimate height varies from 60 cm to 2 m (2 to 6 ft).

Myrica pensylvanica is a much taller shrub with dull green leaves, and, though just as tough as the Gale Myrtle, for me it lacks charm. The leaves are sweetly aromatic, but it does not in this garden produce the white waxy fruit, or I might find affection where now only tolerance exists.

Neillia

Neillia thibetica (*longiracemosa*) is just

one more indication of the richness of the flora of Western China. Here the plant grows in quite dense shade up to 2.5 m (8 ft) high, 60 or 90 cm (2 or 3 ft) taller than in the open border. A moist, loamy soil or a fairly heavy moisture-retentive clay seems quite suitable. The long arching stems bear racemes of most delicate rosy-pink flowers in June. Neilia looks its very attractive best when grown with hosta, Asiatic primulas, ferns, and bamboo.

Stocks can be increased by means of cuttings of half-ripened shoots, or by seed, provided this is reasonably fresh at the time of sowing.

Paeonia

Here must be included only the tree types of peonies, which have grown in a bed across the top of the garden in very wet clay, and full exposure for 11 years, increasing in stature with absolute contempt for even the bleak east wind of spring. All the species listed below can be raised easily from seed, and for anyone with time and the interest, this is the best method.

Paeonia delavayi has proved itself the most thoroughly reliable member of a versatile genus. It is so contented even in the most exposed positions that self-sown seedlings can be found in abundance. Making a shrub anything from 1 to 1.5 m (3 to 5 ft) tall, depending on exposure, with deeply divided leaves followed in late May by a plenitude of dark crimson flowers, this is a very handsome ornament in the garden. The appearance in winter detracts rather from the overall value, resembling as it does nothing more or less than a loose bundle of pea sticks. Be that as it may, I would sorely miss *P. delavayi* if deprived of its company.

Species peonies have always attracted me, and many of them are extremely handsome; *P. lutea* is one which has particular appeal. This seems to be a very variable species, and care should be taken in selecting the best available. The height, too, can vary, the most beautiful form I possess was 1.2 m (4 ft) tall exactly when last measured. The clean crisp yellow flowers, up to 8 cm (3 in) across, show up well against the dark green toothed leaves. Time of flowering varies according to the season, but it is usually early to mid-June.

Parrotia

Parrotia persica was planted quite extensively in the garden because of the reputation the shrub has gained for the brilliance of its autumn colour. Results have in no way justified this initial optimism. Autumn colours so far as the parrotia is concerned have been conspicuous by their absence. A muddy yellow has been the only contribution. Acers, amelanchier, cotoneaster and rhus, all don livery of scarlet and gold, but no sense of shame brings a tinge of scarlet to the leaves of parrotia. In other gardens in Harrogate the leaves of parrotia colour crimson and gold, pilgrimages are made to worship at the shrine, but some evil spirit has decreed that any parrotia under my care the uniform autumn dress shall be an unpretentious yellow. The plant is quite hardy, and in 14 years has made a spreading bush 2 m (6 ft) high and 2.5 m (8 ft) or more across, which does indicate a certain willingness to please. Full sun and a well-drained soil are undoubtedly much to the plant's taste, but as an experiment where autumn tints fail to materialise, try a position in partial shade. The foliage remains green longer, and the frosts of November, at least in this the first year I have tried the experiment, help the colour. Layering is the best method of increase, or seed when this can be obtained in good condition.

Pernettya

Pernettyas, lovely compact evergreen shrubs though they are, are plants only for soils which contain no vestige of lime. One reads that the genus demands a well-drained soil, and this is possibly true of the tender species, but having watched *Pernettya mucronata* making hay with a patch of yellow clay, right in line with the surface run-off from a hard road, I find the demands for perfect drainage purely an affectation.

Opposite: 'John Downie' is one of the best fruiting crab apples

A well-known variety of *Paeonia lutea* named *ludlowii*

Pernettya mucronata is a very handsome dwarf evergreen which rapidly colonises more than its share of the border unless carefully restricted, spreading by means of suckers in a most obliging manner. The small bell-shaped flowers are worthy of note, but it is in the berry that the true worth of this shrub is fully appreciated. These are 1 cm (½ in) wide, and vary in colour from deep red to purple. Specimens grown from seed here have berries in shades from pink-lilac to red and purple, and are pear-shaped, globose and flattened. Named varieties and cultivars exist: *alba* has white berries, but my favourites are 'Bell's Seedling', with large dark red fruits, and 'Hillier's White'. This shrub is remarkably shade tolerant, but only fruits well in full exposure.

Philadelphus

Within the genus *Philadelphus* are contained species and cultivars which seem capable of adapting themselves to almost any soil and situation. In most gardens they are used mainly as border plants, but in the garden at Parceval Hall they flourish under semi-woodland conditions, though lack of sunlight to a certain extent restricts flowering. An ideal soil would be a free-draining loam, but even with heavy clay and full exposure most will give a full recompense of flower in late June and July as a reward for cultivation. 'Beauclerk' is a hybrid with wide, milk-white flowers flushed with cerise, but a philadelphus devoid of scent loses caste, and this cultivar has no fragrance that even searching enquiry can detect. The ultimate height here is around 2 m (6 ft). 'Belle Etoile' is slightly smaller in stature with white flowers tinted maroon at the centre, and blessed with a delighful fragrance.

With erect branches, arching at the tip, *P.* 'Burfordensis' grows up to 3 m (10 ft), and its flowers are cupped around a central crown of yellow stamens. *P. delavayi,* an extremely strong vigorous species up to 4.5 m (15 ft) in height, has shoots flushed dull purple. Individual flowers are up to 4 cm (1½ in) across, produced in racemes during late June, and they fill the air with their fragrance.

Together with the double-flowered 'Virginal', *P. purpurascens* was amongst the first shrubs to be planted on the border laid out in what was then a grass field. They are now 3 m (10 ft) high, making a delightful picture when each branch is covered with pure white perfumed flowers backed by the violet-purple calyx.

The *P.* × *purpureo-maculatus* group has the virtue of being of more compact habit than *purpurascens,* only reaching 2 m (6 ft). In my eyes it gains additional honour being parent of the lovely 'Sybille'. This delightful shrub grows up to 1.5 m (5 ft) in height with arching branches festooned with orange-scented flowers, stained deep purple.

'Virginal' whose double, sweetly fragrant flowers must be the best known of all the genus, is rather large at 3 m (10 ft) for the smaller gardens. Cuttings of semi-mature shoots, or sideshoots 10 to 15 cm (4 to 6 in) long in July and August, root a good proportion if inserted in a sun frame. Hardwood cuttings in December put into a sheltered border outdoors is the method of increase usually adopted.

Photinia

Photinia species may share common characteristics discernable to the botanist; as a gardener they offer a contradiction. Though the evergreen species will grow on chalk and lime soils, those which, like *P. villosa,* lose their leaves in winter, seem to prefer soils which are acid. Over a decade *P. villosa* will make a well-shaped bush, 3.7 m (12 ft) high. Only one factor prevents it from becoming a universal favourite, and that is a positive antipathy to lime. After 15 years *P. villosa* has made a beautifully shaped shrub of 3.7 m (12 ft) or so. Its white flowers in late May are in corymbs, strongly suggesting a relationship to the hawthorn. This is for me a plant of autumn, when the leaves colour brilliant red and gold. The group here is close to the stream, where on October evenings a grey mist hanging over the water makes a perfect background to the glowing red, especially perfect with a specimen of the variety *flava*, whose leaves turn yellow, planted near. Only in favourable summers are there sufficient berries to make a contribution to the overall beauty of the scene.

Cuttings made in October of mature sideshoots, though slow in rooting, provide a useful means of increase. *P. villosa* will also come readily from seed sown after stratification.

Pieris

These require very much the same treatment and soil as rhododendrons. When making a woodland garden some years ago, where the top cover was mostly scrub birch, the species mentioned below exhibited a tolerant good nature which surprised me. Under no circumstances will they tolerate lime in any form, as was found when a topping of limestone quarry waste was put down to provide a hard road through the woodland.

Pieris floribunda is a tough, slow-growing evergreen 1.2 m (4 ft) high at 12 years old. With white flowers opening in April it makes a pleasant contrast if planted against a background of *Rhododendron* 'Mrs G. W. Leak'. *P. japonica* has shinier leaves than *P. floribunda,* a fact which adds much to its beauty during the winter. The flowers are larger, rather like Lily-of-the-valley, carried in drooping racemes. The variegated form which came from Slieve Donard is extremely slow growing, and because it looked so out of character in the more natural setting of the woodland, has made a home for itself in the open garden. The leaves are attractively bicolour, green and white.

Pieris taiwanensis carries long terminal racemes, fully exposed, but in tight bud right through the winter, and opening at the first propitious moment in March. This is my first love amongst the pieris. The species makes a shapely bush of 2 m (6 ft) or more, and the young leaves unfurl copper-bronze in spring.

Cuttings of half-mature side shoots 8 to 10 cm (3 to 4 in) long with a heel of old wood, inserted in September in a peat and sand frame, will usually root a decent proportion.

Potentilla

Any garden which does not give bed and board to at least one of the shrubby cinquefoils must be the poorer for the omission. This is especially true of the *P. fruticosa* cultivars which flower right through from mid-May to October. *Potentilla* 'Elizabeth' is a small deciduous shrub reaching 60 cm (2 ft) in height which can only be described as a floral mushroom. This hybrid makes a dome-shaped intricate network of branches which are decorated with large richly yellow flowers from May to November.

The most widely planted and equally floriferous 'Katherine Dykes' is taller at 1.2 m (4 ft). As with all the *P. fruticosa* cultivars, it will tolerate most soils except those which degenerate into a bog at regular intervals, and any aspect, sun or partial shade, suits it. The flowers are primrose-yellow, but the foliage is less attractive than that of 'Elizabeth'.

'Longacre' is the crown jewel of the clan, a dense intricately woven hummock of branches only 45 to 60 cm (18 to 24 in) high. Even during the winter, when the leaves have all gone, the outline of twig tracery is attractive. The flowers which appear in superabundance throughout the summer and autumn are bright, yet in no way an acrid, yellow.

A hybrid of garden origin, 'Tangerine', offers an alternative colour, for the flowers are copper-yellow. Apparently once the habit of sporting has been acquired, 'Tangerine' intends to continue the experiment, for this summer one branch produced pink blossoms. Potentilla are nothing if not inventive. 'Red Ace' with flowers of vermillion, and 'Princess', a pink-flowered seedling, offer a variation on the yellow, tangerine or white theme. 'Goldfinger' with deep yellow petals has the largest flowers of the cultivars at present growing in my garden. Cuttings in July or September and October will

Right: *Pernettya mucronata* needs a lime-free soil and is a rapid colonizer

Right: *Pernettya mucronata* needs a lime-free soil and is a rapid colonizer

Opposite: Pieris require much the same treatment and soil as rhododendrons. This is the popular *P. formosa forrestii*

provide abundant stock when inserted into a cold frame.

Prunus

The flowering cherries have proved themselves for many years to be in the front rank of flowering trees. No one seeing a well furnished cherry against the blue of an April sky will ever forget the breath-taking picture it creates. Plants possessed of a superlative beauty have an ability to lift the blackest depression. Frost, snow and chill east winds are all forgotten in the moment when the pink and white cascades of cherry blossom unfurl to the warm sunshine.

A deep soil containing some lime is the ideal medium, but certain cherries have adapted themselves to the heavy clay in this area.

Prunus avium, the native wild cherry, always looks at home in the open woodland, or against a background of trees.

When well suited to soil and situation it will make a tree 12 to 15 m (40 to 50 ft) high, but in an open situation 6 to 9 m (20 to 30 ft) would be more probable. In this district the white flowers open in early May. Maybe it is the plant's method of expressing intolerance with the clay soil, but each and every year the leaves are rendered unsightly by heavy infestations of black aphids. Once a tree gets above 4.5 m (15 ft) high, controlling these undesirable visitors becomes quite a problem.

The double-flowered 'Plena' has many-petalled blossoms which are carried over a longer period than those of the type plant.

Seeds sown in pots, after first being stratified, will germinate fairly rapidly, but I find a walk in the vicinity of an established tree yields self-sown seedlings sufficient for my needs.

The purple forms of *Prunus cerasifera* have long been a familiar sight in estab-

lished shrub borders. Their remarkable tolerance of pruning has led in recent years to their utilisation as hedging plants, and excellent they have proved over the seven years we have grown them here. The crimson-purple leaves make a patch of colour right through the summer months, especially if grouped with some of the pale green and glaucous-grey-leaved shrubs such as *Pyrus salicifera* and *Rosa alba* 'Celestial'.

Prunus cerasifera 'Pissardii' ('Atropurpurea') and 'Nigra', having pale pink and deep rose flowers respectively, are the most commonly planted. *P. laurocerasus,* Cherry Laurel, makes an excellent windbreak where room can be spared to permit full development. Where space is limited it can be restricted by hard pruning with secateurs without undue fear of doing permanent harm. I spent the first 22 years of my life in a house with what seemed at the time two or three miles of laurel hedge; finally in fierce revolt against the ever-recurring job of pruning I cut the whole lot down to ground level. In two years the young growths breaking from the roots had made shapely little bushes 1 m (3 ft) high. I can still see the blaze of colour made by the annuals sown between those bushes in that memorable summer of 1947. The beautiful green of the laurel made a delightful backcloth to the display. Out of the dozen or so cultivars 'Rotundifolia', of bushy habit with leaves 13 cm (5 in) long, is handsome as a free-growing bush, and as a hedge. The flowers are white, in spikes 13 cm (5 in) long.

An old professional gardener who loved a good plant, sent me a cutting of *P. laurocerasus* 'Schipkaensis'. It has now made a low, spreading, narrow-leaved bush 60 cm (2 ft) high and 2 m (6 ft) across. The highly polished, dark green leaves look effective used as ground cover under tall deciduous trees. Cuttings taken in August will root easily in a soil-warmed bench.

Prunus lusitanica is, if anything, hardier than the Cherry Laurel, and yet so few people know it when first confronted with a tree in full prime some 6 m (20 ft) high. This really is a handsome evergreen, and coupled with beauty there is longevity; specimens have been recorded 150 years old. Its very dark green leaves are much sought after by flower arrangers. White scented blossoms appear in June, to be followed in season by spikes of dark purple fruits.

The well-known native Bird Cherry, *Prunus padus,* is a familiar sight to all those who make a pilgrimage to the Lake District in May. I remember standing in that most beautiful of all rock gardens, White Craggs, in early morning sunshine after a night of rain. The air was clear, almost fragile, and, looking down from the garden across the woodland below, the white flowers of the Bird Cherry stood out against the dark green conifers with a virginal purity. The peace and stupendous beauty of that rain-washed scene – in the foreground the tapestry of spring in an English garden, and, stretching away into the distance, the quiet loveliness of a Lakeland wood, touched by the magic of warm sunshine. Even now the picture remains undimmed in my memory, though White Craggs has grown lovelier with the years. The flowers of the Bird Cherry are carried on drooping racemes during late April or early May. Several cultivars exist, of which 'Plena', with large double flowers, is the longest in bloom, and the best.

Prunus padus 'Watereri' is the best of the single-flowered types with graceful pendant racemes of flowers 15 to 20 cm (6 to 8 in) long. To date *P. padus* has seemed reasonably contented with our cold wet clay, but I cannot help a certain feeling of unease when comparing our soil with that in the Clappergate garden.

Prunus 'Pandora' throughout a long association spanning 30 years never fails to impress me as an unshakeably good humoured cherry. Each year in April with unfailing generosity the same prodigal display of soft pink flowers wreathes the branches, despite the evil east wind which so often comes to bedevil the plants at this season.

Loveliest of all cherries here is *P.*

Prunus laurocerasus 'Schipkaensis' makes good ground cover

sargentii, growing to 6 m (20 ft) high, with soft pink flowers 4 cm (1½in) across. In autumn, the leaves turn brilliant scarlet, the display lasting in a favourable season for several weeks.

Of the Japanese Cherries I can never have enough; to plant a hillside with these, daffodils and scarlet azaleas is an ambition long cherished, which may in due course be achieved. Space will not permit a complete list of cultivars available, only those reliable in my experience.

'Amanogawa', the completely upright Lombardy Poplar Cherry, is reliable, given good drainage. The lovely specimen here met with an untimely end, when a 5–tonne rock being manoeuvred into position slipped from controlling chains, and smashed it to pieces. For 12 years it gladdened the May-time with semi-double, delicately fragrant pink flowers; now it has been replaced and once again the spring scene by the stream will be complete. 'Fukubana' is a *Prunus subhirtella* hybrid planted out at 2 m (8 ft) high amongst pines of only 1 m (3 ft), and it is still waiting after nine years for the shelter to catch up. The semi-double rose-pink flowers, appear very early in the spring. Again a well-drained soil is essential 'Hisakura' has single rose-pink flowers in May.

Growing in town and country with equal freedom, 'Kanzan' is the most popular of all cherries, and rightly so. The large double flowers are rich pink, and the leaves colour warm orange in October.

'Pink Perfection' was still as full of leaf in mid-November as in mid-summer, not just last year but every year; it has double flowers of bright rose-pink. This is a strong cultivar even in wet clay; the soil in my garden is wetter than most, yet 'Pink Perfection', now 14 years old and 4.5 m (15 ft) high and in the path of the west wind, still refuses to bend a single branch.

In flower 'Tai-Haku' is the acme of loveliness. Snow-white flowers 5 cm (2 in) across against the copper-red of bursting leaves, make this plant outstanding. Only one word of warning, it does, however, need good drainage.

Another I should hate to be without is 'Ukon', with copper-tinted leaves and pale yellow flowers. Seeing it in flower for the first time in combination with the pink forms, so lovely did it look I bought two more.

Pyracantha

Pyracanthas have not proved absolutely reliable: after surviving 14 years undamaged they caught a spring frost, and only two species recovered.

In a well-drained soil *Pyracantha coccinea* 'Lalandei' makes a fine spreading bush. The panicles of cream-white flowers in spring are followed by orange fruits in the autumn. It makes a first-class wall plant, very effective in breaking the hard formality of the masonry. As all gardeners know, walls have little virtue unless covered by plants.

Pyracantha crenulata and *P. rogersiana* do well here on the north wall. The white flowers and evergreen habit are the plants' only claim to fame, for the berries are not faithfully produced every year. The hybrid of *rogersiana* called 'Golden Charmer' is a much better fruiting shrub, though mine is well placed on a south-facing wall so the comparison is hardly fair. *P. crenato-serrata* 'Orange Glow' with orange-red fruits is a vigorous, free-berrying form.

Cuttings taken in mid-August of current season's growth, 5 to 10 cm (2 to 4 in) in length, will usually root if the compost is well laced with coarse sand.

Pyrus

Pyrus salicifolia 'Pendula' makes a lovely small tree of weeping habit. The true beauty will only be discovered when a single specimen is planted with a dark leaved chamaecyparis, and shrubs with red leaves. I use *Berberis thunbergii atropurpurea* and *Cotinus coggygria* 'Notcutt's Variety'.

In soil of average fertility specimens have grown over a decade to 3.7 m (12 ft) in height. In late April their silver-grey leaves and cream-coloured flowers are a feature of the shrub borders.

Trees and Shrubs:
Rhododendron to Weigela

Rhododendron is a vast genus which offers a choice from tiny species, excellent for the rock garden, to magnificent trees with enormous leaves and beautiful flowers. I have spent many engrossing hours in contemplation of the beauty which is a rhododendron, and hope to spend many more without extracting one-tenth of the joy to be had from the growing of these lovely plants. The range is so vast that it is only possible to describe a few of this genus. All have one thing in common – a profound distaste for lime, no matter how the flavour is disguised. The large-leaved species need more shelter than the average garden can afford; some flower early in the year, and this precocity is quite frequently punished by a late spring frost. There are so many to choose from that even the most cautious gardener need have no fear in casting his bread upon the water, in the sure and certain knowledge that his reward will be flowers in profusion.

Rhododendron augustinii proves, to all who have ever tried growing it from seed, that the word species when applied to rhododendrons can mean almost anything. In the best forms, and it is as well to see the plant in flower before buying, the flower colour is a clean blue; in the worst forms a lavender overlaid with magenta. In the open it grows to somewhere between 2 and 2.5 m (6 and 8 ft), but I have seen it aspire to great dimensions in sheltered woodland. *R. augustinii,* shows a ready alacrity to reproduce from cuttings of semi-ripened wood, taken into a sun frame, and made up with a compost of 2 parts of sand and 1 of peat by volume.

In the Northumberland garden I have seen *R. decorum* used as a shelter belt against the east wind. There seem to be several distinct forms, but the white-flowered variety is for me the most delightful. The tallest here reaches 3.7 m (12 ft), and in late April the dark green leaves are almost hidden by a profusion of the pure white, sweetly scented flowers. Nothing is needed to relieve the purity of the whiteness; no art of man can improve on perfection. I first saw *Rhododendron ferrugineum* growing in a limestone rock garden, not the misalliance it at first appeared for the soil specially provided was largely acid. The rust-coloured undersides of the leaves add to the beauty of this compact shrub, which I have never seen more than 1.2 m (4 ft) high. In the best forms the flowers are an unsullied rose-scarlet. Again the plant shows a commendable willingness to root from cuttings made in July.

Rhododendron impeditum is an interesting little alpine shrublet for the rock garden, with grey-green leaves and purplish flowers. In full exposure the growth is tight, compact, densely twiggy, and ideal to give a change of foliage pattern amongst heathers. The Rock form has particularly grey leaves and clear blue flowers.

Rhododendron keleticum is even more ground-hugging than *R. impeditum,* and flowers later, usually in early June. It has small leaves and rich plum flowers.

Rhododendron pemakoense is another truly alpine species from that home of so many excellent plants, Tibet. What a great pity this wonderful country is now closed to the plant collector. In this garden *R. pemakoense* makes dwarf hummocks 30 cm (12 in) or so in height. In mid-May the leaves are completely hidden by the profusion of pink flowers. This species also makes a good pot plant for the alpine house,

Opposite: Deciduous azaleas relish the dappled shade of light woodland

flowering a month earlier with this modicum of protection from the cold. As with the other species described, cuttings form the readiest means of increasing stock.

Rhododendron racemosum is of an iron constitution and flowers best when planted in an open situation.

This is a Chinese species, and will make a shrub 1 to 1.2 m (3 to 4 ft) high with pale pink flowers in late April. Forrest's form is more compact, with bright red flowers.

A small shrub with rich violet-purple flowers and grey leaves shaded rusty brown underneath, *R. russatum* blooms in early May. The combination of colours is beyond criticism, as is the plant's good temper. Either cuttings or seed will prove reliable methods of propagation.

Rhododendron scintillans bears rather more scanty leafage than the others of the section, but this in no way detracts from its beauty. The height is 45 to 76 cm (18 to 30 in) and the flowers are a bright lavender blue. This species tolerates very dry soil, which makes it useful for the steeper slopes in the rock garden.

Rhododendron yakushimanum is such a notable plant it would be my first choice for a small garden. The habit is neat: a rounded hummock 1 m (3 ft) high on specimens 10 years old. The old leaves are dark, glossy green, those on the young shoots a close felted dove grey. When the compact flower truss opens the buds are rose, turning cherry pink, and finally white. The three I grow are sited in full sun, half shadow supplied by a 'Tai-Haku' cherry, and in the dense shade thrown by the house wall. By doing this I extend the season of interest over two months, and still would like the beauty to be preserved even longer.

As for hybrid rhododendrons, their name is legion, and a glance at *The Rhododendron Handbook* will give some measure of their multitude. In general the older hybrids are the hardiest, for with the introduction of species like *R. griersonianum,* a tender plant but possessed of outstandingly beautiful

flowers, and an excellant parent, the modern hybrids have developed just a hint of miffishness, a reluctance to tolerate cold winds which limits their planting to more sheltered situations.

I would willingly supply an overcoat for gems like the *loderi* hybrids, 'Carita', 'Lady Chamberlain', and 'Romany Chai', just to see their beauty. They may prove quite reliable in the open. The woodland here could hardly be described as sheltered, but certainly it does temper winter's blast to a limited extent, and breaks the frost.

Taking the lower-growing hybrids first, 'Blue Diamond' is a wonderfully compact bush of 1 m (3 ft) with lavender-blue flowers. 'Blue Tit', again with *augustinii* blood, is smaller in stature than 'Blue Diamond', and the flowers are of a similar shade. 'Elizabeth' is a low, spreading bush which over four years has belied its *R. griersonianum* blood by emerging unscathed by the cold to open rich deep-scarlet flowers in May. This beautiful flower is rendered even more attractive with a ground planting of *Omphalodes verna,* Blue-eyed Mary, and the native primrose. 'Pink Drift', with *R. scintillans* as a parent, could hardly be anything else but worthy. A neat little shrublet of 30 cm (12 ins) or so in height, it has scented leaves and rose-lavender flowers. 'Yellow Hammer' is another good dwarf which introduces a desirable yellow tone, lest the garden be overwhelmed with pinks, blues, and magenta.

Amongst the taller hybrids 'Britannia' is slow growing; the leaves, paler green, are a distinguishing feature. The bright crimson flowers need careful placing to get the maximum effect. I use the silvery-grey leaved pear to good effect. 'Carita' in all its forms is delightful. I say all because several hybrids carry the name if my experience is any guide. The bell-shaped flowers, pale yellow stained pink, distil a lovely fragrance in May.

'Cynthia' is a vigorous, fairly upright growing and mature specimen; carrying a full complement of rose-crimson flowers in May it is an arrestingly beaut-

iful sight. 'Santillation' is a useful mid-season blooming hybrid, the soft pink florets stained yellow at the centre. 'A. R. Whitney' has even larger trusses opening late June.

A group of five plants of 'Mrs G. W. Leak' were planted 15 years ago, when the Oakwood (part of the woodland) was just a wind tunnel, and each year they have increased in stature and beauty. The flowers are pink with a brown-purple blotch in the throat. They should eventually grow to around 3 m (10 ft) if the specimens here are any guide.

'Pink Pearl' is the most popular and widely planted of the hybrids, and is strong and vigorous with enormous trusses of rose-pink flowers in mid-May. 'Susan' is compact like 'Britannia', but with darker foliage, making a perfect background to the lavender-blue flowers.

Though azaleas should in reality be listed under the botanically correct name of rhododendron, to most gardeners they are a distinct race. Indeed, so far as possible I avoid putting azaleas and rhododendrons in close associations, for neither benefits by comparison.

Rhododendron albrechtii is a most lovely shrub, 1.5 m (5 ft) in height with bright rose flowers 5 cm (2 in) across during April. This species is well worth raising from seed. The resulting progeny may have blooms ranging in colour from the palest pink to almost magenta.

Rhododendron luteum, the so-called common azalea (once called *Azalea pontica*), is in my opinion the most garden-worthy of all, with rich yellow, sweetly fragrant blossoms, and the most spectacular autumn colour. A bed of honeysuckle azalea planted amongst white-stemmed birch makes an exceedingly lovely picture as the leaves turn in October. Propagation is by seed, layers, or cuttings.

One which has probably excited more admiration than any other spring flowering plant is *R. schlippenbachii*. As it comes into bloom rather early, the frost does occasionally catch it unawares, but the gamble succeeds in three years out of four. A shrub 1.5 m (5 ft) high, covered in the delicate rose-pink blossoms, is a vision to lift the spirits from winter to spring in one brief moment of time.

A singularly attractive North American shrub is *R. vaseyi,* with pale pink flowers in May, and leaves which colour scarlet early in autumn.

There are so many hybrid azaleas now available from nurseries and garden centres the would-be customer is spoiled for choice. 'Berry Rose' came into my care more years ago than I can remember. In spite of oft repetition I still find pleasure in the pink and yellow blooms. 'Golden Sunset' has provided me with several offspring, none with primrose yellow and orange flowers of the parent. All my seedlings are well flowered in shades of yellow. 'Royal Command' is more compactly upright in growth and later flowering. The vermillion-red petals look most attractive amongst pale blue iris.

'Hugo Hardyzer', sent to me from Holland, is a deep, brilliant scarlet, a contradictory description if ever there was one. With dark green conifer foliage behind, none of the colour quality is lost.

'Palestrina' is really a *vuykiana* hybrid, but as with a rose, this azalea under any name would be outstanding. Its flowers are purest white, flushed green at the eye and the foliage is bright green throughout the spring and summer.

In flower 'Satan' does nothing to belie the name, since all the flames of the nether regions are combined in one glorious blaze of colour. It is blood-red with just a touch of orange-yellow to lighten the base of each petal.

Equally brilliant, but flowering a few days later, 'Tunis' has orange-red flowers carried with the same profligate abundance.

Gamblers might like to try a mixed packet of seed from the Exbury or Knap Hill hybrids. With a bit of care in the raising, it is possible to get something like 150 plants for under the cost of one mature specimen. No guarantee can be given as to colour, but all I have raised so far would not be disgraced planted alongside the named hybrids. The above list is only a small selection; for further information the reader should obtain one of the many books devoted entirely to the cultivation of the genus *Rhododendron*.

Rhus

Let no one be deceived by the Stag's Horn Sumach's felt-covered young shoots into believing the plant is fearful of getting cold. I provided a choice position for *Rhus typhina* and was rewarded by a forest of suckers which even invaded the lawn. The autumn colour is rich extravagant red, yellow, orange even a hint of purple. The scarlet cone-shaped fruits on the branch tips persist into the new year.

The cultivar 'Laciniata', with finely divided leaves, is more desirable, even if the autumn colour of orange and yellow lacks the stridently aggressive quality of the species. Most soils are acceptable. As for propagation, numerous suckers will provide for all except the very greedy.

Ribes

Ribes includes, of course, the ever-popular flowering currants, which along with forsythias herald the coming of spring in gardens from Land's End to John O'Groats. Common they may be, but the garden borders would be the poorer for their omission.

The Golden Currant, *Ribes odoratum,* I first knew incorrectly as *R. aureum* or Buffalo Currant. The last name conjured up all sorts of romantic pictures in my mind during boyhood, investing the shrub with additional virtues which long association has not erased. Over the years, *R. odoratum* will make a bush of rather sprawling character some 2 m (6 ft) high, its yellow flowers having a pleasant spicy fragrance, followed by black-purple fruits. I grow a form *aurantiacum* which seems more compact in habit at 1.2 m (4 ft). Seed sown in sandy compost during March will germinate readily. Pruning consists of a judicious thinning of old wood in autumn.

Ribes sanguineum is a plant whose drooping, deep pink racemes of flowers make such a brave show in spring whatever the weather. Obviously, when a plant enjoys such universal popularity there are bound to be selected forms to procure, but not all are as adaptable as the type plant, which makes a sturdy weather-proof bush 2.7 to 3 m (9 to 10 ft) high.

Ribes sanguineum 'Atrorubens' has deep crimson flowers, not quite so long in the truss as the type plant, but of excellent colour.

Making a shrub 1.5 m (5 ft) high, 'King Edward VII' is much more compact than the other cultivars, and has crimson flowers against the light green leaves.

Ribes sanguineum 'Splendens' is the form with the longest racemes of rosy-pink flowers, and vigorous growth. Propagation in each case is by means of cuttings made of the current season's wood, about 30 cm (12 in) long, inserted in soil well laced with sand in the open border.

Ribes speciosum is a lovely shrub which should be more widely grown than it is, judging by the number of enquiries I get about my plants when they are in flower. This is a Californian shrub, and in mild winters will keep a few leaves on as a concession to modesty. Those planted around and about the borders have survived 11 years of siege from wind and frost without undue damage, and are now dainty bushes 1.5 m (5 ft) high. The arching branches are hung with scarlet, delicately formed, fuchsia-like flowers in late May. It is a shrub which needs careful siting so the blooms are seen with the sunlight behind them, and then each petal glows with iridescent scarlet.

Cuttings can be made as for *R. sanguineum,* but I prefer the plant to be grown gooseberry-like on a clean 'leg', rubbing out all but the top three buds.

All the species listed should have a little judicious attention to removal of old wood as the specimens mature. *R. speciosum* in particular should have the ends of the branches (which show a tendency to grow towards the ground) lightly tipped back to an upward pointing bud.

Rosa

As with rhododendrons, only the most modest selection of the outstandingly shrubby species of *Rosa* can be given here. The typical English garden means to most people a broad sweep of lawn and roses, for roses combine the three virtues: beautiful flowers, elegant habit in the case of shrubs, and the most delightful fragrance. Other things may be included in the design, but the basic ingredients to the man in the street must be grass and roses.

Rosa × alba, the White Rose of York, has been in cultivation for many centuries; so long, in fact, that the date of introduction is lost in the dust of history. Flowers on the type plant are semi-double, but for me all other forms pale into insignificance compared to the charm of *R. alba* 'Celestial'. Imagine a shrub 1.5 m (5 ft) high with glaucous-green leaves, almost hidden by semi-double intensely fragrant flowers of the most delicate shade of pink. Put a group of pale blue delphiniums alongside, and it only needs a *Chamaecyparis obtusa* 'Nana Gracilis', with whorls of bright green foliage, to complete the picture of perfect colour and balance.

Rosa 'Canary Bird', sometimes listed as a cultivar of *R. xanthina,* I have never seen growing anywhere as well as it does in the Royal Botanic Garden in Edinburgh. Here it makes a shrub 1.5 m (5 ft) high, with arching branches carrying canary-yellow flowers all along the upper surface; a pleasing trait which ensures that none of the beauty is wasted on unappreciative earth worms. This rose does, however, make a positive demand for good drainage, otherwise it sulks in a most sullen manner.

Another of my favourite shrub roses is *R. × cantabrigiensis,* possibly because here it is one of the first to flower. The foliage is light and delicately formed with pale yellow individual blooms 5 cm (2 in) across. Around the bush I plant *Iris sibirica* 'Wedgewood', or similar blue flowers.

The Threepenny-bit Rose, *R. elegan-*

tula persetosa, I collected from an abandoned garden in Yelland which the great Yorkshireman Reginald Farrer helped to design. Several of the cuttings rooted, and now flourish in the sandstone rock garden here. The leaves are small and the tiny flowers, deep coral in bud opening to dog-rose pink, are borne in such quantity and are of so perfect a shape, that one does not object to the lack of size. In autumn the leaves turn a charming red-purple.

I spent the first seven years of my gardening life in the presence of what has since been proved to be the outstanding form of *R. hugonis.* After acquiring several specimens of this species which by comparison were inferior, in desperation I went back there only to find the plant had been removed to make way for a bed of floribundas of a virulent orange-red. However, a batch of seedlings has since given me one plant which promises well, so the 12 years or so of travail have not been in vain, for it is a shrub of great quality, having long slender branches up to 1.5 m (5 ft) high, with fern-like foliage. In early June the branches smother themselves with soft yellow single flowers. Truly a plant to delight the heart of a lover of good roses.

'Marguerite Hilling' came to me as a pink sport from 'Nevada', and certainly it possesses a similarity to that lovely rose. In seven years it has made a graceful bush, 2 m (6 ft) high, with large single or semi-double deep pink flowers 13 cm (5 in) in diameter. The main flush of bloom comes in June, but flowering continues intermittently through the rest of the summer.

To really appreciate just how lovely *R. moyesii* can be, visit the garden at St Nicholas near Richmond. There in the easterly end of the shrub rose border is a large Silver Fir, against which grows what must be surely the patriarch of all *R. moyesii* bushes. In June, through and against the silver of the fir the flowers glow with the rich lustre of newly polished rubies. Then, just as the picture dims in memory, come the large crimson flask-shaped

Rosa moyesii has attractive flowers and fruits

fruits; but add to the silver and scarlet the soft burnished gold of the dying leaves. This specimen must be all of 4.5 m (15 ft) but in this garden 2 to 2.7 m (6 to 9 ft) seems to be the average.

A form of the type species, 'Geranium' is more compact with orange-red flowers and hips, while 'Sealing Wax', another variant, has scarlet-orange flowers and hips. *R. moyesii* is well worth growing from seed, because a rich variety of colour forms will be the reward.

'Nevada' is almost unique in character, being a graceful bush 2 m (6 ft) high. In bud the flowers are pale pink, opening to rich cream, 13 cm (5 in) across, and relieved at the centre by a golden boss of stamens. Occasionally one shoot will show ambition to grow into a tree, growing up yards above the rest; this tendency must be rigorously suppressed, the offender being carefully cut away to preserve the rounded outline which is the charm of 'Nevada'.

Rosa omeiensis pteracantha is really a plant for the large garden where room can be spared for plants with interesting stems, for it is the crimson thorns of this species which are the main attraction. These are short and curved, but 2.5 cm (1 in) wide at the base, and under bright sunlight are blood-red in colour. Hard pruning will encourage the strong basal shoots of young wood which carry the largest thorns.

A mixed collection of Penzance briars will make a first-class boundary hedge for the large garden. Here in competition with that worst of all garden plants, the poplar, they still arch up to 3 m (10 ft), and give their deliciously fragrant blooms with unstinted generosity. 'Amy Robsart', deep rose; 'Lady Penzance', copper yellow; 'Lord Penzance', a bicolour of really pale fawn, yellow and pink tints; and 'Meg Merrilees', crimson, are all first-class hybrids which will grow from cuttings.

In addition to cyclamen-pink flowers, *R. rubrifolia* has glaucous-purple leaves throughout the summer, and in the best forms red-purple young wood. The beauty of leaf continues through the summer and autumn on plants well furnished with young wood, making this an invaluable shrub for those who give leaves their rightful place in the garden landscape. In this garden self-sown seedlings are fairly common, and the best can be chosen for growing on.

Rosa rugosa and its cultivars have proved themselves amongst the hardiest of the roses for northern gardens. Frequently used as a rootstock for the less vigorous cultivars, some of the specimens one sees in gardens are undoubtedly suckers which have broken away undetected, eventually killing the graft.

In the really deep red forms *Rosa rugosa* 'Rubra' makes an outstanding specimen plant to fill a draughty corner. The large single flowers are highly fragrant, and the large hips, in shape resembling an old brandy bottle, are sealing-wax red.

'Sarah Van Fleet' is the best of the rugosas. Its large, semi-double, pale rose-pink flowers, are like those of a well formed camellia in shape. Eventually this cultivar will make a wide, spreading bush of 2 m (6 ft) in height and breadth, but it can be restricted by severe pruning without depleting the flowers. Plant it alongside a frequently used path so that the delicate perfume can be enjoyed to the full.

Rosa 'Schneezwerg', the Snow Dwarf, bears little resemblance to its more robust brethren, and here it makes a dainty shrublet only 1 to 1.2 m (3 to 4 ft) high. The blossoms really are pure white, semi-double opening continuously through June, July and August.

Of the Scotch or Burnet shrub roses, *Rosa pimpinellifolia* 'Frühlingsgold' is first class, though the flowers are only allowed to grace the border for three short weeks, and then no more. Each individual bloom measures 10 cm (4 in) across, being semi-double and primrose yellow in colour. This is a scented rose, and on warm June evenings the air is filled with a most delectable damask fragrance.

'Constance Spry', with the old-fashioned centifolia character and rich fragrance, is able to do duty as shrub or climber. The large soft pink flowers are carried singly in clusters on the arching stems. 'Golden Chersonese', with 'Canary Bird' as one parent, makes a dainty foliaged shrub 1.5 m (5 ft) high. The bright yellow flowers are a feature in June, casting reflections in the still waters of the pool below. A happy piece of accidental planting on my part.

Rubus

In general, plants of the genus *Rubus* need rather more space than the small garden can allow, and some are as invasive as the common bramble. They do, however, thrive in places which few other plants would tolerate for a single season.

Rubus cockburnianus, sometimes listed under the name *R. giraldianus,* is a delightful shrub for open woodland, or a wilder corner of the garden. I am addicted to quiet walks around the garden in the evening, and it is in the moonlight of an October dusk that the glistening white stems of *R. cockburnianus* are seen to best effect. From then on, through the winter, the leafless white stems are invaluable in lighting up the borders until spring is ushered in by the shy flowers of the aconites, hepatica, and daffodils planted around them. When suited, the White-washed Bramble can colonize at a most fantastic rate, as I discovered after planting a specimen on the edge of the kitchen garden.

Propagation offers no problems, you can just dig out the unwanted suckers, but as with raspberries make sure there are some good strong shoots at the base, for the main stem will die.

Rubus deliciosus has two of the qualities which make for a garden-worthy plant, namely beauty and grace. A native of the Rocky Mountains, its branches (unlike *R. cockburnianus*) are thornless, and in June are covered with large white flowers similar to those of the wild rose in shape, with the same illusion of fragile perfection. I tried for many years to get not only a good

photograph of the flowers, but also one that carried some hint of the charm of the plant as well. Last year I did in some measure succeed. In addition it will faithfully remain in its allotted place, not seeking to rampage all over Yorkshire and half the northern counties.

A soil of moderate richness is all the plant asks, and careful removal of old wood, but not every year by any means.

Rubus odoratus is another in the same ground-hogging mould as *R. cockburnianus,* but will exercise more restraint if planted under trees, which will in some measure give competition for food and moisture. In winter it looks very much like the wild raspberries of our native woodlands, but the leaves in summer are large, dark and glossy green, and the rose-purple, sweetly-scented flowers open in July and August.

The suckering habit indicates the method both of increase and restraint.

Salix

The willows offer a wide choice of species ranging in height from only 5 cm (2 in) to 12 or 15 m (40 or 50 ft). Unfortunately, so many owners of small gardens, beguiled no doubt by a vivid memory of graceful weeping branches against a wide expanse of water, plant the tall-growing kinds in their own modest demesne, then spend the rest of their lives fighting to keep a way clear down the front path. There is nothing quite so right for waterside planting as the delicately graceful golden-stemmed Weeping Willow, but it does need a vast amount of space. A sense of proportion is of vital importance, and the scale of planting must be observed in a small garden.

The White Willow, *Salix alba,* has been extremely prolific in the matter of hybrids. It is excellant on moist heavy soils, or near the coast for making a quick-growing shelter behind which to plant the choicer, less tolerant treasures. Allowed to develop it will make a beautiful pyramid tree, glorious in spring as the grey-green foliage breaks. The cultivar 'Chermesina' steals the picture in winter by having orange-scarlet shoots which glint in the fugitive sunshine to lighten the load of leaden grey days.

On some soils *S. × chrysocoma* has a proneness to canker, but so far I have not been bedevilled by this foul condition on any plants under my care. This is a truly beautiful, but very large, tree which loses much of its character if recourse must be made to pruning to keep it within bounds. When the long arching branches are allowed to develop, each terminating in a multitude of bright yellow shoots, then × *chrysocoma* becomes an object for mute contemplation and admiration.

Almost any branch will root; just cut away and push into moist soil.

Salix daphnoides is a very quick growing species, and some plants will make 2 m (6 ft) of growth in their first season. The young shoots are rich violet-purple covered with a wax-like bloom. Growth is fairly upright, unlike the spreading habit of × *chrysocoma*, and propagation is the same.

Salix fargesii has a very un-willow-like appearance, the shiny red-brown coloured shoots in winter, and the large glossy, heavily veined leaves, making this a shrub of considerable character. The deep red buds have a high polish which makes me feel I should go round with a powder puff to tone them down a bit. A specimen I planted eight years ago is only 2 m (6 ft) high, so *S. fargesii* does not quickly outgrow its welcome.

A beautiful slow-growing shrub, *S. lanata* is found wild in certain parts of Scotland. I must confess to a weakness for our indigenous plants, and one day would like to have a corner of the garden devoted entirely to them. The Woolly Willow, with round silver-grey leaves and large upright catkins, is particularly good looking as the leaves unfold in spring. On a dry site it will make a small shrub 1 to 1.2 m (3 to 4 ft) high, on a moist loam I have seen specimens nearly 2 m (6 ft) high and nearly as wide. A branch will develop roots wherever it touches the ground, and nature can be improved on by pegging pieces with a layering pin.

Salix matsudana 'Tortuosa' found sufficient grace of individuality to be included in Mr Bowles's 'lunatic asylum'; a corner of his garden reserved for the peculiarities and oddities of the horticultural world. Odd the shrub may be, but the curiously contorted branches have a singular beauty, especially when the leaves have fallen and the naked twigs are seen against the winter sky. The largest specimen, though admittedly in a windswept corner, has reached 3.5 m (11 ft) in 15 years; not an outrageous rate of growth, and the branches grow up rather than outwards. In any event, these curiously corkscrewed aerial appendages are much sought after by flower arrangers of the Japanese school, so there is no shortage of market for prunings. Twigs pushed into moist sand soon grow roots and can be lined out in spring to grow on.

Sambucus

The Elder or Ellan Tree is a subject of Nordic superstition: indeed, the branches must not be cut until permission has been first asked of the tree, a civility neglected, I have no doubt, on many occasions when foliage is required to back an arrangement. A cup of China tea with dried elder flowers infused in it has a flavour I enjoy, but not only is the taste of the tea improved, for if legend has not misled me, the house should be free of spirits and witches.

The various forms of Common Elder, *Sambucus nigra*, are in most cases too large for the small domain, but where room can be spared, or to shelter an exposed corner, a choice could be made from the following, namely 'Aurea' with brilliant golden foliage, or 'Aureo-marginata', where the leaves are only margined with bright yellow. The cultivar 'Laciniata', with leaves divided into fern-like segments, achieves as a result of this foliage modification a lightness completely lacking in its rather too solid relatives.

Sambucus racemosa, the Red Elder, is the most desirable of all the genus from the ornamental gardener's point of view, but not the type plant, which is a rather too vigorous, overbearing, self-advertising shrub. In *Sambucus racemosa,* however, can be found one of the most lovely of all the golden-leaved plants. It is a slow-growing shrub with beautifully golden leaves, divided into deeply cut segments. I often wonder how a presumptuous rogue with the character of *racemosa* could give rise to a dignified treasure like 'Plumosa Aurea'.

Cuttings taken in September will root readily in the open ground.

Skimmia

Skimmias are attractive slow-growing evergreen shrubs which seem content to grow in either sun or shade whether the soil be acid or alkaline. They dislike badly drained soils, the leaves turning a sickly yellow if this requirement is not met.

Skimmia japonica has the round, dome-shaped Japanese look which suggests stone temples, lanterns, and carefully raked sand. The male forms have well-developed, fragrant heads of flowers which open in spring, just when sneak frosts can stop them pollinating the females, so some protection should be given. This is not selfish pandering to the feminine, but a desire to get the best possible set of the orange-red fruits, which make a bold planting of this tidy evergreen such a spectacle in late autumn. To ensure a good crop of berries it is advisable to grow male and female plants in close groups.

Two improvements on the type plant can be found in the hybrid *S. j.* 'Foremanii', which, unless some extremely hardworking bee has found skimmias a mile away in Harrogate, must contain flowers of both sexes. The last two years it has set very good crops of berries with no help from a male that I am aware of. *S. j.* 'Fragrans' is a deliciously· scented free-flowering male form, and to ease the loneliness of *S. j.* 'Foremanii', a rooted cutting has been· planted alongside it. To enjoy the perfume of 'Fragrans' without the biting east wind eating into one's vitals, a cutting can be pot grown under glass. So obliging is this cultivar that even

first-season cuttings make quite a respectable flower spike. Apart from the puzzling, self-fertile 'Foremanii', the only other skimmia which is self fertile, *S. reevesiana,* unfortunately has a well-expressed dislike of alkaline soils.

Sorbus

There is a glacial valley near my house, along the bottom of which flows a large stream. The sides of the valley are thickly strewn with enormous boulders and around these grow a heterogeneous mixture of trees, including the graceful birch, and a fair admixture of Mountain Ash. The view from the top of this rocky valley in autumn is superb, because of the multitude of colours adopted by the dying leaves. The soft yellow of the birch makes an undertone to the bright scarlet berries of the Mountain Ash, with here and there the sombre green of holly or Scotch Pine. No matter where it is grown, in the wild solitude of some mountain loch, or in the environs of a suburban garden, there is an untamed air about the tree which no amount of cultivation can disguise.

So many species and cultivars exist that only a modest selection can be included here, but of the 40 or 50 different types of *Sorbus* in this garden I have chosen those which grow most easily, though let me hasten to add, none show any sulkiness of character.

The ever popular Whitebeam, *Sorbus aria,* was at one stage almost lost under the overwhelming patronage of *Pyrus,* but is now, let us hope, for the sanity of gardeners, safely restored to its rightful place under *Sorbus.* The upper surface of the leaf is rich shining green in contrast to the white or dove-grey underside. As the leaves ripple in the gentle winds of May, showing first green and then grey, it reminds me of nothing more than the changing colours of the sea under clouded sky. In autumn the leaves colour dull orange and contrast with the scarlet of the fruits.

Several cultivars are in existence, the best of these is 'Lutescens', and the upper surfaces of its leaves are covered

Opposite: Sorbus cashmiriana is a strikingly beautiful species from the Himalayas

Sorbus reducta is an ideal rock-garden shrub

with white hairs. 'Decaisneana' ('Majestica') is larger in leaf and fruit than any other, and my choice if space is ever limited to only one cultivar of the species. All make trees 9 m (30 ft) or so in height.

Sorbus aucuparia, the native Mountain Ash, has given rise to many forms; fastigiate, weeping, some with finely divided leaves, but none lovelier than the type plant, whose bronze-gold foliage and bright scarlet berries colour up so well in early autumn. *S. a.* 'Asplenifolia' has finely divided leaves, lovely in their fern-like grace.

Sorbus aucuparia 'Fastigiata', as the name implies, is erect in habit. These forms can be found growing wild in the woodlands, as can the weeping varieties.

Sorbus cashmiriana is a strikingly beautiful species from the Himalayas, which more by good luck than good management I planted in association with a group of shrub roses. The large glistening white fruits and delicate autumn colouring of the finely divided leaves look perfect against the carmine-red of the rose hips. It makes a rather spreading bush here, but that may be because it grows in a very windy position.

Sorbus decora 'Nana' is one of those shrubs which has first one name and then another inflicted upon it. Originally *americana* 'Nana', to be botanically correct, I believe the poor unfortunate should now be listed under *scopulina*. Under any name this plant is one of the most desirable of all the genus, because of its compactness and relatively small stature; a full grown tree is only 3.7 m (12 ft) high. The large scarlet berries are nested in a fan of dark green leaves, somewhat in the manner of a country bouquet.

Even more compact in growth, *Sorbus reducta* should really be confined to the rock garden where it will make a spreading bush 45 cm (18 in) high. I find some forms make a better display than others which seem reluctant to set even the modest amount of flowers they display in spring. This shrub is considered something of a rarity, but the alacrity with which it comes from seed should overcome this minor problem.

Seed should be stratified and then sown in pans of sandy compost.

On first acquaintance, *S. sargentiana* looks like the result of a union between a sorbus and horse chestnut; the huge sticky buds bear a striking resemblance to those of the 'conker'. The likeness ends there, since this is a sorbus with large leaflets which turn a rich glowing red in the autumn. I have never been permitted to enjoy the full beauty of the orange-red fruits, as they ripen just as the fieldfares appear and strip the bushes overnight.

Sorbus 'Wilfred Fox' is another of those unfortunate orphans who was at first issued under *S. nepalensis;* indeed, I still have it so labelled, but now discover this is incorrect. It has large glaucous-green leaves and fruits of an unusual copper-yellow much coveted by flower arrangers. The overall shape is, however, what makes this tree so attractive.

Spiraea

A charming race, spiraeas are so easily grown that much of their efficacy has been shadowed by the epithet to damn so many good plants, namely 'common'. I cherish a fond regard for any shrub which in addition to being attractive has none of the wilful waywardness of beauty, and grows easily. All the spiraeas like a fairly sunny position, yet will grow in part shade (but only of necessity). Those which flower early in the summer should be pruned after flowering, cutting any weak or debilitated shoots clean away to make room for vigorous youngsters. The later ones can have the flowering shoots cut back to within two buds or so of the base in spring, or, alternatively, where a taller, spreading bush is required, you just remove the old truss.

Spiraea × arguta, popularly known as Foam of May or Bridal Wreath, is the most striking of the early-flowering spiraeas. In the borders it will make a rounded bush about 2 m (6 ft) high, with clusters of white flowers along the branches in April and May. The appearance of a bush in full bloom is much enhanced by an evergreen background, and *Berberis darwinii* is excellent for the purpose.

A dwarf and interesting species, *S. japonica* 'Bullata' was introduced from Japan towards the end of the last century. Its dark green, heavily veined leaves are studded with rosy-crimson flowers in July and August. The height varies according to locality, but 45 cm (18 in) would be a fair average to expect.

An outstanding cultivar is found in *S. × bumalda* 'Anthony Waterer' the flowers being a much gayer crimson, and most effective when used as bold groups at the front of a shrub or herbaceous border.

One of the toughest and most reliable, *S. douglasii menziesii* was banished from the shrub border to open bays in the woodland, because of its suckers invading the preserves of other shrubs. When space is not at a premium, or there is a rough corner to be filled, then the 2 m (6 ft) stems crowned in July and August with 20 cm (8 in) panicles of purplish-rose flowers are well worthy of consideration.

The cultivar 'Triumphans' with brighter coloured flowers in the same shade has the prize for quantity of bloom.

Stranvaesia

A pleasant shrub which after a few years tends to be taken for granted is *Stanvaesia davidiana*. One expects to see year in year out the umbrella-like evergreen shape, topped with cream-white flowers in May, then in September by the crimson fruits. A proportion of the leaves turn scarlet and look most effective against the glossy green of the remainder. This may seem a great deal of beauty to take for granted, but one tends to accept the healthy, vigorous shrubs with only passing approbation, and fuss over the weaklings with loving care, though in truth they have only a modest charm.

The only method of propagation I have succeeded with is by seed, stratified outdoors in sand, and then sown in pans of sandy compost over gentle heat. A well-drained loamy soil with a position in full sun encourages the shrub to ripen a full crop of glorious berries. In my experience growth is fairly slow, in 14 years only reaching 2.1 m (7 ft) by as much through. I understand they do grow up to 12 m (40 ft), but at the present rate of progress I shall not have time to see my plant in maturity.

Stranvaesia undulata is a low-growing spreading species, thought by some botanists to be only a variety of *S. davidiana*.

Symphoricarpos

Symphoricarpos albus is enjoying a renewed burst of popularity for the Snowberry really is nothing more or less than a pernicious weed. Where nothing else will grow it has a use; in pine groves, or under beech trees it will at least relieve the monotony of bare earth.

Symphoricarpos rivularis which is also known as *S. albus laevigatus* is a distinct improvement and a first-class ornamental shrub for the late autumn. At this season the leafless branches are hung with pure white berries in liberal profusion.

'White Hedge', as the name implies, can be utilised as a barrier, but there are so many plants better qualified to function in this capacity that it is used as a free-growing shrub in the border here. The habit is compact, 1.2 m (4 ft) high, with small white berries in erect trusses.

Syringa

To even the non-gardener, the word lilac is linked with that of the rose as typifying the English garden scene. In May and June, when the flowers are fully opened, the air is filled with the delightful fragrance traditionally connected with this lovely flower. Unfortunately, some lilacs are singularly lacking in scent, unless it be that of privet, so these are banished to the outer boundaries; for what is lilac without scent?

The species have charm, and in really brutal conditions are more reliable than the cultivars of *Syringa vulgaris*. Most are strong growing up to 4.5 m (15 ft), so allowance must be made for this when considering their inclusion. Lilacs prefer a soil with free lime, but will grow with equal vigour in acid media, provided the drainage is good.

Syringa josikaea is the Hungarian Lilac introduced to English gardens in the middle of the last century. Growth is very strong and upright, the deep lilac flowers opening in June. As with all the species and cultivars of this genus, pruning consists of removing the dead flower heads once the colour has gone. A finger and thumb pruning is best, or if done with secaturs make sure the buds at the base of the truss are left undamaged.

From China, *S. julianae*, is a delightful shrub making a rounded bush of 2 to 2.5 m (6 to 8 ft), with deliciously perfumed flowers of red-purple.

Syringa microphylla has the happy knack of flowering twice in the year, the first flush coming in late May, the second in August. Usually the overall impression given by lilac is of rather dumpy solidarity, but *S. microphylla* on the other hand has smaller leaves and slender branches; a picture when covered with lilac-pink blossom of delicate grace. One bush in the woodland has reached 2 m (6 ft) in height; in the open 1.2 m (4 ft) is about the average.

According to some authorities *S. patula* (*S. palibiniana*) grows up to 3 m (10 ft) tall but the representatives I grow cannot have been given any notice of this, for they stubbornly refuse to grow above 1 m (3 ft), and make useful dwarf shrubs for the rock garden. The dark green oval leaves contrast with the pale lilac fragrant flowers, which against a light background would look insipid.

Like most of the species, both *S. microphylla* and *S. patula* come readily from cuttings of semi-hard wood in July and August, dibbled into a sand frame.

Sometimes known as the Canadian hybrids, *S. prestoniae* must rank amongst the most resilient of the hardy shrubs. They grow with tremendous

vigour and should be given sufficient room to develop to their full elegant 2.5 to 3 m (8 to 10 ft) 'Audrey,' has plume-like panicles of pinkish-mauve flowers. In 'Desdemona' the rather astilbe-like flowers are a pale mauve, and 'Hiawatha' is the richest colour of all – a good strong red-purple.

Syringa sweginzowii has the sweetest scent of all the species. and makes a tall graceful bush of 3 m (10 ft). The flowers open in June to a beautiful rose-lilac shade. Unfortunately this is a colour which unless sited very carefully loses much of its beauty. Suitable company would be *Berberis darwinii*, the dark green leaves enhancing the delicate pink shades of the lilac. Some nurserymen list a cultivar called 'Superba', and this should be preferred for the deeper pink of the flowers.

The Common Lilac, *Syringa vulgaris*, conjures up memories of the village school which I attended to have the initial rudiments of an education instilled into my somewhat unreceptive mind. A pink and white lilac, which when in bloom filled the air with fragrance. Strange how the sun always seemed to shine, and the air was always soft and full of the perfection of a May day in the dales country. No doubt I am influenced by the memory of these first lilacs which made an impression on the schoolboy mind; be that as it may, the ordinary Common Lilac is still my favourite. Since then an almost endless procession of cultivars from *S. vulgaris* have passed through my hands into this garden, though some have proved ephemeral, tarrying for only a few short seasons and then giving up the struggle against soil or climate. Others have stayed, prospered, and finally established a firm hold on my affections. One thing no Common Lilac will tolerate, and that is bad drainage. Given a suitable soil and a generous dressing of bonemeal each year – a commodity the plants here are positively addicted to – there will be little cause for anyone to complain about lack of vigour or blossom.

'Etna' with panicles of deep purple flowers in mid-June is one of the latest to bloom, but unfortunately when fully open they have the faded look of clothes which have been through the wash too often; in maturity they become lilac-pink. 'Hugo Koster' grows as a stiffly erect bush with huge panicles of purple-crimson flowers in mid-May. 'Marechal Foch' is an old favourite, excellent in the vivid carmine-rose of its flowers, but for the rest of the year it looks tatterdemalion. The lax gaunt shape and sparse leafage make this cultivar a veritable 'artful dodger'. 'Massena' on the other hand has a neat air of respectability which would never give offence. Its flower truss is larger than any single-flowered lilac I have seen, and is of a satisfying shade of deep purple-red.

Next to the white cultivar 'Souvenir de Louis Spath' is my favourite. It has rich dark red flowers and there can be few lovelier pictures than a bronze or copper jug filled with spikes of these.

The double cultivars have never appealed to me as much as the singles because they have a stiff formality which is too unbending in its primness ever to excite affection. The best double white is the old 'Madame Lemoine'. The big truss develops on a long stem, very suitable for cutting and arranging in a deep vase. Enthusiastic floral artists should remember that depletion of the bush one year means fewer flowers the next.

'Mrs Edward Harding' with purple-red flowers is slower growing than most and is suitable for the smaller garden. 'Paul Thirion' has very heavy full heads, rich rosy-red, which open rather later than others in a normal season.

Ulex

Having spent many pleasant afternoons (before work called me from the school room) chasing rabbits from one gorse bush to another, getting plenty of healthy exercise without reducing the furred population appreciably, I often feel that if the Common Gorse were some rarity from the mountains of China, it would receive the homage its beauty warrants. A drive along that lovely valley of the Swale, then over the Stang to Scargill, when the hillsides are bathed in the golden sunshine of gorse in full bloom, must impress even the most reluctant gardener.

To be absolutely in character, *Ulex europaeus* should be planted with heathers, dwarf rhododendrons, and cytisus, all shrubs which carry with them an aura of the windswept hills and quiet reaches of moorland. The gorse is invaluable for those with an exposed coastal side to the garden, especially on the East Coast where the wind cuts like a sliver of ice, laden with salt spray. Inland, a dry, poor soil suits the shrub best; grown hard in this way flowering is encouraged to a greater extent than if the soil were full of rich goodness.

The best form for garden cultivation is *Ulex europaeus* 'Plenus'. A neat, rounded bush with glaucous-green leaves, it is covered in April and May with full double, deep yellow flowers, and then intermittently through the year. A walk round any well gorsed bank where natural regeneration can proceed usually discloses variation in flower form, even some semi-doubles, but I have never found anything so becoming as the full double.

Ulex minor (nanus) is a pleasant little hedgehog for the larger rock garden or dry bank difficult to furnish with anything else. Flowering as it does in September, a good companion in bloom at the same time would be *Calluna vulgaris* 'H. E. Beale'. The deep yellow with the purple of the heath makes a bonnie picture.

To increase stock of any of the species make cuttings of current season's growth during early August, about 8 cm (3 in) is the correct length. Insert them in a compost of 3 parts sand, 1 part loam, and 1 part peat by volume under a sun frame. Like certain other shrubs gorse strongly objects to being force-rooted by bottom heat.

Vaccinium

Another strangely neglected genus is *Vaccinium*. Nothing can be claimed to equal the heather, or for that matter the gorse, in beauty of flower, but the quiet tones of the leaves in autumn,

Ulex europaeus 'Plenus' is the double form of native gorse

and, in the case of the native Bilberry, the excellence of the fruit when covered with pastry give it a strong claim for a place in our affections. Some species are extraordinarily shade tolerant, as witness the way Bilberries carpet the birch woods all over the north of England, where the soil is acid in character. *Vaccinium myrtillus* is the Bilberry – sometimes known as the Whortleberry – to all children who gather the harvest of blue-black succulent fruits in August, oblivious to the bites of midges and other distractions. As previously mentioned, this is an excellent little shrub for carpeting the bare earth under deciduous trees, especially attractive in autumn when the leaves colour dull purple and gold. It grows to between 20 and 45 cm (8 and 18 in) and I run the scythe over the older colonies to keep them bushy.

The Cowberry, *V. vitis-idaea*, is a ground-hugging shrublet which enjoys a soil a good deal moister than the average garden provides, and has an intricate network of wiry stems, clothed in lustrous green leathery leaves. The fruits are dark red, but only 0.5 cm (¼in) across.

Viburnum

Any shrub which is as easily cultivated as the viburnum must deserve special recommendation. This genus includes amongst its species shrubs whose flowers open right through the winter, as well as those more orthodox in outlook that restrict themselves to spring and summer as the time for so serious a business as blossoming.

Winter-flowering plants tend to be rhapsodied about regardless of their quality, but after seeing *Viburnum* × *bodnantense* in full bloom, few would quarrel about its merit. In summer the leaves and manner of growth do not command attention, and beauty of form is a quality the summer-flowering species have monopolised. In winter when the leaves fall the rather angular outline is not unpleasing, but as the first buds open to show the rose-coloured, sweetly scented flowers, then, be the wind like a blast from the Arctic tundra,

in that moment at least it is high summer. Flowering continues intermittently during spells of open weather from November to March, and the petals are frost resistant to a marked degree. A bowl of cut branches in a warm room will fill the air with a perfume which even in a confined space is never oppressive.

Propagation offers few problems. Cuttings of half-mature shoots inserted round the edge of a 13 cm (5 in) pot in a compost of 3 parts sharp sand and 1 peat moss by volume, with a little bottom heat, root in four weeks.

A form of *V.* × *bodnantense* with brighter pink blossom is available under the alluring name of 'Dawn'. I must confess not having noticed any vast difference between the type and cultivar until one day in February 1964. That afternoon was mild for the time of year, and the 'Dawn' was positively covered in flowers whose scent could be enjoyed 6 m (20 ft) or more away. That moment of beauty made me a devoted admirer of this lovely plant from then onwards.

I have only slight admiration for shrubs which need continual attention to keep them free of pests or diseases, since for me there are so many which grow without a lot of fuss, and so why waste time on those reluctant prima donnas? Undoubtedly *V. carlesii* is very handsome, provided the blackfly give one time to enjoy the beauty. More often than not the leaves are rendered hideous by a seething mass of these pests and spraying must be resorted to at fortnightly intervals. Where the soil is right the shrub is a veritable Samson, with stout stems surmounted with clusters of sweetly scented flowers, coral-pink in the bud, maturing to a white of almost unsullied purity. As far as I can discover, the ideal soil is a free-draining loam, preferably containing a little lime; given this the shrub can shrug off the plague with complete disdain. Propagation is as for *V.* × *bodnantense*.

Shrubs with exquisite foliage and beautiful flowers or berries are not conspicuously numerous, in any case what appeals to some people has the reverse effect on others. *V. davidii*, a neatly rounded evergreen shrublet rarely more than 76 cm (30 in) high, has the happy ability of making friends with everyone. The flowers are a dull cream, but the berries are the most vivid shade of turquoise. To get effective cross-pollination, male and female plants should be growing in close proximity to each other. Even without flowers or berries I would still grow *V. davidii* for its innate good temper, and the beauty of its oval evergreen leaves in the aridity of winter. Use it as ground cover under one of the winter-flowering members of the family.

Cuttings root with alacrity from July to November with bottom heat. No soil or situation bothers the plant; wet clay or sand, full sun or shade are all tolerated with equanimity.

Viburnum farreri (V. fragrans) grows 2 to 2.5 m (6 to 8 ft) here, and has an even more angular outline in winter than its offspring *V.* × *bodnantense.* The flowering is extended from autumn to early spring, but the colour is paler, a delicate shell-pink. Soil or exposure make no difference, apart from the habit being more compact and rounded in windswept situations.

Viburnum grandiflorum is the other half of the union which resulted in *V.* × *bodnantense,* but in this case the flowers are carried in bigger clusters, rich carmine in the bud opening to pink. They are not so frost hardy as they should be, and a November freeze-up can put them out of their stride for a season.

The Guelder Rose, *V. opulus,* whose white flowers in flattened heads have been dedicated to the festival of Whitsuntide for generations, is a shrub possessed of a wealth of charm. In flower a full-grown bush 3 to 3.5 m (10 to 12 ft) high is an impressive sight of the June border. As the leaves colour, and the berries glow red amongst them, one again pays homage at the shrine of the Guelder Rose.

As one would expect with a native plant, several forms can be obtained; the best of these is 'Compactum' which flowers and then berries with the same beauty and freedom as the type plant,

but only grows 1 to 1.2 m (3 to 4 ft) high. The other, and better known offspring, is 'Sterile' the lovely Snowball Tree, and how well this describes the globose clusters of sterile flowers! All grow on alkaline or acid soil, but the leafage is not so luxuriant on a badly drained soil, which gives the plant a tatterdemalion aspect on occasions.

Layering offers the surest way of increase with the Snowball Tree; the other two can also be propagated by this method or by seed, but 'Compactum' may not come 100 per cent. true.

One would assume a large-leaved evergreen species with a predilection for carrying its flowers in the naked bud state, to be anything but reliably hardy. However, in *Viburnum rhytidophyllum* can be found an exception to this rather sweeping generalisation. In due course it will make a 3.7 to 4.5 m (12 to 15 ft) shrub, and apart from cold east winds scorching the large leaves on occasions, it exhibits no sign of discontent at all. The soil, be it acid or alkaline, must be well drained, for on a waterlogged soil the roots are beset by fungus, and strong winds complete the process of destruction by blowing the weakened plant out of the ground. Rather dull white flowers in trusses 10 to 15 cm (4 to 6 in) in diameter open in late May, but it is the dark green wrinkled leaves, grey felted underneath, which give this shrub its attraction.

Propagation can be effected by seed sown in the open ground during early April, or by layering.

So far as I am concerned, beauty of form plays a part equal in importance to beauty of flower. Blooms are fugitive, only lasting a brief time, whereas interesting contours or leaves make a perennial contribution to the landscape. A plant endowed with the dual virtues of form and flower is *Viburnum plicatum tomentosum,* with wide-spreading horizontal branches, built up tier upon tier. In May and June, when the upper surface of each branch is covered with flat clusters of white flowers, the shrub is indeed a picture of grace and beauty. I like to use *V. plicatum tomen-*

The beautiful foliage of *Viburnum davidii* forms effective ground cover

tosum as a front piece to conifers of similar style, then cut the angles with a complete contrast by including a weeping birch or cherry in the picture. In autumn the leaves turn a deep red, tinged with purple, a colour which oddly enough looks glorious with a carpet of *Calluna vulgaris* 'H. E. Beale' spread underneath. Pruning is only necessary to emphasise the horizontal branching effect, when an occasional stem becomes endowed with an ambition to the vertical; otherwise only dead or damaged wood should be removed.

Cuttings of half-ripened shoots taken in August will root a reasonable proportion, given some bottom heat. *V. plicatum* 'Lanarth' only differs from the type in having bigger leaves and possibly stronger growth, which is only desirable in a large garden.

Viburnum plicatum 'Mariesii' is the gem in the collection, the branches rise tier upon tier, laden in due season with an abundance of snow-white flowers. This is a shrub capable of fitting into any setting: in the herbaceous border flanked by the blue of anchusa, in the shrub border, or as a specimen on a lawn with only grass as a foil to the beautiful shape which catches and holds the eye.

Vinca

The shady parts of the garden, so long given over to Victorian rock gardens and similar grotesquerie, have now become places of quiet beauty. Many plants enjoy the cool, dappled shade provided by wall or trees, their flowers preserved against fading, endowed with subtle tones in the play of light which filters through from overhead. Unfortunately, shade in some cases means drips from overhanging branches and dry aridity because of greedy roots, and thought must be given to find plants which can overcome these obstacles.

The Periwinkle, emblem of the pleasures of memory and sincere friendship, makes a pleasing evergreen ground cover under the conditions described. *Vinca major* is a vigorous, rampant ground cover for harsh banks or unsightly corners. The flowers, which

are a fine bright blue, can be found at any time from June to September. A form I grow as *V. m.* 'Variegata' has leaves margined with pale yellow, and flowers of palest blue. This plant was acquired from a crumbling 'wall round an old church. Where it had hailed from originally no one could tell me, but the beautiful variegated leaves covered the wall and shrubbery for several yards. The invitation to take a root was extended and accepted and now a healthy colony makes a home in a shady corner of the peat garden.

If *V. major* can be described as the roistering buccaneer of the family, then *V. minor* must surely be the brother who turned to the plough rather than the sword. Smaller, hugging the ground as it spreads, this wee native plant makes just as good ground cover, but without the boisterous enthusiasm of the other. This restraint has not been carried through in other fields, for many different forms exist, some too delicate for the tasks which so often fall to the vinca in less desirable parts of the garden. Only those which are worthy are included here.

Vinca minor 'Alba', as might be expected, has white flowers and a slightly slower rate of growth, but otherwise is quite adequate. In 'Aureo-variegata' can be found a foliage variation of much beauty, the leaves being marked with bands of yellow, against which the blue flowers appear in demure contrast.

I unashamedly desire any plant described as Bowles' variety, from pansies to vincas, and certainly *V. minor* 'Bowles' Variety' does that gentleman of gardening full honour. The leaves, a dark, healthy green, make a perfect foil to the huge azure flowers. Only one small criticism; the plant is not quite so free with blossom in shade as it might be.

Propagation of all vincas is easy by cuttings, self-made layers, or just digging up the parent plant and dividing.

Weigela

There is no doubt that the genus

The vincas or periwinkles will thrive in dry shade

Weigela contains some extremely decorative and reasonably easy-to-grow shrubs, yet somehow I cannot find it in me to eulogise about them. The habit of growth I find positively ugly, and the red-flowered hybrids lack a certain purity in the colouring. However, as 99 out of 100 gardeners I talk to in the course of a year cherish weigela, it must be I who am out of step. No particular preference for soil is obvious except that it be reasonably well drained. Where possible choose an aspect which gets a fair share of the sunlight available, though partial shade for a limited period around midday does stop the flowers fading.

The most suitable form of pruning consists of cutting back each flowering shoot immediately the blossoms have faded to within two or three strong shoots of the base. This has the virtue of stopping the plant developing the rather loose, gaunt character which I find so ugly.

One of the most useful species can be found in *Weigela florida*; a mature specimen usually reaches 1.5 to 2 m (5 to 6 ft) in height, and the foxglove-like flowers are deep pink on the outside, almost shell-pink within. The season is relatively short, commencing late in May or early June depending on the prevailing weather. The form of *W. florida* known as 'Variegata', with creamy-white-margined leaves, is a handsome plant when not in flower. This may seem a contradiction, but the pale pink flowers look insipid against the cream and green leaves. Growth is much slower than in the type, a plant here at 15 years old is now only 1.2 m (4 ft) high.

My favourite amongst the weigelas is the sulphur-yellow-flowered *W. middendorffiana*. In this garden it grows on the north-easterly side of the shrub border, on a shallow soil over yellow clay, and positively radiates health. In due course it makes a pleasantly spreading bush 1 m (3 ft) high by some 1.5 m (5 ft) across, but it can be restricted by judicious pruning. Care must be taken to select a form with good strong yellow flowers, and on the lower lip of each a daub of bright orange. Some cultivars available have a paler colouring, and no orange blotching. Many garden hybrids of weigela are in existence, of these 'Bristol Ruby', with bright red flowers, and 'Eva Rathke', with deep crimson blooms, are worthy of attention. The cultivar 'Lavallei' has crimson flowers with white protruding stamens, and an indestructible vigour.

Propagation can be effected by means of semi-ripe cuttings taken in July, 10 to 15 cm (4 to 6 in) long, and inserted in a sunny cold frame. Hardwood cuttings taken during November will also root in a cold frame.

Climbers

—◈—

Walls perform a variety of functions apart from holding up the roof of house or garage. To the gardener they offer a support and a degree of protection to the shrubs which even before the furniture van has· disappeared over the horizon, are already in imagination planted against them. Even the smaller house and miniscule garden has a considerable area of wall space which when brought under cultivation enables a much wider range, and a greatly increased number, of plants to be included. A point which is not fully appreciated is the walls of buildings offer varying aspects which can be exploited for plants and, in consequence, to the gardener's advantage.

Shrubs, which in their homelands are used to hot dry summers, may be persuaded to grow if given the shelter of a south-facing wall. Similarly, a climber which prefers the cool moist shade of a woodland might discover the same degree of comfort on a north-facing wall. Only those who garden in exposed places where the wind has free play can appreciate just how much the plants must benefit given the protection from cold bruising winds. Shelter is of particular value when growing shrubs with attractive foliage.

Walls are not the only support for shrubs which the garden affords. Fences, trellis, arbors and moribund trees are all subjects for exploitation by those who wish to enjoy the pleasure derived from the cultivation of climbing plants. Most of the climbers are chosen for the beauty of leaf or flower. Occasionally beauty is a secondary consideration, when some unsightly object which spoils the close or distant view needs a mantle of green foliage to act as a disguise. Then vigorous growth becomes 'a prime virtue.

Vigorous climbers can be incorrigible nuisances in some cases if allowed to grow unchecked. Roots block drains or damage foundations, while invasive shoots dam gutters and push under slates and tiles.

Remember also those plants which are self-clinging might do damage to walls if the mortar is rotten. Roots which grow from the undersides of the branches explore every joint and crevice which offers. Removing Virgina Creeper from an old house which a newly married friend had bought without proper examination proved the point most graphically. In addition to a mound of vegetation there was a barrow and a half of mortar to clean up.

Climbing plants can also be used to cover steep banks or provide ground cover under taller growing trees or shrubs. The soil close to a wall is often impoverished to the point of sterility. In most cases the shrubs or climbers installed will be permanent features, making improvement of the soil in subsequent years difficult, and in some cases impossible.

Improve the soil by digging in organic matter as described earlier in the book. In extreme cases I have removed the existing soil to a depth of 45 cm (18 in) where planting was to take place, and replaced it with good loam.

Supports of some sort will be required and these should be efficient yet remain neat and unobtrusive. Fixing them in place it is important to do the minimum damage to the wall itself.

I use a system of angle brackets and plastic-coated wire. These are cheap and efficient, and once the climbers are established the wires become virtually invisible. The wires are fastened to eye bolts with a screw at one end, so once the system is in place correct tension is

Opposite:
Parthenocissus tricuspidata is a Japanese creeper of considerable vigour

arrived at by simply tightening a nut.

Wooden trellis, plastic mesh, and similar should be attached to bobbins or blocks of wood so there is an air space between growing plant and wall.

The choice of plants suitable for wall culture is quite bewildering. Anyone who doubts this should try making a selection from the lists of clematis and roses.

Actinidia

Actinidia kolomikta is the only species from a genus of climbers, originating in Eastern Asia, that I will mention, simply because it is the only one of which I have practical experience in growing. At first this plant filled me with revulsion, I saw nothing in the parti-coloured leaves to excite my admiration in the slightest. Gradually, however, I began to enjoy the changing colours, some leaves wholly pink or white, some only partially so, and others completely green, and certainly in most visitors it produces whole-hearted approval. Grown as a climber on any but a north wall, or on a pillar or pergola, throughout the summer the leaves are both unusual and decorative. The type of soil does not seem to matter a great deal, but in my experience the poorer and drier the mixture the better the leaf variegation. Cuttings of semi-ripened shoots made in July, August, or September root readily in a sun frame or propagating case.

Ceanothus

Shrubs which can be trained to wires, trellis, or similar supports are of particular value on exposed sites. Ceanothus, the Californian Lilacs, are suitable for planting on south or west walls. The evergreen cultivars are best lightly pruned after flowering, while those which lose their leaves are treated in March by pruning back side-shoots to three or four buds of the previous season's growth. For detailed description see the entry in the main tree and shrub section.

Chaenomeles

See tree and shrub section, p. 81.

Choisya

Choisya ternata will grow handsomely, given the protection of a wall, into a dense evergreen foliaged shrub 2.5 m (8 ft) tall. The white citrus-scented flowers earn choisya the popular name Mexican Orange Blossom. Cuttings of half-ripe shoots or ripened wood later in the summer root with ease.

Clematis

Should a survey ever be made to find the most popular climber of all, it would be a pretty safe bet that clematis would be a strong contender for the title. They are, however, far from predictable in their reactions, and they have unexplainable moods; fits of temperament for which there seems no logical explanation. I spoil my clematis unashamedly, and pander to their every whim. Again and again I hear of instances where clematis grow well in one garden, while next door on apparently the same soil and aspect they fail miserably. Do not be misled into thinking clematis difficult, for they are more likely to flourish like the green bay tree than not to grow at all. Most, but by no means all, enjoy a position in full sun, with their roots able to explore a cool, rich compost. The easiest way to supply the right root medium is to work up the site with moist peat, well laced with bone-meal, and topdress annually after planting with the same material. Well-rotted manure and compost will do the same job, of course, but these commodities are difficult to come by, whereas peat is readily obtainable and clean to handle. Poor drainage will kill clematis quicker than any other single factor, and no labour should be spared to ensure that surplus moisture drains quickly out of the root area.

When planting clematis do not be in a hurry over any part of the procedure. The shoots should be carefully spaced out on to some support, wire, or canes, and firmly tied in so there is no danger from wind breakage or twisting of the pithy stems.

There are so many clematis available that choosing a few for the garden is limited only by one's personal taste.

One hardly connects the exotic clematis with high alpine meadows and majestic mountains, yet my first meeting with *Clematis alpina* was in just such a setting. What a picture the delicate, soft blue bells made, interlaced with the rather brick-red blossoms of *Rhododendron ferrugineum!* This is the way I like to grow *C. alpina*, over and amongst dwarf shrubs in the rock garden; azaleas make superb companions. The best form of this species I have so far encountered is 'Columbine' bearing lavender-blue flowers with extra long sepals, giving the plant a curiously elfin air. The normal time of blossoming is in May, but I have one seedling which persists in delaying its entry until June. 'Ruby', purplish pink, and 'White Moth', which opens semi-double flowers, are valuable additons to the *alpina* range.

Grown on a wall, *C. alpina* should be trained out to form a framework of main branches, and then the short growths from these are cut hard back each year in July-August. I like to cut an old framework branch back each year after maturity to get the young shoots as replacements. When the plants are growing free over bushes, removal of dead wood and the worst tangles should suffice.

For a white or grey wall 'Ernest Markham', with petunia-red flowers, makes a pleasing contrast. In this garden the growth is moderately vigorous, and the medium-sized blooms make up for a certain lack of size by sheer weight of numbers. Pruning consists of cutting back to soil level, or when this has been neglected to within 5 cm (2 in) of the base of the previous year's growth, in January.

'Royal Velours', with purple flowers, and 'Ville de Lyon' with deep red flowers, are two more which flower at the same time in July, and require similar treatment to 'Ernest Markham'. The best known and most widely planted of all must be *C.* 'Jackmanii', and few would deny this lovely climber with violet-blue flowers the place of honour it holds in public esteem. The flowers open in abundance during July and August. In 'Jackmanii Superba' the blooms are larger, and glowing violet-purple. Pruning can be done by either cutting the stems back annually in December to within 8 to 10 cm (3 to 4 in) of soil level, or alternatively to within an inch of the base of the previous year's growth.

Clematis × jouiniana I have grown for many years on a north-facing slope to cover a very unsightly stump of an oak tree, felled to make way for some steps. Its tiny flowers are milky white, but carried in riotous profusion during August and September. Apart from thinning out surplus shoots, no pruning seems to be necessary. This is a modest plant in or out of flower, yet very worthy of a corner in the garden.

A genus which enjoys as much affection as clematis must inevitably be possessed of a roistering, rollicking 'Friar Tuck', and this for me is the species *montana*. For sheer *joie de vivre* and willingness to grow, this one would be hard to beat, and for this alone I love it. I have a *C. montana* 'Elizabeth' planted in rough grass at the foot of a gnarled old hawthorn 9 m (30 ft) high. For a year the clematis weighed up the situation, then having come to a decision romped up to the top of the thorn and cascaded over to hang down like some delightful pink-flowered, sweetly scented veil. Chance has it that most years the flowers of hawthorn and clematis open together, pink on white with the grass around filled with the yellow of daffodils. Small wonder that each time I pass the picture holds me entranced.

There are variations other than 'Elizabeth'; *grandiflora* with white blossoms, and 'Pink Perfection' which has the richest colouring of any. As a trained form *C. montana* should have the main shoots spaced out to make a framework, and then the growths that come from these are spur pruned to within 2.5 cm (1 in) of the base immediately after flowering.

Some cultivars hold a special place in the ranks of the genus so far as I am concerned. The first one is a *patens* variety, 'Nelly Moser' by name, having

Opposite: Wisteria are in the top six of best-loved climbers and are very adaptable to training

Flowers and seed heads of *Clematis tangutica* make an attractive display

The catkins of *Garrya elliptica* appear in the winter

pale mauve flowers with a deep carmine bar down the centre of each petal. This was the first climber I ever bought with my own money, and it grew like a weed all over the grey walls of a stone shed at home. Each May came the wealth of flowers, then as a bonus a second smaller bouquet in September. The second, 'Perle d'Azure', 'Jackmanii' group, commands a reserved seat simply because the clear pale blue flowers are so ethereally lovely. In 1965 the first blossom opened on July 28, the frost of October 21 blackened the last one, and there were still buds unopened. The wall on which it grows faces due north, yet the clematis is quite content there in company with *Hydrangea petiolaris,* of which more later.

Clematis macropetala is what I would describe as the Himalayan counterpart of the European *alpina* with lavender blue, semi-double flowers. I grow the species and the pink form 'Markham's Pink' against a low terrace wall. Pruned either hard or light, flowers are displayed abundantly in April or May.

Clematis tangutica whose pendant yellow lantern flowers are followed in due season by silken feathered seed heads offers a colour variation. A species which, like many other clematis, can be raised from seed which is offered in plenty for the harvesting.

'Hagley Hybrid' with rosy-pink flowers will be well suited with a north-west wall. 'The President' is another which in three years since planting has opened a succession of purple flowers from July to late September – an admirable display of character.

Forsythia

Forsythia suspensa sieboldii is another plant of quality, especially on the problem east wall. The shoots are so slender that it is really only on a wall that it has any claim to beauty. Grown in the open, the shoots spread along the ground and the golden flowers are soon sullied by rain splashes from the soil.

The type plant *F. suspensa,* and its variety *fortunei,* are vigorous growers, and the long strong branches must be firmly tied in position or the whole effect is spoilt. The golden-yellow flowers open in April and May.

Garrya

Poets have sung the praises of *Garrya elliptica,* and visitors admire the grossly healthy specimen on the west corner of my house, which receives the full untempered blast of the wind from the moors. The grey-green leaves make this a pleasant foliage plant, and I can find it in me during less critical moments to admire the soft silvery-green catkins, 23 cm (9 in) long, which grace the bush in winter. Let me confess that, though all who see covet my plant, I should have long since given it away if it were not sheltering a rather lovely fern, and some good forms of *Cyclamen hederifolium (C. neapolitanum.)* Soil of heavy clay, well nourished with rotted manure, has suited the shrub absolutely. Once established no tying or pruning is necessary except, if my treatment is any guide, to plunder it unmercifully to provide background arrangements at flower shows.

Hedera

Hedera or ivy is the badge of the clan Gordon, and the plant is under the dominion of Saturn; yet, according to Folkard, to dream of it portends 'friendship, happiness, good fortune, honour, riches and success'. A sprig put into the cask is said to clear clouded ale. A herb of virtue, and useful as well, and in the garden what other evergreen climber remotely compares with the adaptability of ivy? On any soil or situation, in the polluted atmosphere of cities, in the dank shade of woodlands, even under sycamores where not one blade of couch could survive, ivy will spread to make a deliciously evergreen carpet. Being self-climbing it will hide unsightly buildings or soften the stark aridity of brick or stone with a shining evergreen mantle. A great many cultivars are available, but few exceed in quality the different types of the common *Hedera helix*. The tiny *H. h.* 'Congesta', dense and almost painfully slow-growing, is useful in the rock garden, or for growing up terrace walls.

On the north-east wall of my house grows the gay *H. h.* 'Marginata'; the leaves are beautifully proportioned, just long enough to balance the width, each one edged with a creamy-white. At first I thought the bitter east winds were going to prove too much for it, but now it has grown into a shapely specimen some 1 m (3 ft) high, spreading round on both north and east faces, a matter of 1 to 1.2 m (3 to 4 ft).

So adaptable have the various species and cultivars proved I tend to take advantage of their good nature. A mixed planting of the Variegated Persian Ivy, *Hedera colchica* 'Dentata Variegata', with very large cream and grey leaves, competes with a marbled leaved *H. helix* 'Glacier' for pride of place on a steeply sloping east-facing bank. In autumn *Cyclamen hederifolium* push up pink flowers through the carpet of ivy leaves. On the wall of a well, situated at the west end of the terrace, *H. helix* 'Goldheart' enjoys full exposure to sun and wind which intensified the deep gold at the leaf centres.

Hydrangea

Even now I can remember the feeling of blank astonishment when, as a boy, with an awakening interest in gardening, I was told that what I thought was a rather good ivy was really a hydrangea. One does not expect hydrangea – at least small boys do not – to have anything else but blue flowers, and to grow demurely on either side of the front door. To find a specimen so depraved as to scoot 6 m (20 ft) up a wall, climbing by means of its own self-clinging branches seemed almost against nature. Be that as it may, *Hydrangea petiolaris* is a very beautiful climber on any wall, even one which faces due north. I have grown it on lime soils, on sand, and on clay and over an apple tree which refused to bear fruit, without offending one iota the plant's sense of justice. The heart-shaped leaves are nearly hidden during July and August by the big flat corymbs of white flowers. In autumn the leaves go an enchanting shade of lemon.

Jasminum

See tree and shrub section, page 98, for *Jasminum nudiflorum.*

Lonicera

Some plants excite affection wherever they are grown, and even in this age of sophistication, honeysuckle conjures up a memory in the mind of woodland walks, the air redolent with the smell of this delightful climber. Not all the family are possessed of fragrance and I prefer to sacrifice the more exciting flower colours of the scentless cultivars, in favour of those which have this valuable adjunct to beauty. There are not many scented climbing plants, after all.

A woodland setting, where the long stems can wind up a gnarled tree trunk, or through a strong shrub, shows its character to best advantage, but I have them growing also on stonework, especially on the edges of paths where the scent can be enjoyed to the full. As the name Woodbine implies, a cool leafy soil is the most suitable, and a partially shaded situation.

Lonicera × americana is an extremely vigorous species which can be allowed to ramble freely, or by rigorous pruning be persuaded to develop an almost shrub-like character. The delicately scented flowers, first white, then changing to creamy-yellow, make a lovely picture in July and August.

Our own native honeysuckle, *L. periclymenum,* in selected forms offers the best of both worlds of colour and scent. The yellowish-cream flowers, suffused with purple, open at intervals from June to September. In the cultivar 'Belgica' the flowers open in early June; then lest we forget their beauty, the cultivar 'Serotina' has flowers in which red dominates, and these open in August and September.

To prune, shorten back the long side shoots to four or five buds immediately flowering is completed. Soft-wood cuttings 10 cm (4 in) long, taken in July, root quite rapidly in a propagating case in the greenhouse. Where this is impracticable, slightly longer material can be inserted in a cold frame in mid-October.

Schizophragma hydrangeoides needs plenty of sun to flower well

Polygonum

Polygonums are plants I treat with respect until, like the herbaceous species described previously, their invasive properties have been ascertained.

The Russian Vine, *Polygonum baldschuanicum,* is a handsome though rampageous climber, which can be guaranteed to cover any object it is planted against in less time than any other climber I am familiar with. Unsightly buildings, ruined cowsheds, tree stumps, can all be mantled by softened greenery, starred throughout the summer and autumn with white flowers stained with pink. To give some idea of the capabilities of this astounding plant, I know a ruined building some 12 m (40 ft) high that in five to six years was completely covered. In a small garden use careful thought about the siting of so boisterous a climber.

Pyracantha

Pyracantha make notable and distinctive wall plants. In addition to those cultivars described in the tree and shrub section I am trying a mixed planting of 'Mojave' with red berries, and 'Telstar' with orange fruit on the south-facing wall of the garage. The resident blackbirds expressed their approval by devouring the berries immediately they ripened. By protecting the bushes I enjoy the spectacle for a season before giving the birds access.

Schizophragma

Schizophragma might at first sight be easily mistaken for the twin brother of the climbing hydrangea, but they are quite distinct. *Schizophragma hydrangeoides* has not the easy-going propensity of the hydrangea, and is rather parsimonious with its flowers, unless given a fair ration of sunlight. In a favourite situation, on any but a north wall, this self-clinging climber, with pale yellow sepals which appear in July, will prove the equal of any.

Vines

In an effort to avoid confusing myself more than anything else, ampelopsis, parthenocissus and vitis are herded into one place. The botanists can play find the thimble to their hearts content elsewhere. I shall, at least for the present, know precisely who is what.

Ampelopsis brevipedunculata 'Elegans' is the only one that I have grown, and then with shelter on a patio wall. The foliage is mottled white and pink, in fact a pallied imitation of actinidia – a fact noted then acted upon.

Parthenocissus henryana climbs by means of tendrils equipped with suckers, to such good effect that one plant in my care covered a wall 6 m (20 ft) high. The leaves are a soft textured green with silvered veins. In autumn the colour changes to red before falling. Certainly my favourite for the beauty of leaf together with the quality of restraint.

Parthenocissus quinquefolia is the true Virginia Creeper which as a self-clinging climber can cover a 12 to 18 m (40 to 60 ft) wall when suited by soil and situation. As the green leaves turn scarlet with the shortening October days they provide a display which, though short lived, abides in the memory.

Parthenocissus tricuspidata is a native of Japan and China which has been widely planted in this country as Virginia Creeper. It is a Japanese creeper of considerable vigour, scaling walls or any similar supports by means of self-adhering tendrils, outdoing the *P. henryana* quite easily in growth rate. The leaf shape is like some of the maples, with three lobes turning from lustrous green in summer to vivid scarlet in autumn.

There are somewhere in the region of 60 species of vitis including *V. vinifera,* plus a multitude of hybrids. Of these *V. coignetiae* is the most colourfully ornamental of those I have grown. In an effort to hide a rather ugly iron railing some 9 m (30 ft) long I planted a three-year-old layer of this species. In a few years the railings were mantled in foliage. The leaves, dark green with rust-coloured undersides, were restful to the eye. In autumn the purple and scarlet of the dying leaves with the white foam of a waterfall behind made a cameo of the season.

Wisteria

Wisteria are surely in the top six of best-loved climbers whether grown free standing, over a pergola, up and over a tree, or as I prefer to see them, across a south-facing wall, they command our admiration. Once the branches have filled the space available cut all young growth back to three or four buds in late summer.

Racemes of purple flowers are displayed by *W. floribunda* in early summer. There is a white form, 'Alba', and there was a specimen of this, a veritable patriarch of the race, growing through a dead oak some 6 m (20 ft) high in a garden I worked 30 years ago. The sight of a wisteria bridges the gap of years in conjuring from memory the picture of white flowers framed against a summer's sky.

Wisteria sinensis with fragrant, deep lilac flowers is the most widely planted of the genus. One plant in my first garden covered the whole house front. As the flowers opened with the leaves in May the garden was filled with their perfume.

Conifers

———◦❀◦———

Conifers offer so much in form, foliage colour, and general adaptability that their exclusion from the landscape garden leaves a gap that no other evergreen, not even the magnificent rhododendron, can fill.

A proper assessment of the popularity of what are termed dwarf and slow-growing conifers can be made by comparing the number of cultivars available in nursery lists at the present time with those on offer even 10 years ago.

Choosing the right plant to suit a particular situation has been made a lot easier because the majority of conifers on offer are pot or container grown. Those who insist on a bare site being instantly transformed into a garden can, at a price, do so by introducing semi-mature conifers which have been grown in large containers. In the past the size of the plant offered for sale was restricted by the difficulty of transplanting bare-root stock from nursery to garden. The season was also limited to the time when most were dormant, usually between October and May. The most inhospitable weather for a plant to be moved occurs in winter, so that was a further limiting factor. The modern practice of growing plants for sale in containers throughout the whole of their nursery life, allows for planting all the year round at a time to suit the gardener. Just one of the revolutions in gardening practice which has occurred in my life time.

Though conifers will adapt to a wide range of conditions this should not be used as an excuse to avoid cultivating the soil in which they are to be planted. Try to ensure the soil is in a loose, friable condition by digging in compost, moist peat, or one of the special tree-planting compounds at present available which includes a slow-release fertilizer. Plant so that the top of the root ball is some 5 to 8 cm (2 to 3 in) below the finished level of the soil. New roots soon form in the surface layers and this gives firmer anchorage and greater stability. An open situation is the best, particularly for the golden foliaged cultivars. Any doubts I had about the hardiness of some have been dispelled by the way; all those listed have adapted to the business of surviving on an exposed hillside 243 m (800 ft) above sea level. Certainly in winter the garden would lack form and present an ill-furnished prospect.

There are species and cultivars so slow growing that they will grow contentedly for a generation in the modest dimensions of a trough garden. At the other extreme the family includes trees that soar 30 to 36 m (100 to 120 ft), majestic in their perfect symmetrical outline. No matter the size of the garden – be the landscape formal or designed to harmonize with the natural scenery around – there are conifers of the right shape and foliage colour to fit and enhance the picture.

They adapt themselves to any but the most inhospitable soils, and there are few gardens incapable of supporting a selection of these fascinating plants.

The trees suitable only for afforestation or parkland planting will not be included, for space permits the mention only of a select number.

Cedrus

Cedars are trees for the large garden; the lovely *Cedrus atlantica glauca* is fortunately relatively slow growing, and it is so attractive in the metallic grey-blue of its foliage, that to exclude it from consideration would be a little short of sacrilege. Lovely though this

Opposite: A beautiful combination of *Picea pungens* 'Koster' and *Picea brewerana*

141

Although eventually a large tree, *Cedrus atlantica glauca* is slow growing

tree may be, certain demands have to be met; for instance drainage must be perfect, and unless there is shelter to temper the worst wind the whole shape is spoilt. Specimens here after 15 years are only 2.7 m (11 ft) high.

Cedrus brevifolia I now have correctly named, thanks to Mr Hillier's painstaking work with the extremely involved nomenclature of the *Coniferae.* This is a remarkably slow-growing cedar with tiny grey-green leaves. The plant here arches over a rock, and makes a perfect picture with a carpet of thymes and dwarf bulbs. To get the full measure of effect from dwarf conifers the chosen companions must be selected with strict attention to details of proportion. To create a perfect replica of a miniature forest, and then put a Red Hot Poker to tower above it quite shatters the illusion.

The Deodar, most accommodating of all the cedars, needs far more room in maturity than the average garden affords, but *C. deodara verticillata* enables the most modest garden to share the charm of the Deodar without having to sacrifice all the other plants. Over many years *verticillata* may make a small tree, but the largest one I have seen was 3 m (10 ft) high and 32 years old, in that Eden for conifers, the Lake District. *C. deodara* and its forms seem rather more tolerant of wet, heavy soils than *C. atlantica,* but stagnant moisture must be avoided.

Cedrus libani, the Cedar of Lebanon, is in maturity a magnificent sight, with wide-spreading branches giving it a characteristically umbrella shape. There are two perfect miniatures of the gigantic species, both correctly proportioned. *C. l.* 'Nana' makes a rounded bush, and after a quarter of a century might attain 1.2 m (4 ft). I have watched a plant closely for several years but it only grows about 1 cm (½in) each season. *C. l.* 'Sargentii' is a slow-growing jewel, and perfect for pot work. The pendulous branches weep in delicate greenery to the ground. The plant here frightens me nearly to death every two to three years by dropping all its needles; fortunately, before donning sackcloth and ashes, I noticed the fat green buds all ready to burst, for I should miss this lovely shrublet. My plant is only 10 years old and has reached 60 cm (2 ft) high by about 1 m (3 ft) across.

Chamaecyparis

Chamaecyparis contribute a wealth of different forms to the rock garden and the shrub borders. Once again Mr Hillier must have saved many a gardener's sanity, lost as we were in a welter of duplications and synonyms.

Chamaecyparis lawsoniana is useful in the large garden as a boundary screen, or in groups at the end of a sweep of lawn. Though as a hedge on a windswept site Lawson Cypress, once it reaches a certain age, becomes distinctly threadbare and of limited ornamental value.

Chamaecyparis lawsoniana 'Allumii', with its narrow fastigiate habit and glaucous leaves, is used extensively for tub culture, and in the open garden. In hard winters this cultivar comes through unscathed. Over a period of 20 years or so it will outgrow the limits of a small garden.

Chamaecyparis lawsoniana 'Gimbornii' with blue-green foliage tipped with mauve in the winter makes a dwarf rounded bush, and is suitable for consideration where space is limited. *C. l.* 'Minima Aurea' is the form of a Lawson Cypress which receives first consideration in any planting scheme I am involved with. A neat compact globe of soft textured gold. Where there is space for two I include the sea green 'Minima Glauca'.

The most easily recognizable outline is that of *C. l.* 'Wissellii'. The columnar habit is devoid of any apparent stiffness, and the leaves are a deep green, almost black-green, with an overshadowing of grey.

There are so many Lawson Cypress listed, with new introductions arriving each year, personal preference must be the final arbitor.

Chamaecyparis obtusa, though more intolerant of dry alkaline soils than some, has needed only the persuasion of a peat mulch each year to accept a rainfall of 60 cm (24 in) per annum. *C. obtusa* 'Nana' with fan-shaped, slightly cupped sprays overlapping, produces a dome-shaped bush. 'Nana Gracilis' has the same tiered branch arrangement and grows slightly quicker. A plant I had from Blooms Nursery six years ago as 'Nana Lutea' has grown only a modest 10 cm (4 in), a glowing patch of gold even in the bleakest mid-winter. I grow it alongside that utterly admirable, though deciduous purple-leaved miniature *Berberis thunbergii* 'Atropurpurea Nana' and complete the ensemble with a skirt of *Tulipa tarda*.

Chamaecyparis pisifera 'Boulevard', though not in maturity a dwarf, is so outstandingly good natured and compellingly attractive I accept the one limitation that after 20 years or so it may be outgrowing a welcome. Bright, silver-blue sprays of leaves, soft to the touch, with *Crocus susianus,* gold in spring, and pink of *Cyclamen hederi-folium* in August and September, is an expression of harmonious beauty which I enjoy each recurring year.

I said in the chapter on hedging plants that in an exposed situation chamaecyparis get sadly blown about, so it was with some trepidation that a run of 'Green Hedger' was planted out, full in the path of all the westerly winds. Ten years is a very short period of time in the life of a tree which may live for 60 or 70 years, so all I can say is the 90 specimens put in are all strong healthy plants. The dense pyramidal shape is exactly which is required in a shelter plant, and the rich green foliage is a delight the year round, but especially in winter. A group of three or five would make a beautiful focal point, but at 15 m (50 ft) high in maturity this must be a thought only for the owner of a big garden.

Juniperus

Junipers I have seen in the wild only on alkaline soil, amongst outcrops of limestone, and yet they flourish on an acid soil with no indication of discountenance of growth. I think it would be safe to say there is a juniper to fit every garden, from the tall trees to the tiny rock-garden species they have much to offer both in colour and interesting shape.

Juniperus chinensis 'Blaauw's Variety' reminds me of a partially opened umbrella, for the branches grow up vertically and then arch over at the top. One thing mars the overall effect of the blue-grey foliage, and that is the tendency of the lower branches to die, showing rather more of the naked stems than modesty permits.

The Common Juniper, *J. communis,* has given rise to many excellent forms, and it is quite fascinating to grow a collection of these reliable, attractive conifers. *J. communis* 'Compressa' is the perfectly formed miniature. Exactly cone shaped, like a line drawing of an Egyptian torch, glaucous-grey in colour, the growth rate is so slow it will take many years to reach 35 cm (14 in) in height. A plant I have in a trough is 25 cm (10 in) tall, and is at least 15 years old.

Juniperus communis 'Hibernica' is like an outsize edition of 'Compressa' in the rigid erectness of its columnar growth. Strangely enough, this is widely used in a strictly formal setting, and yet does not look out of place in the company of heathers, plants blessed with an almost blatant informality. A poor, well-drained soil ensures that the glaucous-green mantle remains tight and close at the tips.

Juniperus horizontalis with spreading, earth-hugging branches offers hope to all those reluctant gardeners who prefer weed-supressing vegetation as an alternative to all growth-supressing alien concrete. 'Bar Harbor' from an island on the coast of Maine has steel-blue foliage, while the Waukegan 'Douglasii' which I grow alongside it has dark green plumes which turn plum purple in the winter. In 10 years both are only 35 cm (14 in) high with a spread of 1.2 m (4 ft).

Juniperus × *media* has been used as a dumping ground for *J. chinensis* and *J. sabina* hybrids. One might almost describe it as the attic of the juniper family, were not so many of the cultivars very attractive. The best of these is 'Pfitzerana' or Knap Hill Savin which makes such an ideal companion for *Viburnum plicatum* 'Mariesii'. The tiered branching system and dark green leaves make this a good feature plant for the landscape gardener. At 15 years old some have reached 2.1 m (7 ft) with a spread of 2.5 m (8 ft) at the head.

Golden-leaved conifers are invaluable, but I always harbour a suspicion for the first few years after planting them, that they may scorch in a really severe winter. *J.* × *media* 'Plumosa Aurea' has remained unharmed through 10 winters to date, and as this included both 1962 and 1965 the trial has been sufficiently rigorous to remove any lingering doubt. A group of this golden-leaved conifer, *Acer palmatum* 'Atropurpureum' and the soft yellow flowers of *Potentilla* 'Moonlight' has given me endless pleasure, especially in May when all the colours are renewed.

Conifers associate well with many other shrubs, like the evergreen euonymus shown here

'Old Gold' is another golden foliaged form of *J. ×. media,* neat and compact in habit and sufficiently durable to retain the colour all the year round.

Where a completely prostrate shrub is required to hide a manhole cover, to soften the corner of a path, or to cover a sloping bank, *J. sabina tamariscifolia* has no equal. A low, wide-spreading carpet of fresh green, it is, after eight years, no more than 23 cm (9 in) high but almost 1 m (3 ft) wide. Where it is necessary to restrain growth to stop further encroachment, the lower branches can be carefully cut away without any sign of the pruning being obvious.

Shrubs with silver leaves rank with the golden-foliaged plants in importance, and one of the most striking of glaucous-leaved forms is *J. squamata* 'Meyeri'. No two specimens of this conifer show the same outline, each one exhibiting a will of its own in this matter. Some develop a single stem which arches over in a plume at the top and another imitates a cedar in the tiered branching arrangment, but all are slow-growing with their distinguished silvered leaves. They form a natural background for *Narcissus* 'February Gold' and *Erica carnea* 'King George', and for the autumn, where the soil is acid, *Gentiana sino-ornata,* whose blue trumpets combine perfectly with the grey.

Juniperus virginiana 'Grey Owl', as the name implies, is another of the grey-foliaged persuasion; not the metallic grey of *J. squamata* 'Meyeri', but rather the softer colouring of wood smoke on an autumn day. In time this juniper will make a wide, spreading bush 1 m (3 ft) high by 2 m (6 ft) across, but judging by the three in this garden it will take upwards of 16 years to do it.

All the conifers so far described will come fairly readily from semi-ripe cuttings, in July and August, especially if a sun frame can be used to accommodate them. Use a sharp lime-free sand, and make certain they never lack moisture. Hardwood cuttings in September and October are an alternative way of increasing stock, either in a frame or, a surer method, on to a soil-warmed bench. In the case of × *Cupressocyparis leylandii* I have had a better result from cuttings taken in February.

Metasequoia

Metasequoia glyptostroboides caused a sensation in both the botanical and horticultural world when it was discovered growing in west China just after the war. Previously it had only been identified from fossil remains. A moist, but well-drained soil is the most suitable medium for this spectacular, quick-growing conifer. On an exposed site an annual growth of 60 cm (2 ft) is not uncommon in a good growing season. As well as being hardy, it is just as willing to grow on an alkaline as an acid soil. Cuttings of semi-ripened wood root well in a sun frame.

The soft copper-pink of the leaves in autumn is particularly lovely for the Dawn Redwood is deciduous. One might almost add fortunately, for each spring we get the delicate, fragile beauty of the breaking buds. Trees planted 12 years ago are now 5.5 m (18 ft) high, so at maturity we may see the record of 30 m (100 ft) passed. The tallest specimen recorded in its native habitat just topped 36 m (110 ft).

Picea

The spruces (*Picea*) include that most beloved of all trees, the Norwegian Spruce, venerated in millions of homes by children of all ages at Christmas time. The type plant is fit only for forest planting, since it does not make a good specimen tree unless adequately sheltered. Numerous dwarf forms are obtainable and make first-class ornamental trees for the rock garden.

Picea abies 'Gregoryana', a dome-shaped bun of a shrub, is lovely in spring, when the pea-green young growths show bright against the sombre dark shade of the older leaves. In 10 years a bush will be no more than 30 cm (12 in) high by 45 cm (18 in) across.

One would hardly mistake a conifer for a bird's nest, and yet *Picea abies* 'Nidiformis' always gives me the

The foliage of *Metasequoia glyptostroboides* is fresh green in spring and copper-pink in autumn

impression of a chaffinch's nest. The growth is extremely dense, built up in a series of tightly compressed branches, as if someone had sat on top of a Christmas tree and flattened it out. Yet again this is a lovely slow-growing conifer which will take many years to reach 30 cm (12 in) in height.

The easiest conifer to identify from a distance, even in a well planted rock garden, is *P. albertiana* 'Conica'. The symmetrical, cone-shaped outline, and relatively slow rate of growth, 1.2 to 1.5 m (4 to 5 ft) in 20 years, make it an aristocrat of rock garden conifers. I was given a 30-year-old tree; it was dug up, moved three miles, and replanted without any ill effects, but three years later vandals tore out the top. This savage reward of effort has not disturbed the plants equanimity, and now the damage is in a fair way to being repaired.

In my experience cuttings are not easy to root, but perseverance with hardwood material in September will bring just reward.

Visiting gardens is a pleasure many people, amateur and professional alike, indulge themselves in whenever an opportunity offers. Usually on a visit to a new garden one plant makes an impression above all others, so that it becomes synonymous with the name of the garden. There are Newby Hall, and the cedars on the front lawn; Tatton, and the beeches; Holden Clough, and the magnificent specimen of *Picea brewerana*. Why this tree should be so rare in cultivation goodness knows, for it is remarkably beautiful. I saw it first on a glorious day in spring. The slender branchlets were 1 m (3 ft) long, hanging down from the horizontal limbs showing first dark green and then silver-grey when touched by the gentle breeze. Eventually I was given a young tree 1.5 m (5 ft) high, but it had to be dug up there and then, carried on my back a good mile and a half, best suit or no, and then persuaded to fit into a small car. Needless to say, stimulated by the vision of the plant at Holden Clough, all this was accomplished for the price of cleaning a suit. Now after three years

the long slender curtain is developing, and it is my pride of all the conifers.

A fairly moist yet freely drained soil is the best, and for companions the pale orange azaleas and bluebells make ideal ground planting to what should eventually be a 12 m (40 ft) tree.

Seed has proved the best, indeed, the only means of increase so far as I am concerned; cuttings stubbornly refuse to root.

Picea pungens glauca is an exciting small tree with lovely grey-blue needles. Unlike the other Silver Spruce it does not enjoy shade, preferring clear skies above, or it sulks.

A dwarf form, *P. pungens* 'Glauca Procumbens', will bring the same lovely colouring to the small garden, which does not permit the inclusion of the type plant. A specimen in a Lakeland garden at 20 years old was 60 cm (2 ft) high and 1.2 m (4 ft) across.

Picea mariana 'Nana' is a most tempting blue bun of a conifer which so beguiled me after six years of growing it in a trough, that I bought two more for the rock garden. An extremely slow growing and eminently desirable true dwarf.

Pinus

Pines are very much trees of the open country, and one rarely sees them growing contentedly in a smoke-polluted atmosphere. *Pinus cembra* 'Nana' makes a neat bush, almost a forest on its own, forming over the years many leaders, none of which gains sufficient dominance over its fellows to spoil the symmetry. The first plant I acquired as *Pinus cembra* 'Chlorocarpa' turned out to be pure *cembra*, and is now 3.7 m (12 ft) high, so it pays to be careful. In 20 years I expect the true plant to be 1 m (3 ft) or so high by as much across.

Pinus mugo, the Dwarf Mountain Pine, as would be expected thrives in poor soil provided the drainage is good, and in the most exposed situation. The best forms of *P.mugo* are 'Gnom' and 'Mops', of similar character though slower in growth, and are worthy additions to any collection. My plants

Above: Surprisingly *Picea brewerana* is not widely planted

Opposite: Dwarf conifers associate particularly well with heaths and heathers

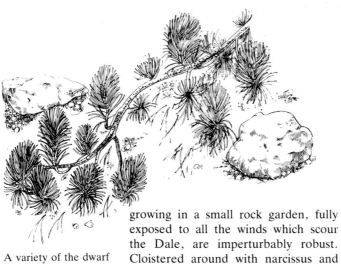

A variety of the dwarf Mountain Pine, *Pinus mugo*

growing in a small rock garden, fully exposed to all the winds which scour the Dale, are imperturbably robust. Cloistered around with narcissus and Dog Tooth Violets, they act the foil and chaperone to the manner born.

Taxus

The yew, unfortunately, has so long been connected with churchyards that most people overlook its value in the garden. *Taxus baccata* is one of the few conifers native to this country, and the dark, sombre leaves which suffer clipping so cheerfully make it an ideal background to the more colourful shrubs and herbaceous plants.

Taxus baccata 'Adpressa Variegata' is a slow-growing form with golden variegated leaves. In 25 to 30 years it will grow into a bush 3.7 m (12 ft) or so tall, and about 3 m (10 ft) across. This is one of those shrubs designed specifically for planting in a wide sweep of lawn.

The Irish Yew, *T. b.* 'Fastigiata', is like a lovely dark green pencil, and is ideal for the formal garden, or to accent the pendulous form of a weeping tree. A grove of these, with one or two of the golden-leaved form, can be a feature of the larger garden.

Taxus baccata horizontalis, which spreads out in a dark green mat, after 15 years has shown no ambition to grow above 30 cm (12 in) high, and yet great determination to cover as much ground as possible. Like all members of the genus it will grow well in shade, and is used here as a ground planting under maples, together with the dark purple *Viola labradorica.*

There are many, many more yews so diverse in form that there must be one to fit all gardens, so it only remains for me to mention the smallest, *T. b.* 'Pygmaea', which I have grown for five years in a trough and which never grows more than 3 mm (⅛ in) each year. A tiny, tightly congested ball of a plant, with no ambition to do anything else but remain that way.

Propagation can be achieved by means of semi-mature terminal shoots of the current season's growth, 8 cm (3 in) long and just firming at the base. A compost of equal parts sand and peat moss, over sharp drainage, should be made up in a sun frame. Regular watering is essential to ensure a good percentage root.

Thuya

The genus *Thuya* (or *Thuja* as some prefer it) includes species for hedges, specimen planting, and dwarf shrubs for the rock garden. *Thuya occidentalis* 'Fastigiata' is a very erect columnar cultivar for the formal areas of the garden, growing up to 8 m (25 ft) high.

For the rock garden or shrub borders few conifers can exceed the esteem enjoyed by *T. o.* 'Rheingold'. During the summer it is golden, but as winter approaches it turns a deep bronze. It is a densely furnished, slow-growing shrub which eventually will reach only 2 to 2.5 m (6 to 8 ft) in height.

Thuya orientalis 'Aurea Nana', loveliest of the American Arbor Vitae dwarf forms, makes a rounded bush of softest green suffused gold in summer. My plant is closely associated with the spring-flowering *Erica carnea* 'Myretoun Ruby'.

The species most widely used for hedging is *Thuya plicata;* it grows quickly, and will stand clipping well, but it is a difficult plant to move unless transplanted very young. On its own it makes a cone-shaped tree, and on well-drained land will make 60 cm (2 ft) of extension growth a year. The foliage is delightfully and characteristically scented.

Dwarf forms include *T. p.* 'Hillieri', a slow-growing cultivar with curiously corded shoots. I have a plant which is 10 years old, and looks 150, yet even in a favourable soil is not yet 1 m (3 ft) high. 'Rogersii' makes a more shapely bush, cone-shaped in outline with bronze-coloured foliage.

I find cuttings of thuya root best when taken in September, when they are just firm at the base, and with a slight heel of old wood. Put them fairly close together in a compost of equal parts sand and peat by volume, made up in a sun frame.

Tsuga

Tsuga are a must, though just two have proved hardy here of the five cultivars tried. Both are so arranged as to grow down over limestone boulders like pale green cascades. *T. canadensis* 'Prostrata' at present, after eight years, is 25 cm (10 in) high by possibly 50 cm (20 in) in spread. The other labelled 'Sargentii Pendula' is the more attractive and has proved more prostrate if slightly faster growing. Close alongside is a *Potentilla* 'Goldfinger'.

A pendulous or prostrate form of *Tsuga canadensis*

Roses

—◦❀◦—

Popular fashion and tastes, linked to a certain extent with publicity, decree that certain flowers should be the mode. Unless the particular plant which enjoys the rather fickle public esteem of the moment is possessed of sterling qualities and singular beauty, it is soon discarded in favour of a new candidate for floral honour. The hybridist, like the fashion designer, is ever seeking to improve on existing cultivars and rightly so, for had this not been the case, we gardeners would still have been restricted to cultivars of *Rosa alba, R. moschata,* and *R. mundi.* In the early days of the 19th century the devotees of the rose cult increased in number as a flood of new roses were introduced, such as the moss, damask, and gallicas which were to reign supreme as the queens of the garden flowers until the hybrid teas and floribundas finally usurped their throne. So through the centuries has the rose held its place in the gardens of Britain, and not even in this the 20th century has it reached the apogee of development.

To hold the affectionate interest of the diverse gardening public so firmly, the rose must be, and indeed is, a veritable paragon of a plant. Possessed of an outstandingly lovely flower, in a wide range of colours, it is extremely adaptable in almost any soil or climate, and excellent as a cut flower and for mass display in the open garden. The only colour which the hybridisers have not succeeded in introducing into roses is a true gentian blue, but this is a deficiency soon forgotten in the bewildering range of self and bicolour blooms advertised in even the smallest specialist rose catalogue.

The ancestry of so many garden flowers reaches so far back as to be lost in the dim, obscure recesses of history.

Fact and legend become so intertwined, as I discovered when trying to unravel them recently, that separating truth from fiction becomes well nigh impossible. The rose, possibly more than any other, holds close the secret of origin, yet remains simple expression of mankind's love for all that is beautiful in natural things.

Site and Soil

Though I hesitate to mention the matter again, in case by oft repetition the theme becomes monotonous, thorough preparation of the soil is essential. Planted at 60 cm (2 ft) apart, a bed can hold several pounds' worth of roses, and it is poor economy to put them into anything but the best soil the wit of man can devise. Drainage is of vital importance, and failing the facilities for a complete system of drains the most effective alternative is to raise the bed above the general level of the surrounding garden. No rose likes to sit with its roots waterlogged for eight months of the year, and tolerant though these shrubs are, the display of flowers is a poor travesty of what it should be. I have been asked so many times to visit gardens, especially in this area, to try to advise on why roses are sickening, only to find water standing round the edges of the beds, and the soil in which the plants are existing settled into a grey jelly, without humus or one sign of a worm cast. On offering an explanation the usual reply is 'but I thought roses liked clay'. No plant will grow as well in a wet soggy clay as it will in a humus-rich loam, well aerated.

Similarly no rose will thrive in a poor, light soil which is not improved by every means which science and the gardener's ingenuity can contrive, as I have discovered in the last 10 years.

Opposite: Through the centuries the rose has held its place in the gardens of Britain for it is not only beautiful but very adaptable

Digging

Double-dig the whole area, taking out a trench 30 cm (12 in) deep, fork well-rotted manure into the bottom to break up a further 25 cm (10 in), then turn another spadeful on to the forked area to leave a further lot of subsoil ready for fork and manure. In this way the soil is broken to a depth of 50 to 55 cm (20 to 22 in) and the subsoil is kept where it should be, down below the topsoil. Were the subsoil to be brought to the top, in most cases, and especially on a heavy clay, the finished product would resemble nothing more in both colour and texture than pease pudding, incapable of supporting the meanest weed, let alone roses.

The improvement in soil condition continues with the annual mulching and feeding – an essential part of the routine cultivations. Ideally the soil should be well supplied with humus and plant nutrients while remaining slightly acid in reaction. Occasional dressings of lime will be required on some soils to maintain a correct balance. Do not over lime as this results in weak growth.

Planting

Roses are usually sent out ready trimmed from the nurseries. No further pruning of the above-ground portion is therefore required until the correct time for the job, of which more later. I do trim the roots just a little even if undamaged, for this encourages the production of the fine white feeding roots which makes certain the bush will soon establish itself in its new quarters. After firming, the finished level of soil should be just above the old soil mark at the base of the stem. In the average garden there is generally a limited choice of site for a rose bed, but where there are several alternatives select the most open, sunny place that offers. Close, sheltered conditions mean poor air circulation, and this leads to mildew problems. Shady places I avoid, except with the newer cultivars with violet, lavender, or deep red flowers which tend to fade in full sunlight. Otherwise grow roses where the sun can coax them to full perfection.

Containerization has with roses extended the planting season over the 12 months of the year; only the weather now calls a halt to what was once a dormant-season operation.

Container-grown roses are too expensive to be sent through the post like bare-root stock and are best collected direct from the nursery. The same care is needed when planting from a container as with bare-root roses. The soil must be in such a fertile condition as to persuade the roots to grow out into it, otherwise they remain where they are. Water the container thoroughly, dig a hole large enough so there is a 10 cm (4 in) gap all round, and the top of the rootball is about 5 cm (2 in) below soil level. Slit down the container so that it can be removed without breaking up the compost around the roots. Fill round and firm as for bare-rooted roses. Should the weather turn dry water all newly planted stock, particularly those which came out of containers.

Distance apart

Planting distances vary according to cultivar. Strong growers will need 76 cm (30 in) each way at least, but on average 50 to 60 cm (20 to 24 in) is quite adequate. Nothing is worse to the eye of a gardener than roses planted so close together that one battles with another for a fair share of light and nutrient. In any case I like to work easily amongst the plants, mulching, pruning, dead-heading, and so on, not be torn to pieces pushing through a jungle of thorny branches.

Pruning

The how, time, and wherefore of pruning is something gardeners have argued about for generations, and will continue to discuss with some heat until the last rose bush vanishes under concrete, brick, or tarmacadam. I have tried every month from November to April. Autumn pruning means having to go over the bed again in spring to cut out further dead wood. If in February the plants get the stimulus of the knife, are coached into growth, and then if

there is a frost in late March it all has to be done again in a state of acute anxiety. Having endured all sorts of pangs and finger-biting tension, I now choose a warm day in March. With the blessing of a warm sun, bird song, and spring on every side, pruning becomes a carefree pleasure, not a bitter trial. Newly-planted roses should be hard pruned, leaving as little top hamper for the establishing roots to support as common sense permits. I take some 60 pence worth from a £1.60 rose, or, an even better description, cut each shoot back to within two or three buds of the base. Where possible prune to an outward-facing bud, and even after these break into bud be fully prepared to rub out any growing in the wrong direction. This initial training is of vital importance in building up a strong, well-furnished bush.

Pruning established hybrid tea roses is adjusted according to the cultivar. Prune 'Peace', or worse still 'Rosy Cheeks', hard, and it will grow at the expense of flowers. On the other hand, 'Admiral Rodney' and 'Just Joey' thrive on the knife, and can be cut down low enough to get a mower over the beds. I must add, however, that in general moderate pruning is the normal application for 'garden display purposes. There are, however, a few general rules which can be given. First remove all weak, dead or diseased wood, since once this is out of the way the general framework of the bush is easier to see.

The remaining shoots are then pruned back to four or five buds on the weaker growths, six or seven on the strong. The aim should always be at an open-centred bush permitting the maximum penetration of light and air.

Pruning floribundas

Floribunda roses require a different technique, though I hasten to add that devotees of the little or no pruning school can expect no approbation from me. Continual light pruning over the years creates a bush which resembles nothing more than a crow's nest on a walking stick; something which sends me into a shaking ague. First-year plants should be cut hard back as for hybrid tea cultivars. The second year, cut the shoots back to approximately half their length. In the third year cut approximately one-third of the old wood hard back to within four or five buds of the base to give a crop of healthy vigorous shoots at or near the base. The remaining one-year-old shoots are cut back to about half their length. The next year these are only lightly pruned and the remaining old wood is cut hard back to give young growth the following year. Treated like this the bush is completely re-furnished every two or three years; a rotation which ensures a continuous supply of young shoots.

Feeding

If the soil has been well prepared newly planted roses should need no feeding

To prune a hybrid tea rose first remove thin weak shoots (1), and then reduce the remaining strong branches in length (2 and 3) according to the vigour of the cultivar

the first year, apart from just a light encouragement of 56 grams per m^2 (2 oz per sq yd) of complete fertilizer. I prefer to split this annual feed into two, one in the spring, the other immediately the first flush of flower fades in early July, rather than putting the full 113 g (4 oz) on at once. Little and often, rather than glut and famine is sound practice. Work the fertilizer in with a garden fork, but only into the top 5 cm (2 in) or the roots will be disturbed.

Mulching

About 10 days to a fortnight after the first spring feed mulch the beds with compost, peat, mushroom manure, or well-rotted farm manure. I get this mulch on before the breaking buds are long enough to be seriously damaged, finding it hard to believe that people who advocate waiting until the soil warms up in May can ever have tried to manoeuvre a fork full of muck between tender rose shoots without knocking them off or going berserk in the process. I do not like to mulch the beds gradually during the summer with mowings from the lawns, especially on heavy clay. In a wet season this settles into a poultice, cutting off air to the soil, growing weeds in profusion, and keeping the soil far too moist.

Deadheading

As the year proceeds the removal of dead blooms should be regularly attended to. Do this with secateurs or a sharp knife, cutting each truss back to a strong bud, so that the breaks come up unhindered by an impedimenta of useless twigs. Suckers may appear from below ground; some weak cultivars are prone to this, usually encouraged by careless digging round the roots. Pull these away from as near to the base as possible.

As previously mentioned, after the first flush give the bushes a further dressing of 56 grams per m^2 (2 oz per sq yd) complete fertilizer, and, if the weather is at all dry, water it in. The way they respond to a little attention of this sort is nothing short of miraculous.

Miniature roses

Though I have grown a selection of the roses classified as miniature since I was 18 years old, the awakening public interest in, and popularity of these compact cultivars has resulted in a host of new ones which are a considerable improvement on those offered in the past. Obviously the owner of a small garden who enjoys growing roses wants to introduce as much variety in flower form and colour as space allows. The scaled-down versions of the hybrid tea and floribunda answer the purpose admirably. In my experience they are less tolerant in regard to soil so are best grown in raised beds. To avoid contrasts in scale, keep these small roses isolated from the conventional kinds.

Container-grown stock transplants from nursery to garden with less risk of loss than bare-root material. The planting is best carried out as soil warms up in spring. These small roses were popular 100 years ago, yet we think of them as modern.

Avoid over feeding – a little complete fertilizer in spring – no more than 14 grams per m^2 (½ oz per sq yd) topped up with two liquid feeds in summer will be sufficient. A mulch of organic matter – finely pulverized bark is suitable – completes the soil care. Pruning is less easy to define. A thin out of dead, overcrowded and a percentage of old wood is all most of them require. The shoots left are tipped back by one-third. Most important, keep a careful check on pests and diseases which can be more debilitating than on bedding roses.

Climbing and rambling roses

Roses of this sort can be used in a number of ways to cover walls and fences, or grown on tripods, pergolas, pillars and even up through trees. The choice of cultivar for a given purpose is the only obstacle the would be rosarian has to surmount.

Only trouble arises from growing a mildew-prone rose on a wall – it needs to be on a trellis where the air can circulate through the branches. Similarly, allowing a cultivar which needs

Opposite: The floribunda rose 'Mountbatten' can be grown as a bedding rose or hedge

Some rambler roses should have all stems that have bloomed cut cleanly away after flowering if young shoots are available to replace them

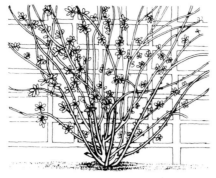

before

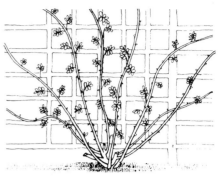

after

regular pruning to scramble up through a tree is not condusive to a long active gardening life.

Thorough preparation of the soil is essential – as described for bedding roses. Feeding and mulching are also the same.

Ramblers are pruned as follows. Remove all stems which have flowered back to a vigorous young shoot. With a cultivar like 'Albertine' this is the usual form. Some ramblers, for example 'Crimson Shower', which grows vigorous young wood from soil level, should have all stems that have bloomed cut clean away if a young shoot is available to replace them.

Once the framework is established climbers should have non-ripened tips cut back to sound wood; old, dead or diseased branches cut clean away, and lateral branches which have produced flowers cut back to within two buds of the main stem.

Pests and diseases

The commonest diseases are mildew, rust and, the pernicious evil, black spot.

Mildew occurs as a white powdery mould on all above-ground portions. Spraying with benomyl or thiophanate-methyl will limit the infection. Use mulches to conserve soil moisture in dry weather and avoid giving the bushes excessive amounts of nitrogenous fertilizer which tends to promote over-lush growth.

Rust is more frequent in occurence than it used to be. Orange pustules on the undersides of the leaves which turn black are the symptoms to look for.

Spray with mancozeb or Bordeaux Mixture.

Black spot is serious in south-west England, a pernicious nuisance elsewhere. Olive-brown or black spots with yellow hollows are visible signs of infection. Spraying with benomyl will in some cases help in a control. Growing resistant cultivars, burning diseased leaves and shoots, mulching and balanced feeding are all measures which will limit the spread of the disease.

Greenfly is the commonest pest and, fortunately, there is a battery of killer chemicals to choose from: systemic insecticides based on dimethoate, or contact slaughterers, fenitrothion or liquid derris.

Propagation

Eventually the enthusiastic gardener will be tempted to try one or all of the various methods which can be used to propagate, and increase his range. As anyone who has neglected dead-heading will appreciate, both hybrid tea and floribunda roses set seed readily. The capsules can be harvested when ripe, then laid in between layers of sand in a pot or box (stratified), and carefully covered with zinc to exclude mice. The boxes are stood outside, since the more they are exposed to extremes of weather the better. Twelve months later the containers can be knocked out, and the seed sown in the normal way. Unfortunately no guarantee can be given as to what these seedlings will be like, so mixed now is the parentage. To reproduce cultivars true to type they must be propagated by cuttings, or

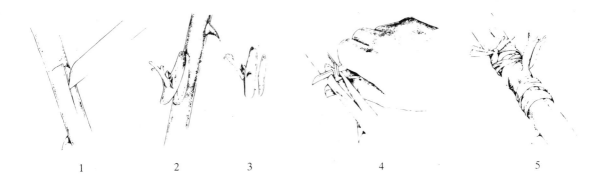

1   2   3   4   5

budding on to a suitable rootstock. Cuttings of stems which have finished flowering, 15 cm (6 in) long, can be made in July and August; remove all the leaves except the top two, and insert in a sandy compost round the edge of a pot or in a sand frame.

Similarly cuttings can be made in September and October, but they should be slightly longer – 20 to 25 cm (8 to 10 in) – prepared in the same way, but inserted in sandy soil in a sheltered place outside.

Budding is usually carried out during July and August on to an appropriate rootstock and is one of the more technical operations, which professional and amateur gardeners alike eventually try their skill on. There are many different types of stock eminently suited to rose budding, and the real enthusiast will try them all to see which grows best on the soil he gardens. The various forms of *canina, simplex, manettii,* and *laxa* are all used in the trade. For the beginner I would suggest *canina,* planted in the autumn on land which is well supplied with organic matter, and free from perennial weeds. Put down in October or November, the stocks are ready for working the following summer.

The actual operation of budding takes place when the bark or rind lifts freely from the wood, a condition easily checked with the 'heel' of a budding knife. The buds are usually selected from shoots which have already flowered, the best material to use coming from the middle of the stick. A check here on the degree of ripeness is to press the thorns gently sideways, when they should break easily.

Select the buds which are fresh and plump, and trim away the thorns and foliage leaving only a small portion of the leafstalk, about 1 cm (½in) as a handle. Scrape the soil away from the base of the stock, for the bud must be inserted as close to the root as possible, and wipe the stem clean with a piece of damp cloth. A T cut is then made in the stem, first the cross-cut to form the top of the T, then the downward slit to form the stem. Then with the heel or flattened ivory end of the knife prize up the two flaps of bark. Bud sticks during this operation should be kept wrapped in moist sphagnum moss or polythene to keep them fresh. Take the bud, using a sharp knife to make a slanting cut 2.5 cm (1 in) below the bud, up behind it and out the same distance above it. A little sliver of wood will be left attached to the bark, which should be flicked or pulled out using the point of the knife. Make certain the centre of the bud is not torn out at the same time as not infrequently happens. Insert the bud under the bark flaps of the T-shaped cut, pushing it down as far as it will go. Any of the bud shield which protrudes above the cross of the T is cut away. Once in position the bud is tied in securely with moist raffia, or one of the rubber budding patches now available. Make certain the bud itself or the leaf stalk are not covered. Apart from routine weed control the stocks are left until pruning time the following March when the whole head is pruned back to about 2.5 cm (1 in) above the bud. Growth should be rapid, as all the plant's energies are concentrated on the bud. The long tender shoots are easily

Budding a rose: a T-shaped cut is made on the rootstock (1), then the bud is removed on a shield-shaped piece of bark (2), after flicking out the sliver of wood (3), insert the bud into the slit (4) and tie it securely into position (5)

damaged so can be tied in to a cane until they firm up.

Choice of cultivars

The thousands of cultivars available make the choice of just a modest collection extremely difficult, and many gardeners prefer to do the choosing at one of the many shows held up and down the country. The colours in the diffused light of a tent, or still worse under artificial light, can be changed almost out of recognition, and may be nearly as misleading in many cases as the colour pictures in the catalogues. Where possible see the selected roses growing out in the open, and then there can be no cause for complaint if the colour does not match into the garden scheme.

Colours must be blended with infinite care, for though no bed of roses could ever be said to achieve the ultimate in ugliness, I have seen some very near misses. A common fault is to buy a mixed collection, and plant them at random over the bed. To have pastel shades mixed with deep colours, orange-red against scarlet, blue-mauve with a bicolour red and yellow, results in colour clashes, and achieves a discontented, disjointed picture impossible to describe.

Use strong colours as the central features in bold blocks, and complement and contrast these with lighter tones as an edging. A garden, and particularly a rose garden, should be a place to relax the mind, not have every nerve jarred by a discordant blaze of colour.

A Selection of Roses

There will not be room here to mention more than a limited number of the cultivars at present available, nor would I care to produce what would be inevitably a catalogue list. Some old cultivars continue to hold a place in spite of the enormous competition from new introductions, and they do so purely on merit, and not because of a sentimental attachment.

Hybrid tea roses

Choosing only 20 varieties of hybrid tea roses from the many hundreds which have added to my enjoyment of summer, to attempt a bias-free distillation from such a cavalcade of beauty and fragrance, required hours of single-minded thought. Now when the decisions are all made, doubts and a sense of disloyalty remain, for in the process of elimination I have discarded cultivars which, just a few years ago, commanded pride of place in the garden and on the show bench. I can only suggest 'The King is dead, long live the King'.

'Admiral Rodney' introduced over a decade ago is a great rose for the show bench. I have personal reason for including it here, for on my soil the flower colour is superb. The petals deep pink fading to palest rose are shaped into the large, high-pointed bloom beloved of exhibitors. My plants grow against a background of glaucous-green-leaved hosta. What this cultivar lacks in quantity of blooms is more than made up for in quality.

Though 'Ace of Hearts' was only introduced in 1981 it is a cultivar which shows real character. The flowers are well formed, the scarlet petals of that texture which one associates with the rose and a fragrance which beguiles rather than assaults. That the blooms last well in water after cutting is a further recommendation.

'Alexander' came to me from Jack Harkness with a special recommendation – and this proved reference enough. It has long-lasting blooms in shades of red and vermilion. Growth is vigorous and the dark green foliage notably disease free.

'Blessings', though introduced in 1968, still holds a place as one of my top 20 roses. A gentle, unassuming bright rose-pink petalled stalwart which year after year adds good contribution with a succession of blooms and a delightful fragrance.

'Congratulations', though it has yet to prove durability to the same extent as 'Blessings', opens large long-pointed buds, singly, on long stems. The colour is soft pink with the merest hint of salmon at the centre, and a pleasing

Opposite: Climbing rose 'Zéphirine Drouhin' will produce blooms between June and October

fragrance as further endorsement. Certainly a cultivar for those who practice flower arranging.

Amongst the increasingly sought after orange cultivars 'Doris Tysterman' is attractively upright in growth with bronze-green foliage. The petals are bright tangerine with a most pleasant perfume. A good bedding rose and useful for cutting.

Yellow roses with a strong enough perfume to be enjoyed without stooping are not common – a good enough reason to include the recently available 'Fragrant Gold' into the list. The deep gold petals are slightly pinked at the edges.

'Grandpa Dickson' is now old in rose-enthusiast terms: I planted it 18 years ago. Pale yellow flowers of impeccable form and sturdy upright growth are qualities not to be despised or ignored.

'National Trust' came to my notice and garden four years after 'Grandpa Dickson'. Seeing the crimson-scarlet of the flowers against a white patio wall made a good first impression which has been reinforced by closer knowledge.

White roses are something of a lottery and need careful evaluation in all the rare and boisterous permutations of weather which summer affords. 'Pascali' is the most elegant and very good for cutting.

Bicolour roses are not my first choice, though I do make exception with 'Piccadilly'. The bright scarlet and gold flowers shared 20 years of gardening on a heavy clay without a wrong word passing between us. 'Rosy Cheeks' another red and gold, offers competition for my allegiance.

Last year I spent a fascinating two days in the birth place of 'Peace'. The Meilland garden sported a long bed of this famous rose which on a glorious summer day was a tone poem of golden yellow, touched with cerise-pink. I grow 'Peace' as a shrub, only pruning enough wood out to maintain health and vigour. The flowers are certainly smaller but the crop is heavier.

'Silver Jubilee' is often presented as a rival of 'Peace' as the Rose of the Century and it is most certainly an exceptional hybrid tea. Peach pink and cream flowers held poised on top of strong vigorous stems ensures for this cultivar an immediate popularity.

'Troika' stood out amongst the 1972 introductions as showing considerable disease resistance. The copper-red flowers are delicately perfumed.

Names need to be chosen with care or they can form an insurmountable handicap which even a quality rose cannot overcome. 'Red Devil' as a name has little appeal, and yet this cultivar has such sterling qualities that it must be included in my list. Light red flowers of perfect form and a delicate fragrance are recompence enough for bringing a 'Red Devil' into the garden.

Though 'Wendy Cussons' has been in gardens for 25 years it shows no decline in appeal, possibly because of the abundant flowers unfailingly displayed each summer. Deep pink petals and a damask fragrance are other contributory influences in my choice.

Amber yellow is not a common colour amongst roses. Combine the colour with a strong scent and a sound constitution and it adds up to a fairly accurate description of 'Whisky Mac'. Another which offers an unusual colour combination is 'Double Delight' – creamy white buds edged with cherry red. Listed as the strongest perfumed of the modern hybrid teas.

'Fragrant Cloud' has large, rather cabbage-like blooms of coral red. They are extremely useful for cutting and the scent from well-flowered bushes on a warm summer evening is an experience to enjoy.

There must be a story behind the name 'Just Joey'. These large, fragrant, copper-orange exhibition type roses with a frilled edge to the petals are distinctive enough to warrant a proper romantic pedigree.

Floribunda roses

For vigour, freedom of flowering and a rich variety of colour tones, cluster-flowered floribunda roses have no equal. Spaced at an average of 50 cm (20 in) apart they will flower from June until October.

Opposite: An attractive combination of rose 'Ballerina' and *Senecio* 'Sunshine'

'Anne Harkness' after three years has proved vigorous and disease resistant. One hazard to be avoided is exposed situations. The stems of saffron yellow blooms are so large they are subject to wind damage.

'Ballerina' in its first year made such an impression that I have kept faith over 20 years. Grown in a tub or best of all as a standard, this is a most cheerful and efficient cultivar. The single pink flowers each with a white eye are carried in gigantic clusters. That it roots easier than any rose from July cuttings was a secret discovered that first season.

To include a nearly new rose in a list of this sort is tempting fate but there are exceptions. 'Beautiful Britain' sold itself to me first on the name, second on vigour, and thirdly with those tomato-red flowers. For five years I passed a bed planted with 40 'City of Leeds' at least three times a day and never tired of the brilliant display of bright orange-red flowers. It is one of the best bedding roses.

Rarely do I consider replacing a rose which fails at the first attempt. 'Elizabeth of Glamis' was an exception. For some reason this cultivar was grazed almost flat to the ground by hares, so the fault was mine rather than the lack of adaptability on the part of the rose. The fragrant flowers are deep salmon red.

'Evelyn Fison' is comparable as a bedding rose with 'City of Leeds'. Vigorous, branching growth topped by trusses of bright red, non-fading, weatherproof flowers are the best of recommendations.

Coppery-orange flowers appeal to both gardeners and flower arrangers which, no doubt, explains the success of 'Fragrant Delight'. Against the blue and steel-grey background of a lavender hedge it is enhanced by the contrasting colours.

'Iceberg' is still the most attractive white floribunda, and versatile in that it can be grown as a bush, bedding, or cut flower.

'Matangi' was the second of what were then known as hand-painted roses

which I planted. The vermilion-red white eyed flowers are not so remarkable as the silver and rose-red variation displayed by 'Picasso', so as I cannot decide between the two a fair decision is to grow both.

Another newcomer, 'Mountbatten', can be grown both as a hedge or bedding rose, a vigorous cultivar with crisp yellow scented blooms which radiate good health.

To mention 'Orange Sensation' is rather like discussing a friend in public. This rose should be grown isolated, ideally in a bed which forms the centrepiece of a smooth lawn. Then the orange-red of the flowers can be enjoyed without the risk of strident discord.

Another long-term acquaintance, 'Pink Parfait' is quite the opposite in colour, the rose pink and cream combination more a cool reflection.

Of 'Queen Elizaabeth' suffice to say that it is excellent as a hedge or as a dot plant in the borders, appearing rather too vigorous when grown with less-ambitious companions. The clear pink flowers are a feature throughout the summer.

'Southampton' with apricot-orange petals is very upright and looks especially appealing when grown with an intermixing of grey foliaged artemisia.

Presents of roses are viewed with some misgiving as I like to choose my own. 'Sunsilk' was a present which proved by accident rather than design just the right colour combination to 'Southampton', with the artemisia as referee.

'Topsi' and 'Trumpeter' are variations on the orange-scarlet theme. 'Topsi' is an exceptionally free-flowering dwarf, while 'Trumpeter' is quite the most eye-catching scarlet of the roses I have grown. That the foliage also remained disease free during the summer of 1980 is a tribute to the shrub's exceptional health.

Miniature roses

True miniature roses are best grown in beds devoted entirely to their culture,

'Picasso' is one of the hand-painted floribunda roses

or as an edging to a pathway, so the flowers do not loose quality by comparison.

'Angela Rippon' is quite tall and the coral-pink flowers are good for exhibition and as a buttonhole.

'Dresden Doll' is like a mossy hybrid tea, very free with its shell-pink flowers.

'Pour Toi' is quite lovely with pure white petals tinged greenish yellow at the base.

'Mini Metro' is rather tall, for it grew 38 cm (15 in) high in a patio display. The vermilion flowers remind me of 'Orange Sensation', they are so bright.

Climbers and ramblers

Reading through a list of the climbing and rambling roses which I have grown in different gardens, offering an extraordinary variation in soils and climate, some names are repeated with surprising regularity.

'Albertine', whose salmon, pink-tinged pink flowers for three weeks in June turned a terrace wall into a cascade of colour, and filled the air with fragrance, is one which holds a place against all comers and has to possess special qualities.

'Josephine Bruce', with velvet textured, deep crimson petals and exquisite scent, typify the romantic history of the rose.

'Handel' for two years had to be persuaded into accepting a sticky wet clay. The creamy white petals edged with pink were reward enough for my labours.

'Maigold' I grew on a trellis which bordered a rose display and trial beds. Twenty well grown 'Maigold' covered in apricot flowers are, indeed, a spectacle.

'Iceberg' grew on the wall alongside 'Josephine Bruce', the white and dark red somehow sympathetic.

'Danse de Feu', like the floribunda 'Orange Sensation', should be grown against a neutral background – dark green of yew is the ideal foil for orange-scarlet, I think.

'Compassion' combines beauty of flower with strong healthy growth. A succession of apricot-pink flowers, spilling their perfume on a June night, has persuaded me into the garden on many an occasion.

'American Pillar' and 'Zéphirine Drouhin' have been in all the gardens I have worked in and in due course will be planted in this one – when the soil is fit to receive them. 'American Pillar' with carmine, white-centred flowers is best grown on a trellis. 'Zéphirine Drouhin' I have grown as a free-standing shrub, on a 2 m (6 ft) high trellis sheltering a rose garden, and on the house wall. Grown on a wall it developed mildew in spite of repeated spraying; elsewhere it showed little sign of infection. Like the marines, it is the first in and the last out. In most years the first pink bloom opened in June and on many occasions I have picked quality flowers in October to smell that most evocative of summer distillations, rose perfume.

'Pour Toi' is a lovely white miniature rose

Bulbous Plants

Though shrubs and herbaceous plants may be the main ingredients in the horticultural cake, bulbs with their delicate beauty are surely the icing which adds the final adornment. Botanists may argue the finer points of difference, but to the average gardener, unconcerned with such niceties as to what is a stem or embryo bud, the word bulb covers tubers, corms and rhizomes as well. Probably the affection for bulbs is acquired during youth, for the freshness of snowdrop or daffodil is linked in memory with the birth of spring and the joyous pursuits of childhood. This short discourse is not concerned with the rare or difficult bulbs, though once the interest is stimulated the gardener will feel tempted to try his or her skill on these. Rather will it speak of the easy genera, which, be the garden never so windswept, sunk in a frost pocket, or suffer from any other adversities without which the practice of the art would be so much easier, will grow and continue to flourish. One thing alone these amiable plants will not tolerate, and that is stagnant moisture. Heavy clay, cold and sand they will make light of, provided the water is kept constantly moving.

Looking back to my early childhood, life seemed to be full of flowers, for my father was an enthusiastic gardener, a devotee of the informal rather than the strict regimentation of bedding schemes. In consequence the garden and woodland was full of bulbs in a myriad different varieties. There were narcissus, snowdrops, tulips, cyclamen, gladioli, muscari, glory of the snow; all delightful, but some cherished more than others.

As a general rule the planting of autumn-flowering bulbs is done in July and August; those which flower in spring, during September and October. There are exceptions of course, since because of risk of fungal infection tulips are better put down in early November, and snowdrops are only installed as the flowers fade, or losses are heavy.

Lilies do not enjoy being planted in a wet cold soil full of hungry slugs in January, and it is far better to pot them and hold them in a cold frame until May. Planted then, success is assured with this most regal of all flowers.

Allium

One would hardly expect to find amongst the relations of the epicurean onions claimants for a place in the ornamental garden, and yet there are some with strong claims for inclusion. *Allium cernuum,* 30 cm (12 in) high, with rose to red-purple flowers, will spread into a healthy colony even in light shade, any soil proving suitable provided it is well drained. The Golden Garlic, *A. moly,* is a friendly little bulb, 30 cm (12 in) high, which I use to furnish a dry bank under a pink hawthorn. Revered in Pliny's day for its magical property, and potency in charms, I never handle the bulbs without a feeling for this antiquity. The yellow flowers usually open in compact umbels on 20 cm (8 in) stems in June and July. Do not give it a choice place, or in time the spreading habit can become offensive.

Alstroemeria

With the increasing popularity of flower arranging, alstroemerias, in particular the Ligtu Hybrids, have become popular. Once established, from June onwards the colony will give a steady succession of flowers in shades of pink, orange, flame, and yellow, on leafy stems 1 m (3 ft) high. Tubers often fail to grow, but seed, space-sown

Above: Ideal for a dry bank, the Golden Garlic, *Allium moly*

Opposite: Daffodils look charming naturalized in woodland glades or in grass

into a deep box, grown on for a year and then knocked out into a trench 10 cm (4 in) deep, with a good layer of sand on the bottom, is a sure way to acquire a stock. Give them a sunny, well-drained position, and all will be well.

Anemone

Anemones usually conjure up a picture of the De Caen and St Brigid hybrids, clutched in hot, eager hands for presentation on Mothers' Day, but these are not sound perennials. *A. apennina* is a plant of light shady woodland, and it was under just such ideal conditions that I first saw it growing, beside a stream running through a silver-birch wood in a Lakeland garden. This charming little plant is perfectly happy in a shady shrub border, and the clear blue flowers are carried on 15 cm (6 in) stems in early April. There are both white and rose forms in cultivation, and a few scattered amongst the blue enhance the picture.

Anemone blanda could almost be described as a smaller edition of *A. apennina,* but this might cast a reflection on its own particular charm. A native of Eastern Europe and the Taurus, it enjoys a rich soil either in sun or in partial shade. A generous planting of the blue, pink, and white forms, in company with the earliest of spring bulbs, will gladden the days of late March and early April. The flowers bloom on stems only 10 cm (4 in) high, and left to themselves will seed with great discretion over the surrounding ground.

There is a shy, modest, yet quite alluring freshness to the flowers of *Anemone nemorosa* which is irresistable. That the plant is native to these Islands and grows in several woodlands which are favourite haunts of mine further recommends it. Two forms of the species, 'Robinsoniana' with lavender-blue flowers, and 'Vestal' with an extra ring of white petals, are worthy of sanctuary in a shady place.

Chionodoxa

Occasionally the arts of poetry and botany combine to produce a name which does justice to the beauty of the flowers, *chion* – snow, *doxa* – glory. In the wild chionodoxas flower against the melting snow. This is a bulb to spread in drifts under spring flowering shrubs, forsythia and azalea, or against the gold of a bank of daffodils, for it is in such a situation that the Glory of the Snow will spread a haze of intensely blue flowers, each blossom showing a point of white at the centre. In time the initial planting will grow from self-sown seedlings, increasing in beauty with each succeeding spring. *Chionodoxa gigantea* will grow 20 cm (8 in) high, and has violet-blue flowers. *C. luciliae* is the jewel at 15 cm (6 in) high, with brilliant blue flowers.

Colchicum

Not quite so poetic, but equally descriptive, is the colloquial name of Naked Ladies for colchicum, herb of the sun, used by the enchantress Medea as a virulent poison. Unfortunately, most of the species must be banned from the small garden, because they produce such enormous leaves in spring. These die away, then in September come the massive goblets of flowers, lovely when naturalised under shrubs notable for autumn colour. There against the saffron and gold background the flowers have a worthy complement to their own outstanding beauty. Grown in grass as they are in Silverwood, Howick, with the blaze of autumn colour all around, it would be hard indeed to deny them the tribute demanded by their charm.

Colchicum speciosum at 8 to 13 cm (3 to 5 in), has flowers in purple, white, or rose. The white is surely one of the loveliest bulbs ever introduced. *C. autumnale* has smaller leaves and flowers of rose or white. As one would expect of a native British plant, it naturalises in grass with commendable ease. Several flowers are produced from each corm: in the species these are lilac; there is a white form 'Album', and a double petalled rose-pink called 'Roseum Plenum'. Hybrids between *speciosum* and other species include

A white form of *Colchicum speciosum* named 'Album'

'Autumn Queen', violet-purple, 'Violet Queen', mauve, and 'Water Lily' with mauve double flowers.

Crocus

With the daffodil and snowdrop, crocuses are flowers of the spring, starring the grass with yellow, purple, blue and white. The flower, according to legend, was born of the love of a youth for a beautiful young shepherdess, after whom it is named. The Romans almost reverenced the flower, strewing their apartments with its petals. Some can be had to flower in autumn and winter, but it is those that usher in reluctant spring which gardeners treasure. There are so many forms it would be impossible to list them all. There are *Crocus aureus* and cultivars in brilliant orange; *C. chrysanthus* and cultivars lovely beyond description, in shades of lilac, blue, yellow, and white; *C. korolkowii,* bright yellow, and *C. sieberi* dainty in the crimson-purple form, but also in blue, white, or gold.

The ground-hugging *C. susianus* shows delicate grey or white feathering on the deep orange ground colour in some seedlings. *C. tomasinianus* is the rampant, cheerful brigand of the race which spreads at such a rate as almost to become a weed, if it could ever be possible for a flower of such elfin grace to do so in its hues of palest lilac to deep glowing purple.

Give the crocus good drainage and they will grow in grass, under trees even, but loveliest on a warm sunny bank so that each cup opens to show a golden or orange heart.

Cyclamen

A collection of the lovely cyclamen species, grown in pots under glass, helps me through the dead grey featureless days of December. Some are hardy, others need a little artificial heat to see them through. The best and most reliable for outdoors is *Cyclamen hederifolium (neapolitanum)*, beautiful in leaf, each one being marbled with silver, and exquisite when the rosy-pink flowers open in September. In some forms the flowers appear before the leaves, and then the leaves remain all winter. A cool leafy soil under deciduous trees suits the plant to perfection. In time, self-sown seedlings will spread the joyous colour all around. There is a white-flowered and scented form.

Where *C. hederifolium* succeeds, *C. purpurascens (europaeum)* with carmine-scented flowers in July, and *C. coum* with deep pink-red flowers in March, would also be worth trying in a well-drained soil. I grew the white form of *C. hederifolium* as an underplanting to a female variegated holly where it has seeded into a carpet of mixed pink and white. Both *coum* and *purpurascens* share a border where they have flowered and seeded for seven years.

The form known as 'Atkinsii' with marbled foliage and dark pink flowers, shows buds in January so is the earliest to bloom with me.

Erythronium

Erythroniums for some unaccountable reason do not enjoy the acclaim that the beautiful lily-like flowers – and in some cases attractively marbled leaves – would warrant. Nearly all grow relatively easily in a well-drained leafy soil. I like to see them planted in grass amongst thinly planted deciduous trees. The loveliest and easiest to grow is the European Dog's-Tooth Violet, *Erythronium dens-canis.* It is a rather ugly name both in English and Latin, and refers to the shape of the cream-coloured pointed bulb. Flowers usually appear in April and are lavender, pink, or white. The leaves are tastefully mottled silver or pale gold on a glaucous green.

A dark petalled Dog's-tooth Violet with purple and silver marbled leaves in association with *Narcissus asturiensis* covers a hillside in Northern Spain to form one of the most sympathetic plant communities. I am trying to reproduce the combination in my own garden, minus the mountain unfortunately.

Another species, *E. tuolumnense,* has settled quite happily amongst the roots of a very venerable oak tree, and each April come the golden-yellow flowers on 30 to 38 cm (12 to 15 in) stems. Two

hybrids, 'White Beauty' and 'Pink Beauty', are also highly desirable garden plants. Initial stock can be bought in, or raised from seed sown in February in a sandy, leafy compost. Planted in the open ground they will spread by offsets, although I suspect 'Pink Beauty' of a certain reluctance in this respect.

Galanthus

I have often wondered why the snowdrop is so often associated with old buildings. Apparently it was dedicated to the Virgin Mary, so this may account for its being planted so frequently near convents and monasteries. Be that as it may this is a universally beloved flower, and always the first bulb to bloom in my garden.

A reasonably well-drained soil, if possible in light shade, is ideal. I have never seen them grow better than opposite a little church on the banks of the River Greta. There in the shade of beech and sycamore the flowers carpet the earth like drifted snow.

Galanthus nivalis, the Common Snowdrop, makes itself at home rapidly. I like to move the bulbs in late April, planting them about 10 cm (4 in) deep. There are numerous cultivars, but for me the best is 'S. Arnott' with enormous white bells, lovely with the early narcissus and the winter-flowering heathers.

Galanthus nivalis 'Atkinsii' is the earliest to flower on strong stems, 20 cm (8 in) high. *G. ikariae latifolius* has broad shining leaves, and prefers a slightly moister soil.

Hyacinthus

Most members of the general public consider hyacinths in terms of bulb bowls and Christmas presents. There are some lovely hardy species, all of which flower in spring. A well-drained soil in a modestly sunny position seems best, or the bulbs run more to leaf than flower.

Hyacinthus amethystinus from the Pyrenees has bright blue flowers on 15 cm (6 in) stems in April. There is a

Galanthus nivalis, the Common Snowdrop, rapidly makes itself at home

white form which is quite lovely. *H. azureus* is available in many cultivars, and it is so tiny it should really be planted on the rock garden, the stems being only 8 cm (3 in) high. It varies in colour from deep blue to white.

Iris

Unfortunately, none of the early-flowering bulbous irises can be regarded as really permanent and regular replenishment is necessary. For those who care to try, *Iris histrioides* and *I. reticulata* cultivars will succeed for two or three years in a well-drained, sun-baked border.

Leucojum

Snowflakes or leucojums suffer from the fact that the early species flower at the same time as the snowdrops, and the Summer Snowflake flowers in May when all thoughts of snow and chill east winds are gone in the riot of colour all around. The two species I shall mention like a moist yet well-drained soil. They are one of the happy breeds which, once introduced, charm their way into one's affections.

Leucojum vernum flowers on 10 cm (4 in) stems in early April; the white-tipped green bells are delightfully fragrant. *L. aestivum,* the Summer Snowflake, is taller at 30 to 45 cm (12 to 18 in) with the same coloured flowers, elegant in their pendant grace. A form grown here as 'Gravetye' is even better than the type.

Lilium

It would be difficult to consider this genus in any detail, for lilies are available in a multitude of forms, some thriving in sun, others in shade, some hating lime soils, others tolerating it. Of one thing I am certain, and that is that there should be at least one or two representatives in every garden. They have the reputation of being difficult: some are very much so, but others grow like daffodils.

The most important aspect of lily cultivation is good drainage, for in common with other bulbs they do not like sitting with their roots perpetually

Leucojum vernum, a spring-flowering Snowflake

in water. On a heavy soil a bed which slopes gently from back to front is ideal. Work the site with coarse sand and well-rotted manure before doing any planting at all. Ideally the slope should include one or two ornamental trees, standards preferably, with no branches below 2 m (6 ft) from the ground. These provide a certain amount of shade for those species which object to growing in full sun. The roots of the trees or shrubs make certain there is no excess moisture to harm the bulbs.

Depth of planting depends on whether the lily is stem- or base-rooting. Basal rooters should go in to a depth of two to three times that of the bulb. *Lilium candidum* is an exception, for the bulbs of this species are only just covered with about 2.5 cm (1 in) of sandy soil, and even then the bulb finishes up on the surface after a couple of seasons unless topdressed. Species which root from the stem should go down at least 15 cm (6 in) although I prefer to plant at 10 cm (4 in) and then topdress as growth proceeds.

When buying bulbs, always insist that they are well furnished with roots. The cheap job lots are usually in such a dehydrated state, rootless and sapless, that it is a waste of effort planting them. The best time to plant is between early December and the end of February, but anyone who has lived through an English winter will appreciate this is when the soil is at its coldest and wettest, with hoards of hungry slugs ravaging any vegetable matter within reach. The best results are achieved by potting the bulbs and holding them in a cold frame until early May. I use fibre pots about 20 cm (8 in) deep; at planting time you just rip the bottom out and put the pot and bulb in undisturbed.

The endless variety of these lovely bulbs makes a choice of just one or two extremely difficult. One thing is certain, anyone who grows them will never thereafter be without a collection in their garden.

Lilium auratum, the Golden-rayed Lily of Japan, I have grown 2 m (8 ft) high with 30 gloriously scented blooms all open together. Each is pure white with a pale golden bar down each petal, relieved on either side by crimson spots. Even the best cultivars only seem to last five or six years before the bulbs break down with virus. Seed is freely set and grows readily, so this is no problem. Bulbs are planted 10 cm (4 in) deep with root shade, and the flowers open in July and August. Visiting a 200 acre lily nursery in Oregon, and walking amongst rows of these magnificent flowers in full bloom, gave me a new awareness of the richness of variety in form and colour achieved by the plant breeders. For 30 years I have grown plants from this same bulb farm, this year is no exception. Names like 'Tiger Baby', bronze shaded, and 'Edith', yellow, will in due course share garden space with those which have been favourites for years.

I met *L. martagon* for the first time in an alpine meadow, and the picture of thousands of the gay blossoms, all fully open in the warm sunlight with snow capped peaks behind, is something I shall never forget.

On an acid soil, at least one as strongly acid as mine, the *martagon* prefers a bed rich in leafmould. At Pickering, on the lime, they grow 60 cm (2 ft) higher in shrub borders or in rough grassland, and self-sown seedlings abound. The type plant has flowers of glossy purple. Colour forms include *album,* white, and *cattaniae,* maroon.

Lilium pardalinum, the Panther Lily, as the name implies has scarlet flowers shaded with orange-yellow, liberally spotted black. This plant has established itself quite contentedly in rough grassland amongst silver birch and rowan. As with the *martagon* it flowers in late June or early July. One of those memories which are gathered and cherished over years is of seeing *L. pardalinum* very early one sunlit morning growing alongside a stream. I had walked since dawn amongst the Giant Redwoods until dwarfed and subdued by the majesty and cathedral-like quiet which seemed to emanate from these superb, centuries old trees; I suddenly came on the lilies. Lovely, nodding,

friendly flowers, the perfect counterbalance to the 91 m (300 ft) high Redwoods.

Lilium regale is probably the most widely grown of all trumpet lilies, and the flowers on 1.2 m (4 ft) stems open in July and are creamy-white, feathered yellow inside, and banded ruby-red on the rib outside. The scent always reminds me of a small garden in Swaledale which I had to pass on my way home from work. The new hybrids, however, are in many ways superior to the type plant, especially in the balance of the inflorescence.

One of the last to flower, around mid-September, is *Lilium speciosum.* The species grows 1 to 1.2 m (3 to 4 ft) high, with white flowers, stained and spotted pink. The petals turn right back to show the glorious colouring to the full. Several forms exist, and again the hybrids, especially those between it and *auratum,* are wonderful garden value. I like to grow them with the late-flowering herbaceous plants, or with autumn-colouring shrubs.

Lilium testaceum is one which enjoys a lime soil. The sweetly scented soft apricot flowers, with brilliant orange-scarlet anthers, open in June and July. The ideal combination of colour is to grow a group of this lily against the feathery foliage of a hard pruned tamarisk in open shrub borders.

Lilium umbellatum should now be known as *Lilium hollandicum,* and I still have the greatest difficulty in acknowledging the change of name. Because many catalogues still retain the first specific I have listed it for convenience of readers under *umbellatum.* This is certainly one of the sweetest tempered of all lilies, growing and spreading with vigour in the most uncongenial soil. Innumerable hybrids have been raised, all having the characteristic upright flowers in yellow-orange or scarlet. The most effective plantings here are against the dark green background of a mature yew. The height varies from 60 cm to 1.2 m (2 to 4 ft), and the only positive demand is for full sun and reasonable drainage. Of the named cultivars 'Alice Wilson', a lemon-yellow, 76 cm (2½ ft); 'Coolhurst', deep orange, 1 m (3 ft); 'Orange King', bright orange with red tips to the petals; and 'Splendid' are all worth attention. To make confusion even worse confounded these are sometimes listed under *L. maculatum*, another of the many reasons why botanists are rated by gardeners to be more of a pest than a plague of aphis.

For the last eight years I have subjected the Orange Lily, *L. bulbiferum croceum*, to the propagation test. Plants grown from seed, bulbils, scales and embryo bulbs which grow at the base of flower stems all suceeded to such an extent I could try them in clay, sand and well-drained loam. They are the most aimiable of lilies, producing each June and July, according to mood and weather, large heads of orange flowers.

Unlike the species which, at least in the course of one gardener's life time, show little variation, hybrids are introduced, receive approbation or for one reason or another are rejected by the gardening public. A select few survive, usually because they adapt most readily to the various soils and situations offered by gardens in this country and elsewhere.

'Enchantment' has for 30 years held a sure place, the upturned, nasturtium-red flowers have enlivened borders world wide. 'Gold Medal' could almost be termed a yellow counterpart to 'Enchantment', though the petals are broader and do not turn back on themselves to quite the same extent.

The Bellingham hybrids grow taller and are best grown amongst shrubs or in groups down a herbaceous border. 'Shuksan' with light orange and red turks-cap flowers is the best known.

Golden or yellow lilies include both new and old. 'Citronella' with pendant reflexing flowers hung candelabra fashion is of a fine yellow shade. 'Limelight' offers a trumpet flower in a deeper yellow shade.

A lot of work is being done in Scotland in the breeding of disease-tolerant hybrid lilies. The modern technique of embryo culture has put a new weapon, if that is the right description, into the hands of the hybridists. Those of the Chris North hybrids I have seen had me envying my neighbours goods.

The list could be extended to several pages for these hybrids are absolutely enchanting and like Oliver Twist one always asks for more.

Narcissus

No chapter on bulbs would be complete without a word on the narcissus around which a hundred legends have evolved, some linking the name with a youth of Boeotia who fell in love with his own face. Proserpine was gathering daffodils when she was seized and carried off by Pluto. Poets sing the praises of this lovely flower through each generation. As gardens contract, the hybridist has increased the size of the narcissus, so that now it is very easy to strike an incongruous note by planting large-leaved enormous flowered hybrids, where the grass-leaved, more delicate flowers would have proved more in character.

A well-drained, deep loamy soil is suitable, and they look charming naturalized in woodland glades. As the years pass they will spread to make a solid carpet of yellow, orange and white each springtime. On no account must the bulbs be planted into freshly manured ground, for this induces coarse growth and in extreme cases lays the plant open to fungal infections.

Seeing narcissus growing wild in Spain almost caused me to re-assess my ideas on suitable soils. The Trumpet Daffodils, *N. pseudo-narcissus*, *N. nobilis* and *N. bulbocodium*, were growing in running bog when I searched them out. I was re-assured when it was explained to me that this condition applies for only four to six weeks. One thing I have proved is many of the narcissus which flourished in the clay soil of my last garden sickened miserably in the very light soil of this, unless I keep them well mulched with pulverized bark.

Narcissus asturiensis is a dainty treasure of a plant, smallest of all the Trumpet Daffodils at 5 to 8 cm (2 to

Opposite: A naturalized carpet of *Anemone nemorosa* and muscari

Narcissus cyclamineus enjoys the moist peaty soil of the gentian bed

3 in) high. In spite of being the smallest it is the earliest to flower, the clear, soft yellow often showing by mid-February. A dressing of pea gravel around the stems stops the flowers becoming soiled in heavy rain.

Narcissus bulbocodium, the Hoop Petticoat, is a little charmer, only 15 cm (6 in) high, with rush-like leaves, and golden-yellow flowers. Dry soil and full sun are essential, or the extra foliage is produced at the expense of flowers.

Narcissus minor is sometimes confused with *N. asturiensis;* the soft colouring is identical, but the blooms open later and the growth is more robust. Indeed, this plant grows happily with Tiger Lilies in the rough grass of the woodland. The plants here are the Farrer's Garden Form which gives them added lustre in my eyes. *N. cyclamineus* enjoys the moisture-retentive peaty soil of the gentian bed, or the damp, grass-overgrown bank of the stream. There in April, against the tender green of the grass, the long narrow trumpets, and the strongly reflexed petals, look more like those of the cyclamen, from which they take their name, than a daffodil.

Two excellent hybrids from the above are 'Peeping Tom', a golden-yellow, my favourite of all daffodils, and 'February Gold' with slightly paler petals.

The intensely fragrant *N. poeticus,* the Pheasant's Eye, is frequently still in bloom in the first week in June, though the banners are becoming rather tattered by then. The petals are pure white, and the corona flat with a crisped edge of bright red. Good drainage is essential, but otherwise the bulb is easy to grow. A point always to be remembered is that narcissi start into growth during August, and planting or lifting and dividing should be done early. Depth of planting varies; as a general rule 5 cm (2 in) for the smaller species, 10 to 15 cm (4 to 6 in) for the florist cultivars.

Narcissus pseudo-narcissus, our own wild Lent Lily with palest yellow petals and lemon trumpet, like the Spanish species, thrives in the wild on damp meadows bordering streams. The Lent Lily holds a special place in the affec-

tions of those who have once seen them turning Farndale into a flower garden for a few brief weeks in spring.

Personal preference rules in chosing from the ever-increasing list of hybrids. 'Beersheba' is an old though still excellent pure white. 'Mount Hood', named after the peak, snow capped when I saw it across the Sand River in Oregon, is a beautiful daffodil. A creamy white trumpet overlaid with a hint of Jersey cream.

'Golden Harvest', 'King Alfred' and 'Irish Luck' are variations on a true yellow theme. Of the small-cup narcissus, 'Fermoy', pale gold and orange, 'Scarlet Elegance', deep yellow petals and orange-red cup, or the lovely all-gold 'Galway', are reliable.

I would keep a place always for 'Golden Harvest' which is so useful as a pot-grown bulb and yet establishes well in the garden, the flowers a deep, golden yellow. 'Fortune' is such another with golden-yellow perianth and orange cup, available now as treated bulbs which can be brought into flower at Christmas.

'W. P. Milner', neat and compact, combines pale sulphur yellow and creamy white in a most agreeable way. I grow this cultivar in close company with *Erica herbacea* 'Loughrigg' which has bronzed foliage and purple flowers.

Sanguinaria

Sanguinaria canadensis, the Bloodroot, I first saw growing in open woodland one warm April evening in the Lake District. The combination of perfect spring weather, the long grassy slope running down amongst the trees to the lake beneath, and on all sides daffodils in abundance, set the scene for the experience. Then around a *Prunus* 'Pandora' I saw a sheet of the most brilliant white. Thinking at first it was a white narcissus I walked across for a closer look, only to stand enraptured at this my first meeting with the Bloodroot. The flowers are short-lived, but of such exquisite purity that where a corner can be found for a few roots nothing but pleasure will come from the labour. A moist soil, rich with leafmould and in light shade, is the most suitable; the rhizomes are planted 10 cm (4 in) deep in the autumn. The best group here, against all expectations, is almost directly under a silver birch, but is given an annual bonus of a dressing of leafmould, which may account for its good temper. The flowers appear before the leaves in mid to late April on 15 to 25 cm (6 to 10 in) stems. There is a double-flowered form even more attractive than the single, but this does need a lot of pleasing in regard to soil.

Propagation is effected by division of the roots just after the leaves die, but care is needed, for the operation must be done quickly and the roots replanted in a bed well prepared with sand and leafmould soil.

The name is derived from the orange-red sap which oozes copiously when any part of the plant is wounded.

Scilla

The scillas are surely linked with the daffodil as the best-loved of all bulbous spring-flowering plants. They grow well in normal garden soil, but to ensure success should be planted in early autumn while the bulb is at rest. A violently acid soil should be given a dressing of lime, although *Scilla hispanica* (which is now known as *Endymion hispanicus*) and the stronger-growing cultivars do not positively demand it. I add a dressing of leafmould to the soil each autumn, and this is all the food they require.

Scilla hispanica grows 15 to 30 cm (6 to 12 in) high, and blooms in May, the colours varying from blue through rose-purple to white. Evergreen azaleas provide a picturesque setting.

In late March *S. bifolia* flowers with sprays of gentian blue, and when contented seeds about in a most obliging manner.

The Bluebell of England, the Hare-bell of Scotland, *S. non-scripta* (correctly *Endymion non-scriptus*), turns the woodlands to a blue-misted fairyland in May. There are both white and rose forms; a cool, leafy, neutral soil is most suitable.

Scilla sibirica has deep blue flowers in March and April, and contrasts well with golden forsythia above it. A form obtainable as 'Spring Beauty' with dark blue flowers forms an attractive contrast to red-leaved maple.

Tulipa

By devious means then to the tulips, richest in colouring of the bulbous plants; bizarre some undoubtedly are, but the species have a grace and charm equal to that of the daffodils. Florists' cultivars could hardly be classed as capable of holding their own unassisted, even under carefully controlled conditions. A few species do maintain a less-than-precarious hold on life, and some like the native *Tulipa sylvestris* may naturalize as I have seen them in a Lancashire garden, amongst the stones of a little-used path. Perfect drainage, and an open sunny position are required; a wet soil encourages fungal rots and the omnivorous slugs.

Tulips are so rich in colour and interest that it is worth going to a bit of extra trouble to provide a suitable environment. Plant the bulbs in November, 8 to 10 cm (3 to 4 in) deep, and in scattered array to avoid the regimentation of a bedding display. One of the best collections I have seen was growing in an exposed windswept garden near the coast. Here on a steeply sloping bank, where thorough ripening was assured, the colours were sparkling.

The species most likely to succeed, *T. fosteriana*, has grown and flowered here for five years, but without increase. Its scarlet blooms with a black blotch, margined yellow, open in late April. A sun-baked crevice of sandy soil will prove the best inducement to good health.

Tulipa kaufmanniana, the Water-lily Tulip, has given rise to many excellent cultivars. The flowers which appear in early April are sometimes so large as to be out of proportion to the size of the plant. The type species is white or prim-rose yellow, feathered scarlet. Cultivars include 'Shakespeare', apricot and salmon, 15 cm (6 in) high; 'Scarlet Elegance', vivid red petals with gold at

Tulipa tarda is happiest on a sun-baked scree

the base, 15 cm (6 in); and 'Gaiety', cream striped scarlet.

Tulipa sprengeri has dark crimson flowers touched with a coppery hue, and when well suited by the soil conditions it will naturalize. In a very stony soil amongst dark purple dwarf iris, *sprengeri* is one of the last tulip species to flower with me.

As I have already indicated, *T. sylvestris* needs stony, poor, well-drained soil. In late April it will display the most graceful clear yellow flowers on 25 to 30 cm (10 to 12 in) stems.

Of *T. tarda* and *T. urumiensis* I can never decide which pleases me more. The former has flat, star-shaped blooms with white-tipped yellow petals, and is happiest in a sun-baked scree. *T. urumiensis* has flask-shaped yellow blooms, feathered olive and red outside. Both are exquisite, and I should miss them in my garden if they failed to appear. Both species seed themselves with surprising freedom for bulbs used to a Central Asian climate.

Both tulips and narcissus can be grown from seed in which case they should be sown in a sandy compost in a frame. It will take approximately three years for the tulips and small-flowered narcissi to come into flower; the large-flowered narcissi take from five to seven years.

Envoi

Few hobbies bring the rewards that can be found in cultivating plants. Equally there must be few houses so situated that it is impossible to grow any plants at all around them. Some people prefer a house on a hilltop with a wide view of the surrounding country; these pay the penalty of high winds, but usually have well-drained soil. Their choice will be restricted in the main to low growing alpines that do not catch the wind or limit the view.

Others prefer the valleys with tall trees and shelter from the worst of the weather; they could pay the penalty of late spring frosts, but will be able to grow tall shrubs, and enjoy the vista unmarred by the winds which tear and destroy.

So be it, each will in time stamp a personality on the garden, and, as the pattern grows, so will the rewards in colour and rich maturity. Contentment, too, for the plants grow only slowly, quieting minds sorely tried by the pace of modern living.

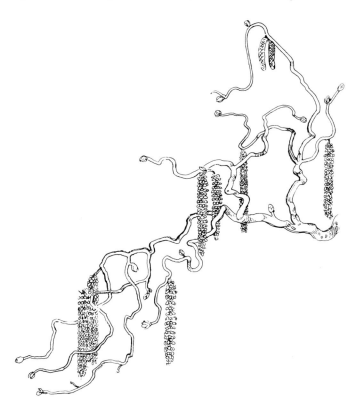

Plants for Selected Sites and Seasons

Full Sun and Dry Soil

Perennials

Name	Height	Comments
Agapanthus	1m (3ft)	Blue lily-like flowers
Echinops	1–1.2m (3–4ft)	Blue globular flowers
Eryngium	45–76cm (18–30in)	Blue flowers
Kentranthus (Centranthus)	45cm (18in)	Pink or white flowers
Kniphofia	1.2m (4ft)	Red, orange or yellow flowers
Oenothera missouriensis	Prostrate	Lemon-yellow flowers
Phlomis samia	1m (3ft)	Cream flowers in tiers
Potentilla	60–75cm (2–2½ft)	Red and yellow shades
Sedum	Prostrate to 60cm (24in)	Pink, yellow or white flowers
Serratula shawii	23–30cm (9–12in)	Lilac-purple flowers
Stachys lanata	38cm (15in)	White-felted leaves
Verbascum	1–2m (3–6ft)	Bold flower spikes; felted leaves

Trees and Shrubs

Name	Height	Comments
Buddleia	2.4m (8ft)	Spikes or ball-shaped flower clusters
Caragana	4.5m (15ft)	Yellow pea-like flowers
Chaenomeles	1–2m (3–6ft)	Pink, red, orange, white flowers
Cistus	1–1.5m (3–5ft)	Rose-like flowers, various colours
Cytisus	Prostrate to 2.4m (8ft)	Yellow, red, white flowers
Euryops acraeus	45cm (18in)	Silver-grey leaves, yellow daisy flowers
Genista	60cm (2ft)	Yellow pea flowers
Potentilla	60cm–1.2m (2–4ft)	Rose-like flowers, many colours
Ulex minor	1m (3ft)	Yellow flowers; needs acid soil

Climbers

Name	Height	Comments
Actinidia kolomikta	3.7m (12ft)	Pink, white and green leaves
Ceanothus	Up to 3.7m (12ft)	Blue flowers

Conifers

Name	Height	Comments
Pinus	1m (3ft) plus	Dwarf species ideal for rock garden

Bulbs and Corms

Name	Height	Comments
Allium	30cm (12in)	Yellow, pink, red, blue flowers
Alstroemeria	1m (3ft)	Pink, orange, flame, yellow flowers
Crocus	10–15cm (4–6in)	Yellow, blue, purple, white flowers
Iris (dwarf)	15cm (6in)	Blue, purple, yellow flowers
Tulipa	15–30cm (6–12in)	Yellow and red shades

Moist, Wet or Clay Soil

Perennials

Name	Height	Comments
Astilbe	60cm–1m (2–3ft)	Plumes in various colours
Caltha palustris 'Flore Plena'	30cm (12in)	Double yellow blooms

Opposite: The blue poppy from Tibet – *Meconopsis betonicifolia*

Hosta	60cm (24in)	Bold foliage
Kirengeshoma	1.2m (4ft)	Pale yellow flowers
Lythrum	1m (3ft)	Spikes or red blooms
Mimulus	30cm (12in)	Yellow, red flowers
Osmunda regalis	1–2m (3–6ft)	Upright light green fronds
Primula	Dwarf to 1m (3ft)	Many colours, some like shade
Ranunculus aconitifolius	60cm (24in)	White blooms
Rheum	1.5m (5ft)	Bold foliage
Rodgersia	60cm–1.5m (2–5ft)	Large, bold leaves
Senecio przewalskii	1.5m (5ft)	Yellow daisies
Tradescantia	50cm (20in)	Blue, purple, white, red flowers; will also grow in light soil
Trollius	60–75cm (24–30in)	Yellow globe flowers

Trees and Shrubs

Aralia elata	3m (10ft)	Straight thorny stems; bold foliage
Cornus alba and cvs.	3m (10ft)	Red stems
Holodiscus	3m (10ft)	Feathery panicles of flowers
Salix	1–18m (3–60ft)	Some have colourful stems

Shady Conditions

Perennials

Aconitum	1–1.5m (3–5ft)	Blue hooded flowers
Bergenia	30cm (12in)	Pink, white flowers; bold leaves
Dicentra	30cm (12in)	Pink flowers; moist soil needed
Digitalis	1–1.5m (3–5ft)	Pink, yellow flowers in bold spikes
Helleborus	60cm (24in)	Pink, red, purple, white, green flowers
Meconopsis	1m (3ft)	Blue poppies; moist soil
Pachysandra	30cm (12in)	Evergreen ground cover
Polypodium	30cm (12in)	Evergreen ferny fronds
Pulmonaria	15–45cm (6–18in)	Blue, pink flowers
Saxifraga fortunei	45cm (18in)	Cream-white flowers; moist soil
Tiarella	30cm (12in)	Ground cover, cream blooms
Tolmiea	30cm (12in)	Ground cover; plantlets on leaves

Trees and Shrubs

Acer palmatum and cvs.	To 9m (30ft)	Good autumn leaf colour
Aucuba	2m (6ft)	Large evergreen leaves, often variegated
Buxus	1–3m (3–10ft)	Evergreen, often used as hedging
Hydrangea	1.5m (5ft)	White, pink, red, blue, moist soil
Hypericum	45cm–1m (1½–3ft)	Yellow flowers; moist or dry soil
Ilex	3m (10ft) plus	Red or yellow berries, green or variegated foliage
Ligustrum	3m (10ft) plus	*L. ovalifolium* and 'Aureum' used as hedging
Mahonia	2m (6ft)	Yellow flowers; excellent evergreen foliage
Neillia	2.4m (8ft)	Rose-pink flowers; moist soil

Prunus laurocerasus	60cm–2.4m (2–8ft)	Evergreen; white flowers
Pyracantha	3.7m (12ft)	Red, orange, yellow berries
Rubus cockburnianus	3m (10ft)	White stems
Skimmia japonica	1m (3ft)	Evergreen; red berries
Symphori-carpos	1.2–2m (4–6ft)	White berries
Viburnum davidii	76cm (30in)	Turquoise berries; elegant foliage
Vinca	Prostrate	Ground cover; dry or moist soil; blue, purple or white flowers

Climbers and Wall Shrubs

Forsythia suspensa	2.4–3.7m (8–12ft)	Yellow flowers; wall shrub
Garrya elliptica	2.4–3.7m (8–12ft)	Green catkins; wall shrub
Hedera	Often indefinite	Green or variegated leaves; climber
Hydrangea petiolaris	6m (20ft)	White flowers; climber
Lonicera	4.5–6m (15–20ft)	Cream, yellow flowers; cool soil; climber
Parthenocissus	12m plus (40ft)	Good autumn leaf colour; climber
Polygonum baldschuanicum	12m (40ft)	White flowers; climber
Pyracantha	2.4–3.7m (8–12ft)	Red, orange, yellow berries; wall shrub

Conifers

Taxus baccata cvs.	Prostrate to 3.7m (12ft)	Green or gold evergreen foliage

Bulbs and Corms

Anemone	15cm (6in)	White, blue, pink, cool moist soil

Cyclamen	10cm (4in)	Pink, red, white flowers; cool moist soil
Erythronium	15–30cm (6–12in)	Pink, yellow, white, light shade
Galanthus	15cm (6in)	White flowers; light shade
Lilium	1–2m (3–6ft)	Flowers of many colours; light woodland; well drained soil
Narcissus	15–60cm (6–24in)	Yellow, white flowers; ideal for woodland
Sanguinaria	15–25cm (6–10in)	Light shade; cool moist soil; white flowers
Scilla	15–30cm (6–12in)	Blue flowers

Lime-hating Plants

Trees and Shrubs

Calluna vulgaris cvs.	To 75cm (30in)	Some have coloured foliage
Clethra alnifolia	1.5–3m (5–10ft)	White, fragrant flowers
Cornus canadensis	15cm (6in)	White flowers; ground cover
Enkianthus	1.5–3m (5–10ft)	Pale yellow or red flowers
Erica	Mainly prostrate	*E. herbacea* grows in alkaline soils; red, pink, white, purple flowers
Gaultheria	60cm–2m (2–6ft)	Pink, red, purple or white berries
Kalmia	60cm–2.4m (2–8ft)	Pink, red flowers; needs shelter
Myrica gale	60cm–2m (2–6ft)	Resinous-scented leaves
Pernettya	60cm (2ft)	Red, pink or white berries

Photinia villosa	3.7m (12ft)	Good autumn leaf colour
Pieris	2.4m (8ft)	White flowers; red young foliage
Rhododendron	30cm–3.7m (1–12ft)	Wide range of flower colour; evergreen and deciduous
Ulex europaeus 'Plenus'	2.4m (8ft)	Spiny; double yellow flowers
Vaccinium	Prostrate or 45cm (18in)	Black or red berries

Plants which Benefit from Wind Protection

Perennials

Dicentra	30cm (12in)	Pink, red flowers
Iris (tall bearded)	1m (3ft)	Flowers of many colours
Rodgersia	60cm–1.5m (2–5ft)	Large bold foliage
Verbascum	1–2m (3–6ft)	Yellow spikes; often felted leaves

Trees and Shrubs

Acer japonica and *A. palmatum* cvs.	To 9m (30ft)	Good autumn leaf colour
Ceanothus	To 3.7m (12ft)	Blue flowers
Chimonanthus	3m (10ft)	Pale yellow flowers
Choisya ternata	2.4m (8ft)	Evergreen, white scented flowers
Hebe	30cm–1.2m (1–4ft)	White, blue flowers
Hydrangea	To 2m (6ft)	Blue, pink, white, red flowers
Jasminum revolutum	2.4m (8ft)	Yellow flowers
Kalmia	60cm–2.4m (2–8ft)	Pink or red flowers

Rhododendron (large-leaved species)	Depends on species (some tree-like	Flowers in many colours; magnificent foliage
Viburnum rhytidophyllum	3.7–4.5m (12–15ft)	Large deep green leaves, felted below

Climbers

Schizophragma hydrangeoides	6–9m (20–30ft)	Pale yellow sepals; self-clinging

Conifers

Cedrus atlantica glauca	15m (50ft)	Metallic grey-blue foliage

Plants Noted for Autumn or Winter Colour

Perennials

Aster	30cm–1.2m (1–4ft)	Autumn blooms of many colours
Bergenia	30cm (12in)	Foliage tints in winter
Helleborus	60cm (2ft)	Winter flowers of various colours
Physalis	60cm (2ft)	Orange seed pods in autumn
Sedum spectabile	25–45cm (10–18in)	Pink, red flowers, autumn
Solidago	30cm–1m (1–3ft)	Yellow flowers, autumn

Trees and Shrubs

Acers	Depends on spp.	Autumn leaf colour
Amelanchier	6m (20ft)	Autumn foliage colour
Berberis	1–2m (3–6ft)	Autumn colour from berries and foliage
Calluna	To 75cm (30in)	Autumn flowers; often winter foliage colour

Cornus alba and cvs.	3m (10ft)	Red or yellow stems in winter
Cornus mas	3.7m (12ft)	Yellow flowers in winter
Cotinus	3.7m (12ft)	Brilliant autumn leaf colour
Cotoneaster	Depends on spp.	Autumn berries, red/yellow
Crataegus	4.5–6m (15–20ft)	Red berries; autumn leaf colour
Erica herbacea	Prostrate	Red, pink, white winter flowers
Euonymus	2.4m (8ft)	Autumn fruits and leaf colour
Hamamelis	3.7m (12ft)	Yellow flowers in winter
Ilex	3m (10ft) plus	Red/yellow berries
Jasminum nudiflorum	3.7m (12ft)	Yellow flowers in winter
Mahonia	2m (6ft)	Yellow flowers in winter
Malus	4.5–6m (15–20ft)	Large fruits in autumn
Parrotia	3.7m (12ft)	Autumn leaf colour
Pernettya	60cm (2ft)	Red, pink, white berries
Pyracantha	3.7m (12ft)	Red, orange, yellow autumn berries
Rhus	3.7m (12ft)	Brilliant autumn leaf colour
Rosa spp.	Depends on spp.	Often have autumn hips
Rubus cockburnianus	3m (10ft)	White stems in winter

Salix	1–18m (3–60ft)	Coloured winter stems in some species
Skimmia	1m (3ft)	Red berries in autumn/winter
Sorbus	Depends on spp.	Autumn berries and leaf colour
Stranvaesia davidiana	12m (40ft)	Crimson fruits; scarlet autumn leaves
Viburnum × bodnantense	2.4m (8ft)	Pink flowers in winter
Viburnum farreri	2–2.4m (6–8ft)	Shell-pink flowers in winter
Viburnum opulus	3–3.5m (10–12ft)	Autumn leaf colour and berries

Climbers and Wall Shrubs

Garrya elliptica	2.4–3.5m (8–12ft)	Green catkins in winter; wall shrub
Partheno-cissus	12m (40ft) plus	Brilliant autumn leaf colour; climber
Vitis coignetiae	18m (60ft)	Large leaves, colour well in autumn; climber

Bulbs and Corms

Colchicum	8–13cm (3–5in)	Rose, purple, white flowers in autumn
Cyclamen hederifolium	15cm (6in)	Rose-pink flowers in autumn

Index

Page numbers in italics indicate illustrations

Acer:
  capillipes 72
  hersii (A. grosseri hersii) 72
  griseum 72
  japonicum cvs. 72
  negundo 'Variegatum' 72
  palmatum & cvs. *70,* 72–3
  platanoides & cv. 73
  pseudoplatanus & cv. *71, 73*
Aconitum:
  'Bressingham Spire' 25, *25*
  napellus hybrids 25
  wilsonii 'Barker's Variety'
    25–6
Actinidia kolomikta 134
Aesculus:
  indica 73
  parviflora 73
  pavia 73
    'Atrosanguinea' 73
Agapanthus Headbourne
    Hybrids 26
Alchemilla mollis 29
Allium:
  cernuum 165
  moly 165, *165*
Alstroemeria Ligtu Hybrids
    165–6
Amelanchier 73–4
  canadensis 74
  lamarckii (A. × grandiflora)
    74
Ampelopsis brevipedunculata
    139
Anemone:
  appenina 166
  blanda 166
  cultivars 26
  De Caen hybrids 166
  hupehensis (A. japonica) 26
  × *hybrida* 26
  × *lesseri* 26
  nemorosa & cvs. 166, *173*
  St Brigid hybrids 166
  *sulphurea, see Pulsatilla alpina
    apiifolia*
annuals: in mixed border 25
Aquilegia 24
  hybrids 26–7
  vulgaris 26
Aralia elata 74
Arbutus unedo 74
Aster:
  alpinus & vars. 27
  amellus 27
  × *frikartii* 27
  thomsonii 27
Astilbe:
  chinensis pumila 27
  crispa 27
  hybrids *27*
Aucuba japonica cvs. 74–5
Auricula, *see Primula auricula*,
Azalea 116–17
  deciduous *112*
  For species and hybrids, *see*
    Rhododendron

Barberry, *see* Berberis

Beech: hedge 20
Berberis:
  candidula 75
  × *carminea* cvs. 75
  darwinii 75, *75*
  hookeri 75
  linearifolia 75
  × *stenophylla* & cvs. 22, 75–6
  thunbergii & vars. 76
  verruculosa 76
  vulgaris & cvs. 76
Bergenia 29
  cordifolia 27, 27–8
  crassifolia 27
Betula:
  costata 76–7
  jacquemontii 77
  pendula & cvs. 77
  platyphylla szechuanica 76
Bilberry, *see Vaccinium
    myrtillus*
Birch, *see* Betula
Bird Cherry, *see Prunus padus*
Bird's Eye, *see* Veronica
black spot 156
Bleeding Heart, *see Dicentra
    spectabilis*
Bloodroot, *see* Sanguinaria
Bluebell, *see Scilla non-scripta*
borders:
  change of concept 25
  herbaceous 25
  mixed 25, *66–7*
  shrub 71
Bouncing Bet, *see* Saponaria
Box, *see* Buxus
Bridal Wreath, *see Spiraea ×
    arguta*
Broom, *see* Cytisus, Genista
Buckeye, *see* Aesculus
budding, 157, *157*
Buddleia:
  alternifolia 77, *77*
  davidii & cvs. 77
  globosa 77–8
  × *weyerana* 'Sungold' 78
Buffalo Currant, *see Ribes
    odoratum*
bulbous plants 165–76
Butter Blobs, *see* Caltha
Buxus sempervirens & cvs. 78

Californian Lilac, *see* Ceanothus
Calluna vulgaris cvs. 78–80
Caltha palustris & cv. 28
Campanula:
  carpatica & cv. 28
  lactiflora & cvs. 28
  portenschlagiana 28
  poscharskyana & cv. 28–30
  turbinata 'Jewel' 28
Caragana arborescens 80
Carpinus betulus & cvs. 80
Catmint, *see* Nepeta
Cat's Eye, *see* Veronica
Ceanothus 134
  americanus 81
  'Autumn Blue' 81
  'Cascade' 81
  'Ceres' 81
  coeruleus 81
  × *delilianus* 81

Ceanothus continued
  dentatus 81
  'Gloire de Versailles' 81
Cedar, *see* Cedrus
Cedrus:
  atlantica glauca 141–2, *142*
  brevifolia 142
  deodara verticillata 142
  libani & cvs. 142
Centranthus, *see* Kentranthus
Cephalaria tatarica 30
Chaenomeles:
  hybrids 81
  speciosa (C. lagenaria) & cvs.
    81
Chamaecyparis:
  lawsoniana & cvs. 23, 142–3
  obtusa & cvs. 143
  pisifera 'Boulevard' 143
Cherry, *see* Prunus
Cherry Laurel, *see Prunus
    laurocerasus*
Chimonanthus 81
Chinese Lantern, *see* Physalis
Chionodoxa:
  gigantea 166
  luciliae 166
Choisya ternata 134
Cistus:
  × *corbariensis* 82
  laurifolius 82
Clematis 134–6
  alpina & cvs. 135
  'Ernest Markham' 135
  'Hagley Hybrid' 136
  'Jackmanii' 135
  'Jackmanii Superba' 135
  × *jouiniana* 135
  macropetala & cv. 136
  montana & cvs. 135
  'Nelly Moser' 135–6
  'Perle d'Azur' 136
  'Royal Velours' 135
  tangutica 136, *136*
  'The President' 136
  'Ville de Lyon' 135
Clethra alnifolia & var. 82,
    82
climbers 133–9
  support for 133–4
club root 19
Colchicum:
  autumnale & vars. 166
  hybrids 166–7
  speciosum 166
Columbine, *see* Aquilegia
conifers 141–9, *144*
  dwarf *147*
container-grown plants: planting
    20
Coreopsis verticillata & cvs. 30
Cornus:
  alba 82, *83*
    'Sibirica' 82
    'Spaethii' *78–9, 82*
  canadensis 82
  kousa 82–3
  mas & cvs. 83
Cortaderia selloana 73
Corylus:
  avellana 83
    'Contorta' *83, 83*

Cotinus:
  coggygria & cvs. 83
    'Royal Purple' *78–9*
Cotoneaster:
  adpressus & var. 83–4
  bullatus 84
  congestus 84, 85
  'Cornubia' 84
  dammeri 84, 85
  divaricatus 84
  henryanus 84
  horizontalis 84, 85
  'Hybridus Pendulus' 84–5
  microphyllus thymifolius 85
  nitens 85
  salicifolius & var. 85
  simonsii 22, 85
  × *watereri* 85
Cowberry, *see Vaccinium
    vitisidaea*
Crab Apple, *see* Malus
Cranesbill, *see* Geranium
Crataegus (Hawthorn) 22, 85–6
  monogyna & cvs. 86
  oxyacantha & cvs. 86
Crocus:
  aureus & cvs. 167
  chrysanthus & cvs. 167
  korolkowii 167
  sieberi 167
  susianus 167
  tomasinianus 167
× *Cupressocyparis leylandii* 23,
    145
Cyclamen:
  'Atkinsii' 167
  coum 167
  *hederifolium (C.
    neapolitanum)* 19, 167,
    168
  purpurascens (C. europaeum)
    167
Cytisus:
  × *beanii* 86
  × *kewensis* 86
  multiflorus 86
  × *praecox* 86
  purpureus 'Atropurpureus' 86
  scoparius & cvs. 86–7

Daffodil, *see* Narcissus
Daphne:
  mezereum 87
  retusa 87, *88*
Dawn Redwood, *see*
    Metasequoia
Day Lily, *see* Hemerocallis
Deodar, *see Cedrus deodara*
Deutzia:
  'Perle Rose' 87
  scabra & cv. 87
Dicentra:
  eximia 30
  spectabilis 30, *30*
Digitalis:
  ambigua 30–1
  purpurea 30
Doctrine of Plant Signatures 55
Dog's Tooth Violet, *see*
    Erythronium dens-canis
Dogwood, *see* Cornus
'dool tree' 71

Index

Doronicum:
  carpetanum 31
  'Miss Mason' 31
drainage 16–17, *16*
Dutchman's Breeches, *see*
  Dicentra spectabilis

Echinops:
  humilis 'Taplow Blue' 31
  ritro 'Veitch's Blue' 31
eelworm 45
Elder, *see* Sambucus
Ellan Tree, *see* Sambucus
Endymion:
  hispanicus 175
  non-scriptus 175
Enkianthus:
  campanulatus 87–9
  cernuus & var. 89
Erica:
  herbacea (*E. carnea*) & cvs.
    89, *89*, 174
  terminalis 89
  vagans & cvs. 89
Eryngium:
  alpinum 31, *31*
  amethystinum 31
  maritimum 31
Erythronium:
  dens-canis 167
  tuolumnense 167
    'Pink Beauty' 169, *169*
    'White Beauty' 169
Escallonia hybrids 89–90
Euonymus 143
  alatus 90
Euphorbia 24
  epithymoides (*E. polychroma*)
    31
  griffithii 31–2
  heptagona 31
  sikkimensis 32
Euryops acraeus 90, *90*
Evening Primrose, *see*
  Oenothera
Exochorda:
  giraldii 90–1
  korolkowii 91

Fair Maids of France, *see*
  Ranunculus aconitifolius
Flowering Currant, *see* Ribes
Foam of May, *see* Spiraea ×
  arguta
Folkard: *Plant Lore* 97
Forget-me-not, *see* Myosotis,
  Veronica
Forsythia 71
  × *intermedia* cvs. 91
  suspensa & vars. 136
Foxglove, *see* Digitalis
frost pockets, 18, *18*
Fuchsia:
  cultivars 91
  magellanica & var. 91

Galanthus (Snowdrop) 165
  ikariae latifolius 169
  nivalis & cv. 169, *169*
Gale Myrtle, *see* *Myrica gale*
Garrya elliptica 136, *136*
Gaultheria:
  hookeri 93
  miqueliana 93
  shallon 93
Genista:
  hispanica 93
  lydia 94
  pilosa 94
Gentiana:
  acaulis 34
  asclepiadea & var. 32
  'Inverleith' 34
  lutea 32
  septemfida 31, *33*, 34
  sino-ornata 34

Geranium:
  grandiflorum 34
  ibericum 34
  macrorrhizum 'Ingwersen' 34
  pratense 34
  psilostemon (*G. armenum*) 34
  renardii 34
  sanguineum 34
  lancastriense 34
Girl in a Boat, *see Dicentra
  spectabilis*
Globe Flower, *see* Trollius
Golden Garlic, *see Allium moly*
Golden Rod, *see* Solidago
Goodbye to Summer, *see*
  Saponaria
Gorse, *see* Ulex
Granny's Bonnets, *see* Aquilegia
Grant Scabious, *see* Cephalaria
  tatarica
greenfly 156
Guelder Rose, *see* Viburnum
  opulus

Hamamelis:
  japonica & cvs. 94
  mollis & cv. 94
Harebell, *see* Scilla non-scripta
Hawthorn, *see* Crataegus
Hazel, *see* Corylus
Heath 147. See also Erica
Heather 19, *147*
Hebe:
  brachysiphon 95
  buxifolia 95
  ochraecea (*H. armstrongii*) 95
Hedera:
  colchica cv. 137
  helix cvs. 136–7
hedges 20–3, *21*
  growing plants under 19
Helleborus:
  atrorubens 34
  corsicus (*H. lividus corsicus*)
    34–5
  orientalis & cvs. 35
Helmet Flower, *see* Aconitum
Helvetius 55
Hemerocallis cvs. 35
herbaceous plants: in mixed
  border 66–7
hilltop site 15–16
Holly, *see* Ilex
Holodiscus discolor ariaefolius
  95
Honeysuckle, *see* Lonicera
Hornbeam, *see Carpinus betulus*
Horse Chestnut, *see* Aesculus
Hosta:
  fortunei 35, *36*
  sieboldiana 'Elegans' 35
  undulata 35
humus 18–19
Hyacinthus:
  amethystinus 169–70
  azureus 170
Hydrangea:
  arborescens 'Grandiflora' 95–7
  cinerea 97
  macrophylla 95, 97
  petiolaris 97, 137
Hypericum:
  androsaemum 97
  calycinum 97
  elatum 97
  patulum & cv. 97–8
    'Hidcote' *96*, 98

Ilex:
  × *altaclarensis* cv. 98
  aquifolium & cvs. 98
  hedge 22
Inula hookeri 36
Iris:
  bearded 36, *41*
  douglasiana 36

Iris continued
  histrioides 170
  innominata 36
  pseudacorus 50
  reticulata 170
  sibirica & cvs. 25, 36
iron 19
Ivy, *see* Hedera

Jack of the Buttery, *see* Sedum
Japanese Angelica Tree, *see*
  Aralia elata
Japanese Maple, *see* Acer
  palmatum
Japanese Quince, *see*
  Chaenomeles
Jasminum:
  nudiflorum 98
  officinale & cv. 98–9
  revolutum (*J. humile
    revolutum*) 98
Jerusalem Cowslip, *see*
  Pulmonaria officinalis
June Berry, *see* Amelanchier
Juniperus:
  chinensis 'Blaauw's Variety'
    144
  communis & cvs. 144
  horizontalis & cvs. 144
  × *media* cvs. 144
  sabina tamariscifolia 145
  squamata 'Meyeri' 145
  virginiana 'Grey Owl' 145

Kalmia:
  angustifolia & var. 99
  latifolia 99, *99*
  polifolia 99
Kentranthus ruber 36
Kerria japonica 99
Kingcup, *see* Caltha
Kirengeshoma palmata 32, 36
Kniphofia:
  hybrids 37
  tuckii 37
  uvaria 37

Laburnocytisus adamii 99–101
Laburnum anagyroidea 'Vossii'
  100, 101
Ladies' Pendant, *see Dicentra
  spectabilis*
Lady of the Woods, *see Betula
  pendula*
Lambs Lugs, *see Stachys lanata*
Lawson Cypress, *see*
  *Chamaecyparis
    lawsoniana*
Lent Lily, *see* Narcissus
  pseudonarcissus
Leucojum:
  aestivum & cv. 170
  vernum 170, *170*
Liatris spicata 37
Ligularia przewalskii, see
  Senecio przewalskii
Ligustrum:
  ovalifolium & cv. 22, 101
  sinense 101
Lilac, *see* Syringa
Lilium (Lily) 165, 170–2
  auratum 170–1
  Bellingham hybrids 172
  bulbiferum croceum 172
  candidum 170
  'Citronella' 172
  'Enchantment' 172
  'Gold Medal' 172
  hybrids 172
  'Limelight' 172
  martagon 171
  pardalinum 171
  regale 171
  'Shuksan' 172
  speciosum 171
  testaceum 171

Lilium continued
  umbellatum (*L. hollandicum,
    L. maculatum*) & cvs.
    171–2
lime 19
Linaria alpina 42
Ling, *see* Calluna
London Pride, *see* Saxifraga ×
  urbium
Lonicera:
  × *americana* 138
  nitida 22, 101
  periclymenum & cvs. 138
  rupicola 101
  syringantha 101
Loosestrife:
  Purple, *see* Lythrum
  Yellow, *see* Lysimachia
Love Flower, *see* Agapanthus
Lungwort, *see* Pulmonaria
Lyre Flower, *see Dicentra
  spectabilis*
Lysimachia:
  punctata 37
  vulgaris 37
Lythrum salicaria & cvs. 37

Macleaya cordata 38
Magnolia:
  denudata 101–2
  sieboldii 102
  × *soulangiana* 92, 102
  stellata 102
Mahonia:
  aquifolium 102
  bealei 102
  japonica 102, *102*
Malus 102–3
  × *aldenhamensis* 103
  'Golden Hornet' 103
  'John Downie' 103, *104*
  'Lemoinei' 103
  'Profusion' 103
  × *purpurea* 103
  'Simcoe' 103
  tschonoskii 103
Maple, *see* Acer
Marsh Marigold, *see* Caltha
May Blobs, *see* Caltha
Meconopsis:
  betonicifolia 38, *178*
  cambrica 38
  grandis 38
  quintuplinervia 38–9
Metasequoia glyptostroboides
  145, *145*
Mexican Orange Blossom, *see*
  Choisya
Michaelmas Daisy 27
mildew 156
Mimulus:
  cupreus 39
  luteus 39
Monkshood, *see* Aconitum
Moses-in-the-bulrushes, *see*
  Tradescantia
Mountain Ash, *see* Sorbus
  aucuparia
Muscari 92, *173*
Myosotis alpestris 39
Myrica
  gale 103
  pensylvanica 103

Naked Ladies, *see* Colchicum
Narcissus (incl. Daffodil) *164*
  asturiensis 172–4
  bulbocodium 172, 174
  cyclamineus 174, *174*
  hybrids 174
  minor 174
  nobilis 172
  poeticus 174
  pseudo-narcissus 172, 174
Neillia thibetica (*N.
  longiracemosa*) 103–5

Nepeta:
× faassenii 39–40
mussinii 39
New Jersey Tea, see Ceanothus
americanus
None-so-Pretty, see Saxifraga ×
urbium

Oenothera missouriensis 40
Osmunda regalis 40

Pachysandra 40
Paeonia:
delavayi 105
herbaceous 41
hybrids 42
lactiflora & vars. 40–2
lutea 105, 105
mlokosewitschii 42
veitchii woodwardii 42
Pampas Grass, see Cortaderia
Papaver:
alpinum 42
orientale & cvs. 42–3, 44
Paper Bark Maple, see Acer
griseum
Parrotia persica 105
Parthenocissus:
henryana 139
quinquefolia 139
tricuspidata 132, 139
Pasque Flower, see Pulsatilla
vulgaris
Pea Tree, see Caragana
Peony, see Paeonia
Periwinkle, see Vinca
Pernettya mucronata & cvs.
105–6, 108
Philadelphus:
'Beauclerk' 106
'Belle Etoile' 106
'Burfordensis' 106
delavayi 106
purpurascens 106
× purpureo-maculatus 106
'Virginal' 106
Phlomis samia 43
Phlox:
douglasii & cvs. 43
paniculata & cvs. 43–5
subulata & cvs. 45, 45
Phormium cookianum (P.
colensoi) 45
Photinia villosa & var. 106–7
Physalis alkekengi 45–6
Picea:
abies cvs. 145–6
albertiana 'Conica' 146
brewerana 140, 146, 146
mariana 'Nana' 146
pungens 'Erich Frahm' 78–9
glauca & var. 146
'Koster' 140
Pickaback Plant, see Tolmiea
Pieris:
floribunda 107
formosa forrestii 109
japonica 107
taiwanensis 107
Pinus:
cembra 'Nana' 146
mugo & cvs. 146–8, 148
planting 19–20
Plant Lore 97
Plume Poppy, see Macleaya
Polemonium:
caeruleum & var. 46
pauciflorum 46
reptans 'Blue Pearl' 46
richardsonii 46
Polygonum:
affine 46
baldschuanicum 138
campanulatum 46–7
vaccinifolium 47
Polypodium vulgare 47

Poppy, see Papaver
Potentilla 14, 107–8
atrosunguinea (P.
argyrophylla
atrosanguinea) 47
fragiformis 47
fruticosa cvs. 107
herbaceous hybrids 47–8
'Moonlight' 69
shrubby hybrids 107–8
tonguei 47
Prickly Comfrey, see
Symphytum asperum
Primula 19
amoena (P. altaica) & cv. 48
auricula & cvs. 48
beesiana 48–9
bulleyana 48–9
candelabra 49–50, 50
'Delight' 50
denticulata 28, 49
florindae 49
japonica 49
pubescens 48
pulverulenta 49
rosea 49–50
vulgaris 50
privacy 20
Privet, see Ligustrum
Prunus:
'Amanogawa' 111
avium & cv. 108
cerasifera & cvs. 108–10
'Fukubana' 111
'Kanzan' 111
laurocerasus & cvs. 110
lusitanica 110
padus & cv. 110
'Pandora' 110
'Pink Perfection' 111
sargentii 110–11
'Tai-Haku' 111
'Ukon' 111
Pulmonaria:
angustifolia & cv. 51
officinalis 51
Pulsatilla:
alpina apiifolia (P. alpina
sulphurea) 26, 51
vulgaris & vars. 51, 51
Pyracantha:
coccinea 'Lalandei' 111
crenato-serrata 'Orange Glow'
111
crenulata 111
'Mojave' 138
rogersiana & cv. 111
'Telstar' 138
Pyrus salicifolia 'Pendula' 111

Ranunculus aconitifolius 51–2
Red Valerian, see Kentranthus
Rheum palmatum tanguticum 52
Rhododendron 19
albrechtii 116
angustinii 113
'Berry Rose' 116
'Blue Tit' 114
'Britannia' 114
'Carita' 114
'Cynthia' 114
decorum 113
'Elizabeth' 114
Exbury hybrids 116–17
ferrugineum 113
'Golden Sunset' 116
griersonianum 114
'Hugo Hardyzer' 116
hybrid azaleas 116–17
impeditum 113
keleticum 113
Knap Hill hybrids 116–17
'Lady Chamberlain' 114
luteum 116
'Mrs G. W. Leak' 116
'Palestrina' 116

Rhododendron continued
pemakoense 113–14
'Pink Drift' 114
'Pink Pearl' 100, 116
racemosum 114
'Romany Chai' 114
'Royal Command' 116
russatum 114
'Santillation' 114–16
'Satan' 116
schlippenbachii 116
scintillans 114
thomsonii 71
'Tunis' 116
vaseyi 116
'White Diamond' 114
'Whitney' 116
yakushimanum 114, 115
'Yellow Hammer' 114
Rhus typhina & cv. 117
Ribes:
odoratum 117
sanguineum & cvs. 117
speciosum 117–18
Rock Rose, see Cistus
Rodgersia 24
aesculifolia 52, 52
pinnata 52–3
Rosa (Rose) 150, 151–63
'Ace of Hearts' 159
'Admiral Rodney' 153, 159
× alba 118
'Celestial' 75, 118
'Albertine' 163
'Alexander' 159
'American Pillar' 163
'Amy Robsart' 119
'Angela Rippon' 163
'Anne Harkness' 162
'Ballerina' 161, 162
'Beautiful Britain' 162
'Blessings' 159
'Canary Bird' (R. xanthina
'Canary Bird') 118
× cantabrigiensis 25, 118
'City of Leeds' 162
climbers 155–6, 163
'compassion' 163
'Congratulations' 159–60
'Constance Spry' 119–20
cultivars 159–63
'Danse du Feu' 163
deadheading 155
development 151
diseases 156
'Doris Tysterman' 160
'Double Delight' 160
'Dresden Doll' 163
elegantula persetosa 118
'Elizabeth of Glamis' 162
'Evelyn Fison' 162
feeding 153–5
Floribunda 160–2
'Fragrant Cloud' 160
'Fragrant Delight' 162
'Fragrant Gold' 160
'Golden Chersoniese' 120
'Grandpa Dickson' 160
'Handel' 163
hugonis 118
hybrid tea 159–60
'Iceberg' 162, 163
'Josephine Bruce' 163
'Just Joey' 153, 160
'Lady Penzance' 119
'Lord Penzance' 119
'Maigold' 163
'Marguerite Hilling' 118
'Matango' 162
'Meg Merrilees' 119
miniature 155, 162–3
'Mini Metro' 163
'Mountbatten' 154, 162
moyesii 118–19, 118
'Geranium' 119
'Sealing Wax' 119

Rosa continued
mulching 155
'National Trust' 160
'Nevada' 119
omeiensis pteracantha 119
'Orange Sensation' 162
'Pascali' 160
'Peace' 153, 160
Penzance briars 119
pests 156
'Piccadilly' 160
pimpinellifolia 'Frühlingsgold'
119
'Pink Parfait' 162
planting 152
distances 152
'Pour Toi' 163, 163
propagation 156–9, 157
pruning 152–3, 153, 156
'Queen Elizabeth' 162
ramblers 155–6, 156, 163
'Red Devil' 160
rugosa 119
'Rubra' 119
'Rosy Cheeks' 153, 160
'Sarah Van Fleet' 119
'Schneezwerg' 119
'Silver Jubilee' 160
soil 151
site 151
preparation 152
'Southampton' 162
'Sunshine' 161
'Sunsilk' 162
'Topsi' 162
'Troika' 160
'Trumpeter' 162
'Wendy Cussons' 160
'Whisky Mac' 160
'Zéphirine Drouhin' 158, 163
Rose of Sharon, see Hypericum
calycinum
Roseroot, see Sedum rosea
Royal Fern, see Osmunda regalis
Rubus:
cockburnianus (R.
giraldianus) 120
deliciosa 120
Rudbeckia:
fulgida 53
'Goldsturm' (R. sullivantii
'Goldsturm') 53
speciosa 53
Russian Vine, see Polygonum
baldschuanicum
rust 156

Sage, see Salvia superba
St John's Wort, see Hypericum
Salix
alba & cv. 120–1
× chrysocoma 121
daphnoides 121
fargesii 121
lanata 121
matsudana 'Tortuosa' 121
Salvia superba & cvs. 55
Sambucus:
nigra & cvs. 121
racemosa cv. 121–2
Sanguinaria canadensis 174–5
Sanguisorba:
obtusa 55
officinalis 55
Saponaria officinalis 55–6
Satureia:
hortensis 56
montana 56
Saxifraga:
burseriana 56, 56
fortunei 56
'Wada's Variety' 58
hostii 56
oppositifolia 56
retusa 56
× urbium 56–7

Index

Scabiosa caucasica & cvs. 57
Schizophragma hydrangeoides
    138, *138*
Scilla:
  bifolia 175
  hispanica 175
  non-scripta 175
  sibirica 175
screens 20–3
Scrophularia nodosa 'Variegata'
  55, 57
Sedum:
  cauticolum 57
  maximum 'Atropurpureum'
    60
  rosea 60
  spectabile & cvs. 60, *60*
  spurium 'Glow' 60
    'Weinstephener Gold' 60
  telephium 'Autumn Joy' 60–1
Senecio:
  przewalskii 59, 61
  tangutica 61
Serratula:
  shawii 61
  tinctoria 61
Shad-bush, *see Amelanchier*
  canadensis
shade 19
shrubs 71–131
  growing plants under 19
  in mixed borders 66–7
  planting 20
Sidalcea cultivars 61
site 15
  getting to know 17
Skimmia:
  japonica & cvs. 122
  reevesiana 122
sloping garden 16
Snowball Tree, *see Viburnum*
  opulus
Snowdrop, *see Galanthus*
Snowflake, *see Leucojum*
Snowy Mespilus, *see*
  Amelanchier
Soapwort, *see Saponaria*
soil:
  acid and alkaline 19
  types 18–19
Solidago:
  canadensis 62
  hybrids 62
Sorbus:
  aria & cvs. 122–4

Sorbus continued
  aucuparia & cvs. 124
  cashmiriana 123, 124
  decora 'Nana' (*S. americana*
    'Nana') 124
  reducta 124, *124*
  sargentiana 124
  'Wilfrid Fox' 124
Speedwell, *see Veronica*
Spiderwort, *see Tradescantia*
Spindle, *see Euonymus*
  europaeus
Spiraea:
  × *arguta* 124–5
  × *bumalda* 'Anthony
    Waterer' 125
  douglasii menziesii 125
  japonica 'Bullata' 125
  'Triumphans' 125
Spotted Laurel, *see Aucuba*
Spruce, *see Picea*
Stachys lanata 62, *62*
Stag's Horn Sumach, *see Rhus*
staking 20
Stonecrop, *see Sedum*
Stranvaesia:
  davidiana 125
  undulata 125
Strawberry Tree, *see Arbutus*
Summer Savory, *see Satureia*
  hortensis
Sycamore, *see Acer*
  pseudoplatanus
Symphoricarpos:
  albus & var. 125
  rivularis 125
  'White Hedge' 125
Symphytum:
  asperum 62
  peregrinum 62
Syringa 125–7
  josikaea 126
  julianae 126
  microphylla 126
  patula palibiniana 126
  prestoniae & cvs. 126
  sweginzowii & cv. 126
  vulgaris & cvs. 126–7

Taxus:
  baccata & cvs. 148
  hedge *21*
Thermopsis montana 62
Thuya:
  occidentalis cvs. 148

Thuya continued
  orientalis cv. 148
  plicata & cvs. 23, 148–9
Tiarella trifoliata 62–4
Tolmeia menziesii 64, *64*
Tradescant, John 64
Tradescantia virginiana (*T.*
  sandersoniana) & vars.
  64
trees:
  growing plants under 19
  planting 20
Trillium 9
  grandiflorum 63, 64–5
  sessile 65
Trollius 14
  × *cultorum* 65
  europaeus & cvs. 65
  yunnanensis 65
  'Wargrave' (*T.y.*
    stenopetala) 65
Tsuga canadensis & cvs. 149, *149*
Tulipa 165
  fosteriana 175
  kaufmanniana & cvs. 175–6
  sprengeri 176
  sylvestris 175, *176*
  tarda 176, *176*
  urumiensis 176

Ulex:
  europaeus 127
  'Plena' *127*, *127*
  minor (*U. nanus*) 127

Vaccinium 127–8
  myrtillus 128
  vitis-idaea 128
Venetian Sumach, *see Cotinus*
  coggygria
Verbascum 54
  chaixii 65
  nigrum 65
  olympicum 65
  phoeniceum 65–6
  thapsiforme (*V.*
    densiflorum) & cvs. 66
Veronica 66–9
  chamaedrys 68
  exaltata 68
  gentianoides 68
  incana glauca & vars. 68
  longifolia & vars. 68
  shrubby, *see Hebe*
  spicata cvs. 68

Veronica continued
  teucrium & cvs. 68–9
  virginica & var. 69
Viburnum:
  × *bodnantense* & cv. 128, 129
  carlesii 128
  davidii 128–9, *129*
  farreri (*V. fragrans*) 129
  grandiflorum 129
  opulus & cvs. 129
  plicatum cvs. 129–30
  rhytidophyllum 129
Vinca 130
  major & cv. 130
  minor cvs. 130
Vines 138–9
Viola cornuta alba 87
Virginia Creeper, *see*
  Parthenocissus
Vitis coignatiae 139

Wallflowers 19
Wall Pepper, *see Sedum*
walls: effect on wind 17–18
Wedon's Tears, *see Tradescantia*
Weigela 130–1
  'Bristol Ruby' 131
  'Eva Rathke' 131
  florida & cv. 131
  'Lavallei' 131
  middendorffiana 131
Welcome-home-husband-
  though-never-so-drunk.
  see Sedum
Whitebeam, *see Sorbus aria*
Whortleberry, *see Vaccinium*
  myrtillus
Willow, *see Salix*
wind 15–16
  prevailing 17
  unpredictability 17
windbreaks 17–18
Winter Savory, *see Satureia*
  montana
Wisteria 137
  floribunda & var. 139
  sinensis 139
Witch Hazel, *see Hamamelis*
Wolf's Bane, *see Aconitum*
Wood Lily, *see Trillium*
  grandiflorum

Yew, *see Taxus*